Social Work Management and Leadership

Management and leadership are increasingly important within the organization and delivery of social care services, and they now form part of the post-qualification framework for social workers. Yet, whilst there is a relatively broad understanding of management concepts and their application in social care, their foundations often go unchallenged both by students and managers. Furthermore, leadership is open to a wide range of interpretations and is often ill-defined, with the expectation that we share a common understanding of the term.

This text promotes an appreciation of the development of management and leadership thinking and the different themes which inform current ideas. It considers these topics from a range of theoretical standpoints in order to stimulate readers to consider their own experience and expectations of management and leadership. It then demonstrates how these standpoints might promote innovative approaches to management and leadership within social care organizations and ways in which such organizations might then develop. The aim of this challenging text is to encourage critical and informed reflection on current practice.

Social Work Management and Leadership is essential reading for students of management and leadership in social care as well as being an invaluable resource for managers who simply wish to consider new approaches to their practice.

John Lawler is Senior Lecturer in Public Sector Management at the University of Bradford, UK.

Andy Bilson is Professor of Social Work at the University of Central Lancashire, UK.

Social Work Management and Leadership

Managing complexity with creativity

John Lawler and Andy Bilson

Routledge
Taylor & Francis Group

LONDON AND NEW YORK

First published 2010
by Routledge
2 Park Square, Milton Park, Abingdon, Oxon OX14 4RN

Simultaneously published in the USA and Canada
by Routledge
270 Madison Avenue, New York, NY 10016

Routledge is an imprint of the Taylor & Francis Group, an informa business

Typeset in Garamond by Prepress Projects Ltd, Perth, UK,
Printed and bound in Great Britain by TJ International Ltd, Padstow, Cornwall

British Library Cataloguing in Publication Data
A catalogue record for this book is available from the British Library

Library of Congress Cataloging-in-Publication Data
Lawler, John.
Social work management and leadership: managing complexity with creativity/John
Lawler and Andy Bilson.
p. cm.
Includes bibliographical references.
1. Social work administration. 2. Social case work—Management. 3. Social service.
I. Bilson, Andy. II. Title.
HV41.L335 2010
361.3068'4—dc22
2009018958

ISBN10: 0-415-45905-2 (hbk)
ISBN10: 0-415-46703-9 (pbk)
ISBN10: 0-203-86628-2 (ebk)

ISBN13: 978-0-415-45905-1 (hbk)
ISBN13: 978-0-415-46703-2 (pbk)
ISBN13: 978-0-203-86628-3 (ebk)

John dedicates this book to Pam, Anne and Adam and his Mum, Eileen, for all they give and for who they are, and to the memory of his Dad, Norman.

This book is for Anna and Emma, who are my future and never require management, and for Jen: as luck would have it, it just so happens that you provide all the leadership I need. Andy

Contents

Figures

Boxes

Preface

We have worked together over a number of years on a range of projects both in academic writing, management training and in other areas, sharing a particular interest and concern with developments in social work practice and organization. This book is the latest result of our work. It is the outcome of continuing discussions and deliberations over developments in social work management and the increasing topicality of leadership in this area. Our deliberations are based on our personal experience of management and social work practice and organization as well as on our research within organizations.

The book has been a genuine collaboration throughout its writing with each of us taking the initiative for its development at different stages but jointly contributing throughout. Our individual expertise and interest has meant that each of us has taken primary responsibility for particular sections but with the thinking and writing always being refined and developed on the basis of continuing discussion. Andy's expertise and experience meant that he took the lead role in the construction of those elements of the book focusing on management and on systems thinking in particular, whereas John's experience caused him to focus more on leadership and individual experience of organization. We have been influenced by many different writers and many different approaches to management and leadership. The book represents the current stage of our thinking, though this continues to develop. Thus it will always be a 'work in progress', not a final conclusion. Similarly the practice of social work management and leadership is always a work in progress, representing continuing adaptations in social work and social care organizations. The book is intended to stimulate students, social workers, and their managers and leaders to consider fresh ways to improve the delivery and experience of social work services. As our collaboration develops we hope to continue to develop ideas which contribute to the understanding of social work services and their improvement.

1 Introduction

> It is not to the handful of hapless, if sometimes inexperienced, front-line staff that I direct most criticism for the events leading up to Victoria's death. While the standard of work done by those with direct contact with her was generally of very poor quality, the greatest failure rests with the managers and senior members of the authorities whose task it was to ensure that services for children, like Victoria, were properly financed, staffed, and able to deliver good quality support to children and families.
>
> Lord Laming, The Victoria Climbié Inquiry (DH, 2003a: 4)

> metaphors only create partial ways of seeing, for in encouraging us to see and understand the world from one perspective they discourage us from seeing it from others.
>
> Gareth Morgan, *Images of Organization* (1986: 31)

This book provides an overview of management and leadership theories and their implications for social work management practice. In doing this we have chosen to present a range of theories and approaches because we see that ideas from earlier eras, even those developed to manage the Prussian army, persist in the structures and management approaches of today's organizations. We also believe that there is no one right way or one golden key to better management. Our approach is not dispassionate or neutral because we believe that theories are important, that they shape the way we see things and what we do. Like Gareth Morgan in the extract above, we see that theories encourage us to see things from a particular perspective and in doing that hide other ways of seeing. We therefore want to invite you to reflect on the theories and approaches that shape the way you do your work. In order to do this we believe that it is important to understand the theories you use and their practical implications.

Our approach is also not dispassionate or neutral because we believe that some approaches are better suited for social work than others. We are particularly concerned that the command and control managerialism that has become a central feature of many social work organizations frequently achieves its goals and targets at the expense of the flexibility and responsiveness that we would want from services. We believe that goals and targets do not have to be a straitjacket and can be achieved without the need for the rigid or authoritarian approaches that they sometimes encourage. We know that good management and leadership makes a real difference to the work that is done in organizations and to the quality of the services that are provided. We also know that theories can help managers to do their job better.

In some respects this is a challenging book. It challenges what we believe to be dominant theories underpinning (sometimes unknowingly) much current management and leadership practice. It challenges the reader to consider alternative perspectives in analysing management and leadership in social work. As it presents a range of perspectives, some more controversial than others, it also presents an intellectual challenge to the reader. Finally, it challenges managers and leaders, current and potential, to reflect on their own knowledge, experience and interpretations and to consider how they might incorporate a range of perspectives into their own practice.

Social work management is not easy. Social work is a very complex field of work operating in an increasingly politicized and turbulent environment. The social situations of service users are open to different political analyses. Social work activities in themselves can at times be seen as political in the ways in which they might challenge current power dynamics in society. Furthermore, social work organizations are, quite correctly, open to the direct scrutiny of locally elected politicians and are influenced by and must respond to changes in policy at both national and local levels. As a consequence, social work management and leadership cannot be easy. We are concerned that some of the practices promoted for use by social work managers were developed to get better performance out of assembly line production. We believe that social work managers need a range of tools and approaches and particularly ones that are designed for use in such a complex and contested area. We also believe that social work requires managerial and leadership approaches that are appropriate to the ethical and moral nature of social work practice and that can deal with the inherent contradictions of managing a service that aims to protect vulnerable people, empower its users and challenge their oppression.

Finally, we are aware that social work managers will want not only to understand theory but to see how these theories are applicable to their day to day practice. We will therefore consider the application of the theories we have discussed and provide examples relevant to some of the key issues and themes of current social work management. We will now look at the managerial context of social work before going on to give an outline of the contents of the rest of the book.

The managerial context of social work

In recent years there have been a number of clearly discernable trends in approaches to management and leadership of human services organizations in both the public and non-governmental sectors. These trends appear to have an international validity, at least across English-speaking countries, though the timing of their impact may vary from country to country. Three main trends are briefly introduced here: marketization; managerialism; and postmoderniza-tion. In later chapters we will discuss some of these issues in more detail as well as providing access to management and leadership theory and approaches that provide different possibilities to deal with their shortcomings.

Marketization

The first of these trends is the marketization of human services. This is seen in a trend in the latter part of the twentieth century amongst western demo-cratic countries, most of which promoted substantial public sector reform. This change was one in which governments sought to move from the direct provision of utilities and services, to purchase these services from a market or quasi-market (see for example Osborne and Gaebler, 1993; Troy, 1999). This change has not been without its critics. Thus, in their study of six local authori-ties looking at the changes in the purchasing of older people's services in the 1990s, Martin *et al.* conclude:

> What we hope we have shown, however, is the way in which the constant spectre of restricted budgets, combined with the transformation of social work into a managerial role of correctly carrying out bureaucratic proce-dures, has given rise to organizational environments where the needs-led, client-centred approach of professional social work as envisaged in the 1990 NHS and Community Care Act is at best subsidiary to the core objec-tive of minimizing cost, and at worst no more than a myth.
>
> Martin *et al.* (2004: 484)

Marketization necessitated a significant shift in relationships between agen-cies, including a more significant role for the independent sector; a changing role for service users, social work users especially, with more involvement in the planning, delivery and evaluation of services being seen as key. Indeed there has been a significant change in the term by which service users are known: from clients, to service users, to customers. This has been accompanied by increased importance of 'choice' for service users, reinforcing the position of service users as consumers in the market rather than as part of a more general citizenry and certainly no longer seeing them as a passive recipient of state-determined services.

During these changes, the restrictions on budgets, an increasing consumer orientation and the aspiration to involve service users, together with the emphasis on performance management, have led to considerable tensions for social work managers and practitioners.

Managerialism

Alongside this there has been a second trend, the rise of 'managerialism', which stands in contrast to earlier concerns with the development of professionalism and professional service, in which senior professionals were seen as the key figures responsible for the delivery of high-quality social work services (Lawler, 2000). 'Managerialism' refers to the development of the interests of management in how organizations are managed, stressing the role and accountability of individual managers and their positions as that – managers – rather than any other role or identity such as senior professional or administrator. The essence of managerialism is the belief that many organizations have a great deal in common, be they in the public, commercial or independent sector and, given this, people equipped as managers should be able to operate effectively in any domain – in other words there is a belief in the transferability of these skills to other managerial contexts. The trend to view all public services as operating within local and wider markets reinforces the importance of the role of manager in this respect. Thus there is an emphasis on management skills as being more crucial than professional or technical skills. Accountability for success or failure lies at the door of each individual manager, who operates within strategic guidelines and is therefore responsible for the achievement of certain objectives.

Commentaries on the development of managerialism have lead to the recognition of a 'New Public Management' (McLaughlin *et al.*, 2002). Flynn (1990), writing at the time when managerialism was still relatively novel in the public sector, summarizes managerialism thus:

> The managerialist ethos which has developed is based on the view that managers have 'the right to manage', which means that they should be in control of the organizations which they run and they should be very proactive . . . It is this view of managers as controllers which underlies many of the managerial reforms in the public sector. Administering systems which are in a steady state, and doing so by arriving at a consensus among managers of various departments and with trade unions is not considered to be real 'management' . . . Part of the managerial ideology is that there is no difference between running a factory and running a hospital.
>
> Flynn (1990: 177–8)

The trend of managerialism continues and is an issue to which we return in Chapter 2.

Postmodernization

These changes in social work management and in public service management are occurring alongside a number of significant and wider changes in our society. O'Brien and Penna (1998) argue that we are now in a period of 'postmodernisation' which leads us into a new era. By 'modern' we are referring to a continuing process from the Enlightenment onwards, whereby our understanding of the world becomes ever clearer and our capacity to understand

and develop technological means of gaining control over our world, through the application of rational thinking, is strengthened. The current period, with its recognition of increasing complexity and discontinuity rather than relentless continuity, does not see the rejection of all that is 'modern'; rather it sees the intensification of some modern ways of thinking and their translation into management practice, together with changes in orthodox social and organizational practices. This intensification of modernism is evident in the increase in three particular processes: rationalization, differentiation and detraditionalization. Processes of rational examination and explanation are intensified. A prime example of increasing rationalisation is the intensive examination of social work service delivery which has been termed 'McDonaldization' (Dustin, 2007), which we discuss in Chapter 6. Differentation can be seen in the way service providers seek to distance themselves from other organizations offering similar services, to establish their own 'unique selling points' in relation to their users. Detraditionalization can be seen in changes in family structures, in changes in bureaucratic structures and the emphasis on cross-sector partnerships, and in involvement of service users in very different ways from the more traditional approaches to participation.

O'Brien and Penna discuss how these changes occur within four more general processes of postmodernization: namely political and economic decentralization; localization; fragmentation; and desocietalization (O'Brien and Penna, 1998). As with the rise of managerialism these are not necessarily conscious and planned developments; rather they result from the complex interplay of politics, economics and culture. There are many ways in which these processes manifest themselves: in the delegation of services to regional and local levels (decentralization); in the involvement of local users in the planning and delivery of services (localization); in the separation of different aspects of service rather than the provision of a holistic or comprehensive, generic service (fragmentation); and in the focus in the individualization or customization of service provision, rather than focusing on wider social concerns (desocietalization).

Implications for management and leadership in social work

The above trends have had significant influence on the nature of social work and placed particular demands on its leaders and managers. As we see from the quotation from Lord Laming at the head of the chapter, when mistakes are made, the management of social work services comes under public scrutiny and with greater levels of criticism than seems to be the case for other similar professions. At the same time the expectation from managers is high, as evidenced by the following quote from the UK Department of Health and Department for Education and Skills (DH/DFES 2006: 55): 'It would be difficult to create learning organizations, retain staff and change the way that staff work without visionary leadership and effective people-management'. In addition the three trends above are associated with a call for a certain approach to management and leadership, which is responsible not only for the day to day management of services but also for major programmes of change. Thus the Social Care Institute for Excellence (SCIE) has provided a workbook for managers on governance in social work which states (Simmons 2007: 13) under the heading *Leadership and Management*:

> Leadership is essential in changing attitudes and involving all staff in social care governance. Leaders need to have a strategic vision and an understanding of social care governance. They will determine the culture, structures and resources required to take this agenda forward. Corporate leadership is about ensuring there is a competent workforce, clarity about roles and responsibilities, clear structures which address current and future service needs and accountability regarding relevant legislative requirements. Controls and assurances should be in place to manage anticipated risks linked to achieving strategic and operational objectives. Professional leadership is essential to support sound decision-making and improving practice and the service.

We will argue in later chapters that this emphasis on superhuman leaders and managers taking charge, changing attitudes and culture in a managerial context of clear lines of accountability, vision and strategic objectives and structures for control and assurance, stems from a range of theories and approaches to management that we classify as *Rational-Objectivist*. We will go on to argue that these generally reflect approaches that do not fit well with the particular context and nature of social work organizations in the twenty-first century and we will offer a range of perspectives that we classify as *Reflective-Pluralist* that provide different and challenging insights.

About this book

There is a plethora of texts on both management and leadership but relatively little on management in social work and even less on leadership in this context. However, each of these issues has risen in prominence in social work recently, with leadership now forming an important element of policy advice across the UK public sector and within social care. Management and leadership are increasingly concerns within the organization and delivery of social care services and in the UK form part of the post-qualification framework for social workers. Whereas there is a growing understanding of management concepts and an increasing awareness of their application in social care, there tends to be an emphasis on classical management theories that were developed more for managing industrial organizations, though they are widely used outside that context. At the same time leadership is open to a wide range of interpretations and is often ill defined with the unspoken assumption that we share a common understanding of the term. This text aims to promote an appreciation of the development of management and leadership thinking and the different themes that inform current ideas on those topics. Furthermore, it considers these topics from a range of theoretical standpoints in order to stimulate readers to consider their own experience and expectations of management and leadership. It then demonstrates ways in which these standpoints might be used to analyse the work, management and leadership within social care organizations and ways in which such organizations might then develop.

The principal objectives of this book are that it:

* develops an awareness of management and leadership concepts and their application within the social care environment;
* encourages a critical view of the concepts of management and leadership;
* challenges readers to apply leadership and management approaches appropriate to their own contexts;
* encourages a reflective view, in line with requirements of continuing professional development.

The book has eight chapters. Following this introduction Chapter 2 initially considers recent developments in management of social work. This particularly focuses on marketization, managerialism and governance. This analysis underpins the need for a framework to understand the different approaches to management and leadership. Our framework divides organizational theories and management approaches into four sections using a 2×2 matrix and splitting them, on one axis by whether they relate to the role of individual leaders and managers or to the organization as a whole, and on the other by whether they are reflective-pluralist or rational-objectivist, which terms we define and discuss in the chapter.

In Chapter 3 we discuss leadership theories, many of which will be familiar to those with even a passing knowledge of management theory. Such approaches include a focus on individual jobs and how they are best designed, through individual personality traits of leadership, to transactional and transformational approaches.

In Chapter 4 we start to encounter approaches to leadership that are reflective-pluralist and focus more on individual, subjective interpretations of management and leadership and apply a range of philosophical perspectives exemplified by existentialist and social constructionist thinking.

Chapter 5 returns to the rational objective sector of organizational theories covering classical management theories and developments in bureaucracy; strategic management and management by objectives; and later developments that take on board the need to develop human resources including socio-technical systems, human resource management and learning organizations.

Chapter 6 includes discussion of theories of management that fall within the reflective-pluralist sector including Soft Systems methodology; Complexity Theory; Postmodernism; Critical Systems Theory; and organizations considered as networks of conversations.

In Chapter 7 we look more specifically at some of the key challenges and areas of practice for social work management and leadership and how a reflective-pluralist approach can shed new light on them. These are: women in social work management; managing organizational change; organizational culture; joined-up working and whole systems approaches; managing practice; and evidence-based practice.

Finally, in Chapter 8, we consider the way ahead for managers and leaders who wish to apply the approaches we lay out throughout the book and what they say about an ethics for social work management and leadership. Throughout these chapters we will give examples of how these theories have been or might be applied to social work organizations and assess the overall strengths and weaknesses of different approaches.

Conclusion

This introduction has outlined our aim to introduce a range of theories and practices for social work management and leadership. We also want to help to encourage critical reflection in readers by providing a framework to understand and assess the underpinnings of current practice and to explore alternatives. The developments in social work organizations in recent decades have, we feel, emphasized particular rational and bureaucratic approaches at the expense of approaches that promote flexibility and responsibility. We hope that the introduction to theories and approaches given in the following chapters will provide different ways of seeing and understanding the nature of management and leadership in organizations. We have chosen to introduce a range of theories because we agree with Karl Popper (1972: 265), who said:

> Whenever a theory appears to you as the only possible one, take this as a sign that you have neither understood the theory nor the problem which it was intended to solve.

2 Governance, markets and managerialism; and a framework for alternative approaches

For obvious reasons, much public administration and public-policy research explores the politico-administrative potential for improvement of state welfare services such as education, scientific research and healthcare. However, despite substantial efforts in these fields, clear-cut answers are still lacking. The traditional question is whether public or private provision yields the best outcome for these services, but criticism of both forms has surfaced in recent governance literature. The common basis of criticism is the experience of both state and market failures and the notion that the boundary itself between the public and the private is blurred.

Andersen (2005: 891)

This chapter will start by considering the current situation of social work management. It will explore key trends that shape the world of managers and leaders and suggest that the time is ripe for considering alternative theories and approaches. We will argue that the current trends of marketization, managerialism and governance provide a modernist and instrumental perspective which does not fit well with the essentially moral and emotionally charged arena that is social work. At the same time most of the many texts on management, matched by a considerable and increasing literature on leadership, also take a modernist and instrumental view of both topics, largely focusing on how organizations might be improved through the application of specific sets of techniques, behaviours, structures and processes. Such texts have much to offer but tend to be uncritical and non-reflective in considering some of the less immediately obvious dynamics of organization. Despite the growth of this literature on organizations and management, there is only limited literature on management and leadership in public service organizations and very little indeed more specifically on social work.

Social work training places an increasing emphasis on developing a critical understanding in qualifying social workers, of the dynamics of the context within which they operate. Similarly continuing professional development in social work emphasizes reflective practice and reflective learning. However, this emphasis on critical understanding is less evident for those who become social work managers. This is not only because of the lack of a specific literature for social work management but also because management literature itself is largely uncritical (Ford and Harding, 2007). Thus we believe that it is important in these chapters that we make a variety of perspectives more readily available and consider their relevance for management and leadership practice in social work organizations. In this way we hope to create a fuller understanding of the theory and practice of management and leadership in social work for the benefit of all stakeholders.

We will start by considering the trends in governance, marketization and managerialism and their implications for social work management and leadership. This will provide our justification for a framework for categorizing different theories and approaches so that their underpinning assumptions and their focus can be better understood. We will then present the framework and how it relates to a wide range of managerial and leadership theories and approaches. This in turn will form the basis for our discussion in further chapters of a range of different approaches and demonstrate our preference for a more pluralist and reflective approach.

Governance, markets, managerialism

Significant developments over the past two decades affecting social work have included these three prominent elements. First, there is an increasing concern with governance, which relates to the provision of consistent and high-quality services, the maintenance of safe practice and clarification of accountability. Second there is the increasing marketization of public services, whereby the open market is seen to be the best mechanism for providing services to meet consumer needs. Third, as discussed in the opening chapter, there have been significant and continuing extensions of managerialism. The focus of these has been described as being 'the attempt to achieve greater control over social work practice. Such change was deemed necessary to make providers more accountable and to ensure consistency of access to services' (Kirkpatrick, 2006: 18).

Alhough it is possible to view these developments from a number of different perspectives already, perhaps unsurprisingly, there are efforts to restrict the perspectives to a dominant one that we will later classify as rational-objectivist. Why we consider this to be unsurprising is that it is easier from the management point of view to see these issues in relatively simple terms so that they can be dealt with, managed, in practical ways: itself a facet of managerialism. Other perspectives, more critical of such developments, do see expression, as we will demonstrate below. However, this is usually done to highlight some of the potentially adverse impacts of such developments or to highlight the power dynamics operating currently and to emphasize the need to acknowledge the impact of such developments on the less powerful. Some of the rhetoric surrounding these policy developments includes that they will create benefits for the less powerful. However, the critical comments indicate the complexities of the process which managerialized efforts to standardize and proceduralize tend to overlook. Our discussion below considers the continuing impact of marketization and then managerialism, after considering developments in governance.

Governance

The idea of governance of social work and particularly the call for 'better governance' is one that is being heard throughout the English-speaking world. Thus in British Columbia in April 2008 we see the headline 'Act Strengthens Governance for Social Workers'. So what is governance? Governance is one of those terms (like leadership) that are assumed to have a common interpretation but are difficult to define in a precise way, especially here in the context of social work. It has been defined as 'a framework within which Health and Personal Social Services organisations are accountable for continuously improving the quality of their services and taking corporate responsibility for performance and providing the highest possible standard of clinical and social care' (DHSSPS, 2001: 2). To that extent it involves every aspect of the organization. Governance is primarily concerned with providing high-quality, safe services and places responsibility for its maintenance on all employees concerned with service delivery (Simmons, 2007: 3). Its interpretation is therefore important for social work as a whole and for the different contexts in which social work services are delivered. The dominant view is that such improvements in quality can best be produced through having robust structures, clear lines of accountability, standardized routines for practice and reporting, effective methods of quality management and processes for risk assessment. Simmons (2007) outlines a framework for social care governance and the SCIE in England has published this as a workbook for implementation. In the guidance on implementing this framework there is, despite its laudable intentions, rather a prescriptive or 'recipe' approach that ignores some of the complexities and contradictions in approaches and, in ignoring them, also ignores ways in which to deal with them. For example, she states that:

> Clear structures need to be in place to support the implementation and monitoring of social care governance. These structures define clear lines of accountability, roles and responsibilities. The processes identify what needs to be done.
>   The following processes should be in place:
>
> * risk management
> * incident reporting and near misses
> * dealing with poor practice
> * registration and regulation
> * post-registration training and learning
> * complaints and compliments
> * supervision
> * recording.
>
> Simmons (2007: 13)

It will be seen from the above that the approach to governance being put forward in this document by the SCIE essentially assumes that the complex arena of social work can be governed through hierarchical and linear accountability structures and through increasing proceduralization where problems exist. This represents the dominant view of management in social work, in which top-down initiatives, increasing proceduralization (even of professional aspects of the work such as assessment) and ever-increasing use of targets seem to be a rapidly growing feature.

Marketization

Wilson *et al.* (2008) refer to marketization as: 'The political and socio-economic process whereby whole areas of social life that were once kept beyond the reach of the market by governments have been opened up to market forces' (2008: 31). The implications of this are that services previously designed, delivered and managed by the state at both local and national levels have been opened up to the market mechanism of competition. Although this does not necessarily mean the privatization of services or the operation of completely open markets, it results in regulated or 'quasi-markets' (Le Grand and Bartlett, 1993) in which services or elements of service are open to competition from a range of different providers, which may or may not include commercial organizations. Thus privatization may be part of the process, but in many cases it means that different bodies in the commercial, public and independent sectors can compete in providing all or part of an erstwhile public sector service. There are restrictions here, though, which do not appear in open markets, and there are differences in how such quasi-markets operate. Thus entry to and exit from the market are more restricted; payment for services is not on a direct cash basis; and services are commissioned (bought) on behalf of certain groups of users. In this way the individual user of the service may not be the one who is paying for the service (though the implementation of 'personalized care' in England and Wales is enabling this in some areas). The commissioner is obliged to 'buy' services from somewhere because of a legal responsibility for the delivery of certain services and thus is unable to decide not to purchase, or to defer purchase until another time. Thus the role of customer in such quasi-markets is problematic: is the main customer the commissioner or the 'end user' of services? If the latter, it is not easy to see parents involved in child protection cases as customers, or those subject to restrictions of liberty because of acute mental health problems, or elderly people who become a significant risk to themselves or others.

In order for such quasi-markets to operate there had to be structural changes in public services, including social work services, most notably in separating those who provided services from those who bought them on the users' behalf. Whereas in previous professionally based services the professional would make an assessment of need and then either deliver services directly or arrange for others to do so, the function of provider and 'purchaser' had to be separated, which needed significant changes to the structure and processes of social work organizations – indeed these were key to establishing social work as a 'business' (Harris, 2003).

Managerialism

In our introductory chapter we discussed the rise of managerialism in social work services. In some respects we can see marketization as being a complementary development but it is also possible to argue, as does Harris (2003), that managerialism and marketization are contrary forces. They can be viewed as complementary in that, if emphasis is to be put on efficiency of operations and the importing of management techniques from the private sector to the public, then there needs to be a greater focus on costs and indeed costing of elements of services, and a further logical extension of that is the need to have both a market focus and a customer focus as part of the organization's overall strategy. The underlying ethos is that the market is the most effective way of delivering services. Thus they operate together in taking public services more towards open market models of operation. The alternative view is that marketization places customers at the focus of all activity: responding to customer demands (demands as defined by customers rather than needs as defined by professional workers); providing customers with choices over how their demands are met; and tailoring services to those individual demands. Managerialism on the other hand is focused on efficient use of allocated money as it cannot generate further revenue through increasing customer demand, as would be the case in a strictly commercial exchange. In addition, it has a focus on ensuring that services are provided at least to minimum standards to communities or groups of relevant people. In practice, Harris argues, there is conflict between demand side (customers) and supply side (managers) and the managerial agenda has taken precedence. He cites a range of evidence to demonstrate managers' increased awareness of finance and the development of quasi-markets, to illustrate the dominance of the supply side, whereas there is much less evidence to demonstrate that social work organizations have altered markedly as a result of consumer pressure and demand. He argues that the rhetoric of the market and customers is still strong but that it is the managerial rather than the market agenda that dominates and has had most effect on the delivery of social work services. He concludes 'if social workers/care managers had taken seriously the rhetoric and rationale of the market and ignored the state rationale for managerial control, they would have been guilty of raising false expectations for service users of how the system operated' (2003: 53).

According to Kirkpatrick in his review of the impact of managerialism in social work, the results have been far greater attempts to regulate the activities of front line social workers. This has included greater reliance on social workers following increasingly strict procedural guidance and achieving targets, which requires an increasing amount of their time to be spent in administration. In this way, social work has become proceduralized and regulated, with the opportunities for professional decision making restricted in comparison with previous practice.

> There is now mounting evidence of rising levels of stress and demoralisation in the social care workforce and to record levels of sickness and absenteeism [sic]. There is also a trend towards work intensification and deteriorating relationships between junior and senior professionals. In the long term this state of affairs may have a damaging impact on the nature and quality of services provided by [social work departments]. Historically these services were dependent on a sense of professional vocation and a willingness to work 'beyond contract'. The risk today is that management reforms are undermining this ethos and will 'weaken still further the local and moral economy that still prevails and, arguably, still sustains the best social work practice' (Langan 2000: 167).
>
> Kirkpatrick (2006: 19)

Summary

It will be seen that governance, managerialism and marketization have been implemented through a top-down command and control approach. In taking this approach there are other stakeholders who might previously have been seen as having a powerful voice whose influence is now restricted, particularly professional workers. Professional work inevitably involves an element of subjective assessment, which now takes a much less influential part in the design and delivery of services. One might see the possibility for a greater influence from other, less powerful voices in the development of markets in care, particularly the voices of service users and caregivers. However, as we noted above, because quasi-markets operate in somewhat artificial ways in comparison with open markets and the position of vulnerable people might not sit easily with the role of customer, such developments restrict the participation or engagement of those less powerful voices. On the face of it, consumerism might appear to give users greater power but this tends to be limited for most service users. The other important comment to make in relation to this approach is that the proceduralization of work routines – specifying what steps in the procedure need to be followed at each stage in the process – can be highly appropriate for dealing with predictable and regular processes whose outcomes are certain. Some aspects of social work may indeed lend themselves to this, for example ensuring all essential administrative steps have been taken in admitting a person to a mental health facility. However, we know that much of social work, particularly its outcomes, is not certain and depends to a large extent on the commitment of both the social worker and the service user and their individual perspectives, experiences and motivations. Although there are benefits in improving accountability and transparency and in acknowledging the perspective of service users, governance, managerial and market developments attempt this through increasing rational control and disempowerment of social workers. Kirkpatrick (2006) acknowledges the need for dialogue between policy makers, managers and professionals, and users, implicitly the better to access their individual experience and needs, but is reserved about the extent to which this will provide an effective counterbalance to the top-down governance, managerial and marketization processes.

We believe that this increasing bureaucratization and top-down control of social work is based on an understanding of organizations and management that involves increasing rationalization and promotes a lack of trust in individual workers. In what follows we will argue that other approaches to management and leadership of social work organizations are possible and desirable. We will discuss how other approaches can be applied that will improve the quality and effectiveness of services whilst valuing the contributions of all those working in the organization. To make such a change does not require huge investments or changes in structure, as the main thing that needs to change is the assumptions we make about effective management. In the next section we will outline a framework that allows us to understand the nature of the assumptions behind theories both formal and informal, of management and leadership. We believe that the reflection that such a framework enables, and the opening up of alternative approaches that it entails, can be powerful instruments in making changes that will enable the possibility of new forms of management.

The basics of our framework

We will now introduce our conceptual framework for this book. We feel that it is important to establish this framework to try to organize the many and varied theories and approaches to management and leadership in order for us to understand them in relation to each other. So trying to organize what we already know, and perhaps categorize it, is itself an aid to finding our way round this varied terrain. We will also chart the different developments within management and leadership and identify the different approaches and reasons for them. Doing this equips us better to understand the range of approaches, the different foci of various approaches and their relative merits. On that basis we are in a stronger position to compare and contrast approaches and to consider how elements of different approaches can be synthesized to inform better management and leadership practice. The framework assists us both to distinguish the foundations and principal concerns of different approaches and to relate the different approaches to one another.

So a framework itself is useful but what dimensions to use to classify different approaches? We have decided on a 2×2 matrix – not uncommon in social science! Because of the complex nature of the range of organizational/management/leadership theories and the varied topics that each includes and excludes, it is not easy to identify summary dimensions and describe them fully with a neat label. Still we feel it is useful to attempt such a summary and, after much deliberation over how to label our dimensions, we have chosen those of rational-objectivist at one end of the vertical axis to reflective-pluralist at the other, and from individual to organizational as the continuum on the horizontal axis (Figure 2.1).

The reasoning behind using this matrix is as follows. First, much management literature, throughout the twentieth century in particular, is characterized by a fascination with rational planning and attempts to make organizational operations more predictable and thus manageable; that is, the literature is replete with attempts to manage uncertainties out of any organization through the application of rational thinking and the use of 'scientific' methods. Examples of this include how Henry Ford tried to deal with unpredictabilities affecting his business by regulating those uncertainties – buying rubber plantations to ensure a supply of raw material, buying a shipping line and building a railway for similar purposes, and encouraging purchase of Ford cars by employees to smooth uncertainties in demand (Daft and Marcic, 1995). His approach to organization typifies the scientific approach to management and organization, which we will expand upon in due course. However, alongside such applications of the rational approach, the twentieth and twenty-first centuries have been witness to considerable changes – social, political, technological etc. (Giddens, 1999) – which appear to render organizations less predictable and more uncertain. The standard rational approaches to dealing with such developments are of limited value, as they emphasize managing uncertainty out of the organization.

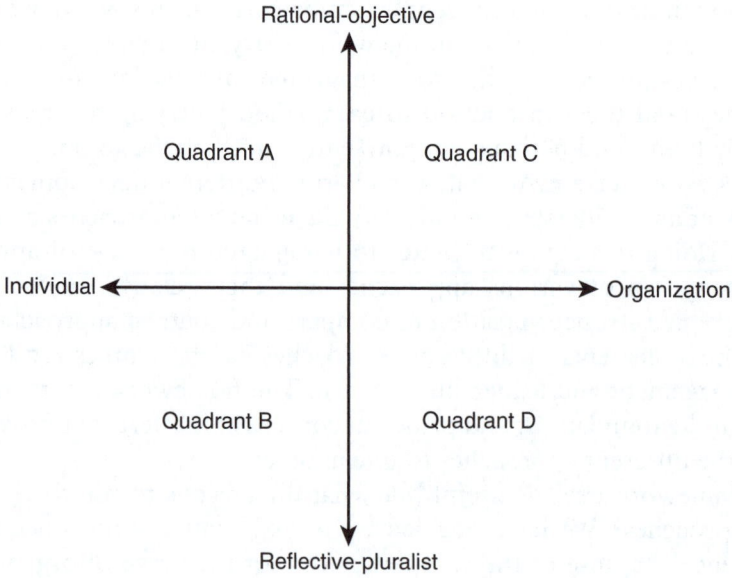

Figure 2.1 The 2×2 matrix for categorization of management and leadership theories.

If organizations are to survive and be effective in these circumstances they have to become more flexible to adapt to such changes, and more tolerant of uncertainty per se. In many respects we can see a change from attempting to manage uncertainty *out* of organizational processes to an acceptance of the need to manage *with* uncertainty. The increasing interest in, for example, risk management, is one such pointer – an explicit acceptance of uncertainty.

A second reason for developing the framework is that the management and leadership literature includes a divergence in the focus of approaches. This ranges from literature that focuses on the individual manager or leader as prime actor or agent in organizational life at one end of the continuum, to approaches that focus not on the leader or manager but on the structure and processes occurring within the organization as a whole, including those occurring in its social and economic context. For example, an approach that seeks to identify the personality traits of individual leaders we see as lying at the individual end of this spectrum, whereas a 'whole systems' approach to organizational change lies at the other.

Utility of the framework

So we have outlined the general need for a framework and provided a rudimentary rationale for the chosen dimensions. We will now explain in more detail the overall utility of this framework. There are several reasons for identifying different approaches and mapping them into the framework. In the first place, much management and leadership literature is relatively lacking in critique of management and leadership theory and in particular it has a 'managerialist' focus. Thus, for example, Ford and Harding (2007: 477) state that, despite considerable numbers of publications, and with a few notable exceptions, '[t]his vast body of work has . . . an almost total absence of any critical analysis'. We believe this framework enables a more critical view of the literature as a whole and of its component parts. By 'critical' in this context, we mean that we can examine some of the taken-for-granted assumptions underpinning certain approaches and begin to question how robust those assumptions might be. This includes considering 'the legitimacy and efficacy of established patterns of thinking and action' (Alvesson and Willmott, 2003: 3). As in social work theory, we also see the necessity for drawing on theories from the broader social sciences in order better to understand management and leadership. So the consideration of different approaches and their classification begins with an examination of the foundations of each approach. In doing this we hope to open up or exteriorize the assumptions sustaining each approach, which often go unquestioned. This promotes both an awareness of the range of approaches and their differences and the opportunity to reflect on these. This in turn, we hope, will stimulate reflection on managerial and leadership practice.

We hope that the framework also assists in the analysis of different approaches by exposing and discussing the commonalities and differences of their underlying assumptions. The Leadership and Management Standards documentation (GSCC 2005: 4) in England and Wales places specific emphasis on reflection and learning, in highlighting that good social care managers 'provide an environment and time in which to develop reflective practice, professional skills and the ability to make judgments in complex situations'. So the aim of our framework, and indeed of the book as a whole, is to stimulate readers not only to reflect on the assumptions that underpin different theoretical and practical approaches to management and leadership but to identify and reflect on the assumptions which inform their own management and leadership practice.

Other frameworks

Some time ago, Burrell and Morgan (1979) produced a seminal text in which they discussed many and various sociological theories and their application to the study of organizations. In that text they highlighted the different ontological bases and epistemological approaches often implicit in such approaches. The framework they used to locate the different approaches took the form of a 2×2 matrix, the axes of which were sociology of regulation versus radical change as one dimension, and subjective against objective perspective as the other. The authors have developed their thinking separately, Morgan going to write a further important text (Morgan, 1986, revised 2006) considering the application of a number of metaphors to the study of organizations, and Burrell authoring other texts with a theme of radical organization theory (e.g. Burrell, 1997). Their original text is still held in esteem and their approach has been developed further and is echoed in the works of others. Within the context of social work particularly, Whittington and Holland (1985) use the same framework to consider theories of social work. In later publications Howe (1987) and Payne (2005) also see value in applying and adapting this framework to social work, to help develop our understanding of social work organizations. A similar approach has been developed by Poulter (2005), again within the social work context. The dimensions he uses to analyse theory and practice in social work are slightly different, in that one is free will against determinism and the other is conflict versus consensus, but the overall approach has strong echoes of Burrell and Morgan.

Our framework thus has similarities with that of Burrell and Morgan and the others inspired by it. It is attempting to draw a wide range of different approaches together for consideration and reflection. Our overall aim is to bring to light the theories on which management and leadership practice is based, to enable further reflection and learning. Much of this basis might not be recognized as 'theory' as such by managers, leaders or practitioners, as it is picked up and applied through practice and communication with others often in very informal ways. Nevertheless we believe it is 'theoretical' in that it forms the informal theories we use to understand the world of management, leadership and organizations. The scope of our work is significantly narrower than that of the above authors, focusing as we are on social work management and leadership rather than more broadly. We share though with Burrell and Morgan the aim of reflection and learning. We share their view of the importance of considering different theoretical viewpoints in order to provide us with insights into our own:

> In order to understand alternative points of view it is important that a theorist be fully aware of the assumptions upon which his [sic] own perspective is based. Such an appreciation involves an intellectual journey which takes him outside of the realm of his own familiar domain. It requires that he becomes aware of the boundaries which define his perspective. It requires that he journey into the unexplored. It requires that he become familiar with paradigms which are not his own. Only then can he look back and appreciate in full measure the precise nature of his starting point.
>
> (Burrell and Morgan, 1979: xi)

The framework we are using to understand leadership and management is explained in the sections below.

Examining the dimensions of the framework

Our starting point is that what we regard as knowledge in the areas of leadership and management is influenced by the underpinning assumptions of each respective perspective. In broader social terms, the way these influence *what* we know and *how* we come to know it is reflected in Habermas's argument (1972) that there is no such thing as neutral knowledge: knowledge is always created from a position of interest and is never entirely value-free in spite of the intention to present 'knowledge' as objective and neutral. Much work concerning management and leadership – research, practitioner writing and policy – may claim to be objective and neutral but much of it is written consciously or otherwise from the perspective of the organization – with furthering the organization's interests as the main priority. Thus it focuses on how organizations can be managed more effectively rather than, say, how they can accommodate conflicting positions and meet a wider range of interests, which may mean that the organization as a whole would operate at a sub-optimal level.

Each of our chosen axes represents different perspectives, reflecting diverse assumptions based on underpinning theoretical and philosophical roots. It is important to understand the varied foundations of each approach, as the assumptions made directly influence the application of the approach. For example, if our basic assumption is that organizations need strong charismatic leaders (an individual approach) our response to the organizational difficulties will be different from if we believe that organizations are best managed by effective structures and clear lines of accountability (an organizational approach). Similarly, if we believe that the more we get to know of organizations through experimentation and research (a rational-objectivist approach) the better we will be able to control them and predict both their internal operations and the outcomes of their activities, then our actions will be different from those taken with the view that organizations are a combination of diverse interests, possibly even competing (a reflective-pluralist approach), and that their activities cannot entirely be controlled or outcomes entirely predicted.

We will detail below the different underpinnings along the rational-objectivist and reflective-pluralist dimension by considering the poles of this dimension. We recognize that in looking at the extreme ends of the dimensions we create a dichotomy. We feel it is better to view each dimension as a continuum rather than as a binary divide. However, we feel that presenting it this way here offers the reader the possibility of seeing the range of the differences that occur across the dimension.

The reflective-pluralist and rational-objectivist dimension

In Box 2.1 we illustrate the differences between the ends of the continuum we use for the reflective-pluralist and rational-objectivist dimension of our framework. This shows the underpinnings of this dimension by considering its poles or extremes. This dimension concerns many of the fundamental debates about poststructuralist and postmodernist versus modernist perspectives. Approaches categorized as rational-objectivist embody a more realist position (or critical realist position, Bhaskar, 1998 [1979]) that assumes that an external stable and knowable reality exists, independently of the observer and his or her actions. This is necessarily so, as without such a position the rational use of management theory epitomized in this pole is not tenable. The other pole of this

---

Box 2.1   Comparison of underpinnings of the poles of the rational-objectivist and reflective-pluralist dimension of the framework

	Reflective-pluralist	*Rational-objectivist*
Epistemology/ ontology	Pluralist/relativistic, observer dependent	Realist, observer independent
View of management practice	Situated, locally variable	Transferable, independent of context
Views of change	Unpredictable, conflictual, emergent	Predictable, planned, managerially determined
Orientation	Social, emotional, reflective	Rational, linear, bureaucratic
Ethical position	Constructivist, feminist, compassionate concern	Utilitarian

dimension covers many different sociological and philosophical conceptions that conclude that there are many socially constructed realities and individually perceived realities, each experienced as real, with real consequences for our actions. Taking this viewpoint can help fundamentally to reconsider the nature of management and leadership practice and promote critical reflection to give a powerful tool for new forms of cooperative action.

Thus the major underpinning and difference between these two poles relates to a view of reality that differs in the fundamental attitude to the nature and stability of the external world. Other differences stem from this fundamental difference in view. At the extremes of this continuum the views of management practice itself are fundamentally different. In the approaches classified as rational-objectivist it is assumed that managerial practices can be developed that are relevant to practice in a range of settings and contexts, that is, they are intended as being universally applicable. Thus techniques or practices that are successful in one context are easily transferable to others. It is a matter of the correct classification of the type of problem in order to identify an approach to its solution. In contrast those approaches classified as reflective-pluralist stress the importance of context and see managerial practice as locally situated. The classification of organizational dilemmas is problematic because one person's view of the nature of the dilemma has no more grounding than that of someone who sees it differently. At this pole management needs to be sensitive to the key role of the organizational environment and particularly local culture, in shaping practice (Lawler and Bilson, 2004).

A further difference that stems from these different underpinnings relates to the approach to and understanding of change in organizations: what it is and how it might occur. From the position of the rational-objectivist pole, organizations are often seen to be essentially stable objects, similar to machines, and change can be achieved through manipulation of the parts. In this approach change is often treated as being structural and instrumental, that is, to achieve specified and predicted aims. Thus attempts to make a difference to outcomes focus on providing new procedures, new working practices, clear job descriptions, clear lines of accountability and so on. Thus change is a matter of logic and planning and is rational and not emotional. From this viewpoint managers can independently plan for and apply changes to the system with relatively predictable outcomes. At the other pole, some theories would suggest there is no or little consensus about the need for and direction of change with a range of often competing views about it. Other theories point to the unpredictability of the responses of organizations to attempts to change it. Approaches to change from this perspective use processes of reflection to guide rather than design future actions. The orientation of approaches that are reflective-pluralist is towards collaborative action, since change is usually seen to be emergent and cannot be comprehensively planned in advance and then applied to the organization. In Box 2.1 the differences in the foundations of these approaches are summarized.

The individual–organization dimension

We have opened up then some of the complexities along the rational-objectivist to reflective-pluralist dimension. What of the individual–organization axis? Is that similarly open to different perspectives? The answer to this is yes, in that there are competing views of what constitutes individuals and the extent to which we can ever view individuals separate from their temporal and geo-social context. Our individual–organization axis is similar in some respects to the approach of Hughes and Wearing (2007), who note the range of theories that consider the different micro, mezzo and macro 'levels of experience' in organizations (2007: 28). We illustrate the focus of different approaches along this continuum in Box 2.2.

There is also a considerable range of views over what constitutes the 'self' that the individual can be seen to represent. Similarly organizations are subject to a range of views, from the realist approach that organizations are independent, coherent bodies, to postmodern perspectives that view organizations, if they can be said to 'exist' at all, as complex sets of constructions and relationships, reflective of different interpretations of power dynamics. However, we cannot easily apply the same concepts to this horizontal axis as we have for the vertical. This might become over-complicated and detract from the prime aim of the framework, namely trying to simplify and locate different perspectives within an accessible framework.

In examining these different approaches, we are encouraging critical reflective thinking and learning, which in themselves inform self-reflective practice and development in management and leadership. Reflection emphasises the individual-subjective perspective as a counterbalance to the instrumental

---

Box 2.2 Comparison of the different focus of analysis/experience in the individual–organization dimension of the framework

Individual	*Organization*
Individual and independent thoughts and feelings	Collective strategy and networks
Individual action	Organizational structure and coordination
Individual attitudes, motivation, characteristics	Organizational policy, climate and culture
Inter-personal relationships	Intra- and inter-organizational relationships
Individual experience and perception	Organizational history and life stage
Individual job, skills and development	Organizational processes of recruitment, reward and development

rationality that typifies much if not most of the managerial literature. What we mean by that is this latter literature employs a largely linear, cause–effect rationality that is instrumental in developing improved operations for the benefit of the organization. Exploring other, subjectivist and pluralist, approaches enables us to analyse the operations and outcomes of organizations in more sophisticated ways. Thus we see exploring possibilities as being an important facet of learning both for individuals themselves and, when aggregated, for organizations more broadly.

Exploring the four quadrants of the framework

This section will now consider each of the four quadrants defined by our matrix (see Figure 2.1) and give more detail of how the theories and approaches have been allocated to them. Since Burrell and Morgan's work (1979) appeared there has been discussion of the problems of 'paradigm incommensurability' (e.g. Jackson and Carter, 1991), of the mutual exclusiveness of different approaches and the problems that creates for theory and practice. Our intention here is neither to present an exhaustive list of different approaches nor to try an over-ambitious reconciliation of different approaches, nor yet to combine approaches. Rather it is to open up the possibilities of thinking and analysis in a variety of ways, to provoke questions and to highlight assumptions with the aim of promoting learning. This we believe will help to inform professional practice and to develop management processes. The ultimate aim is to assist in the organization and delivery of effective human services to address human need in the social work context. With that in mind, our intention is not to be diverted into discussions of the difficulties of combining different methodological or theoretical traditions but to highlight that there are more theoretical approaches available to us, to inform our learning and practice, than might often be acknowledged, given the dominance of rational-objectivist approaches. We are aware of the criticism that Burrell and Morgan's work does not provide a comprehensive review of all theoretical positions (see for example Flood, 1990) nor would we hold such a high ambition for our work here. Our chosen theoretical approaches reflect our interest, developed both in practice and in our academic work, in theories that we believe to be important in providing useful and significant perspectives for management and leadership in social work. To that extent they are our selection, not an attempt to list all relevant approaches.

We feel that reflective-pluralist approaches have been frequently overlooked in the managerial world of operational effectiveness, star-rating of authorities or similar performance measurement, and the performance and audit culture more generally. Our view is that there is often a big difference between the perspectives of professional practitioners and that of their managers – even though many of the latter have come to management from practice. It might be thought that management and leadership theories and social work theories have little in common. Our view is that they are more closely linked than is often realized and that, for social workers, some of the approaches we use here will be familiar from their own training and practice: the same theoretical roots perhaps but with a different application to management rather than social work practice. Given the human interaction necessary both in management and leadership and in social work this should be no surprise, though it might still be so for some people!

Although the approaches within the quadrants we have delineated have certain commonalities in our view, we must acknowledge they have differences too. In some cases there are significant areas of difference or contention between theoretical approaches which we have grouped together (e.g. between social constructionism and existentialism). It is important for the reader not to assume a complete coherence within each quadrant. The difficulties of trying to reconcile different approaches are recognized (e.g. Gregory, 2003). Gregory's phrase to describe accepting different theoretical approaches to examine situations is 'discordant plurality' (p. 138). This indicates a willingness to accept both tensions and synergies between approaches in our analysis and plans for the future. Dealing with such tensions we believe will be familiar to anyone with either experience of social work or of management as both parties have a pragmatic imperative because of the practical focus of their work with people. So, although each quadrant does not necessarily present a cohesive set of accounts, the approaches within each will be less obviously contradictory than approaches in other quadrants.

Figure 2.2 shows our framework including the different managerial and leadership approaches and theories that we have selected as being relevant to social work management and leadership. We will now briefly discuss each quadrant in turn and the approaches to be found there. This will only be a brief introduction to the fuller discussion of these issues in the four following chapters, each of which will deal with one of our quadrants in turn.

Quadrant A: rational-objectivist and individually focused

This refers to approaches that are founded on rational bases, which attempt to objectify knowledge in an impersonal, detached manner and which take the individual manager or leader as the focus or unit of analysis. In Burrell and Morgan's framework, that quadrant which focused on the objective perspective and theories of control was seen as the site for much management and organization theory. In our framework, this quadrant will see the predominant approaches to management and leadership in social work. The rational element is one, in management and organization terms, that has a foundation in approaches from the Scientific Management school of theorists, most notably F. W. Taylor. There is an assumption here that through taking an objective, scientific approach including data gathering, information processing and analysis, and logical decision making, a 'best way' of determining the solution to organizational dilemmas can be arrived at. Such approaches prioritize the rational,

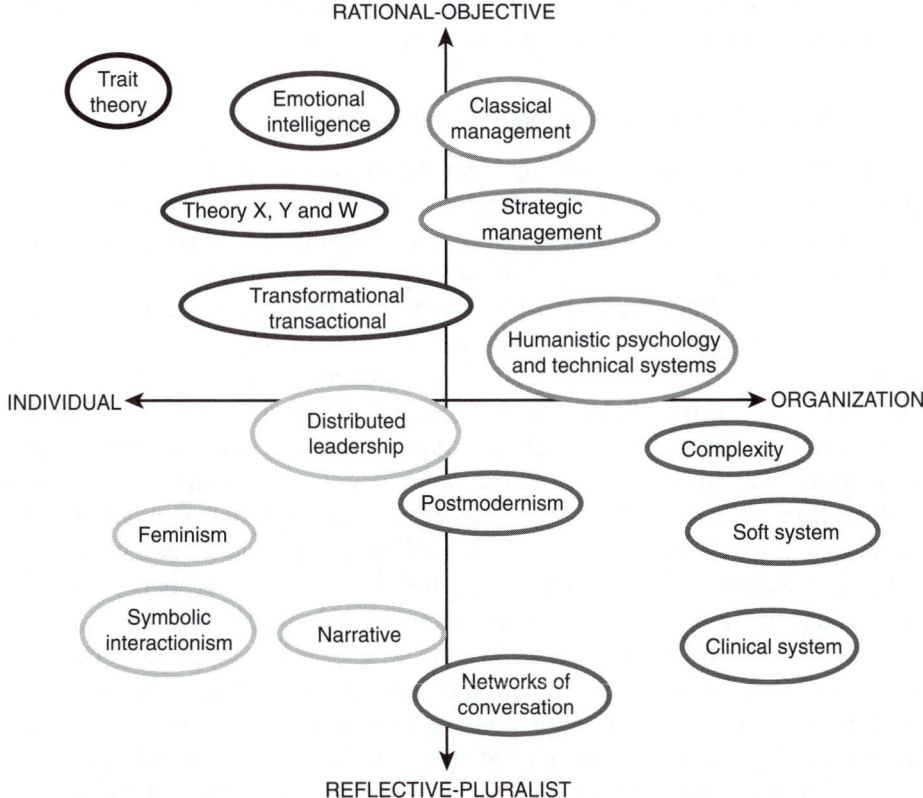

Figure 2.2 The framework showing selected managerial and leadership theories and approaches.

detached perspective. This area of focus is characterized by the 'manager as expert' assumption: s/he has the knowledge to bring to bear on issues of job design and execution etc. to ensure effective operation of the organization or one particular part of it. Much research in management, leadership and organization can be seen to fit comfortably in this quadrant, with the continuing search for general solutions to problems, universal applications of theories. In relation to more recent approaches to leadership, much of the 'heroic leader' work is situated here. Leadership is seen as residing in key individuals within the organization. Approaches that identify the key essential characteristics of effective leaders belong here.

Much of the work in this area could be seen as characterizing modernism and managerialism. By this we mean that progress in understanding organizations and enhancing the effectiveness of their operations is seen to be brought about through the increasing application of rational analysis. The development of competency frameworks comes into this category – the identification of universal qualities and skills necessary to carry out particular roles and tasks from rational analysis. Within the context of social work, developments such as the PQ Framework for Leadership and Management fit here.

Quadrant B: reflective-pluralist and individually focused

This quadrant includes approaches that again focus on the individual but depend less on the search for predictability through rationality characterized by Quadrant A. In our case here, we are discussing not activities or modes of thinking that are necessarily individually biased or irrational, but rather approaches that acknowledge a wider range of rationalities, accept a degree of unpredictability or uncertainty (sometimes a great degree) and also accept that uncertainty is a factor in itself. This perspective is at issue with universal prescriptions and proscriptions. It sees the individual as separate, active and unique, the assumptions on which this quadrant is founded being therefore unlike those that underpin Quadrant A, in which individuals are regarded largely as homogenous and relatively passive organizational actors. This quadrant allows multiple perspectives, which all have legitimacy: the managerial and the non-managerial; the professional and the non-professional; the service provider and the user. No one perspective necessarily is privileged over others. It accepts that individual perspectives on the same phenomenon may, and probably do, differ. Within the organizational context the manager then ceases to be expert. S/he may still be relatively powerful in the organization on the basis of hierarchical position but less so because of technical or professional knowledge. So the manager is no longer 'expert' in his/her role but 'sense maker'.

A range of approaches to management, leadership and organization fall into this category but they are both numerically fewer by far than those in Quadrant A and less influential/popular. Many such approaches would be categorized as 'interpretive' under Burrell and Morgan's scheme noted above. So approaches influenced by phenomenology such as social constructionism and existentialism and their application to management, leadership and organization would fit here, as we detail later.

Quadrant C: rational-objectivist and organizationally focused

This quadrant includes those approaches that focus on the organization as the main unit of analysis and demonstrate a concern with objective views and rational thinking. Models in this quadrant are likely to be developed from positivist methodologies, with the belief that greater understanding of group and system dynamics will lead to the potential for greater regulation and predictability of organizations and, thus, heightened certainty.

Early theorists, later to be described as the Classical Management School, such as Weber noting characteristics of effective bureaucracies, and Taylor asserting scientific management, fit easily here. Approaches here also include those that look at strategic approaches to managing organizations (e.g. Strategic

Management theory, Management by Objectives). We have also included some of the early uses of systems theory and humanistic psychology, which focus on creating better means of increasing the effectiveness of organizations. Thus we consider in Chapter 6 human resource management, socio-technical systems and the learning organization. These latter examples are closer to the reflective-pluralist quadrant to be discussed below.

Other approaches that fit in this quadrant, but are not specifically discussed in Chapter 6, include those that value interpersonal action and interaction above individual perspectives and seek to identify generalizable principles about group and organization dynamics that enable the predictable management of both. Other approaches to systems within this quadrant would include, for example, 'hard systems' approaches such as Operational Research, Systems Analysis and Systems Engineering (see Jackson, 2003: 16). Approaches to group dynamics would include models of groups or teams such as the approach taken to identifying team and task roles as developed, for example, by Belbin (1981).

Quadrant D: reflective-pluralist and organizationally focused

This section considers approaches that take an organization-level view and embrace the concept of a plurality of perspectives and interests. In sum such approaches accept a more uncertain view of organizations than in Quadrants A and C. Assumptions that inform theories in this quadrant include the belief that more can be learned about systems and organizations through further research but that unpredictability and uncertainty are endemic features of organizations and will always be important factors regardless of how sophisticated management and leadership techniques become. Despite an increasing understanding of system dynamics, we will never have completely predictable human systems. In Quadrant D the management theories and approaches acknowledge that uncertainty and difference will always be present; for example there will always be varied perspectives on managerial objectives, change etc. from different parties in any organizational activity. Managerial activity will always lead to some unpredictable and unintentional consequences. This is tolerated, accounted for and expected in quite a different way from a Quadrant C approach, which would attempt to manage out the uncertainty over time, as more knowledge is gained about system and organizational operations.

We consider a range of newer systems theories including Soft Systems Methodology (Checkland and Scholes, 1990), Critical Systems Theory (Jackson, 2003; Midgley, 2000) and Complexity Theory (Stacey, 2007) with its focus on complex adaptive systems. Other dialogical approaches have a more constructivist philosophy and see organizations as networks of conversations (Bilson and Ross, 1999) placing a particular focus on the role of emotions in organizational life. In addition we can see that approaches drawing on postmodernism (e.g. Boje and Dennehy, 1999), with their focus on valuing conflict and voices of oppressed groups, fit very well within this quadrant.

Summary

We thus acknowledge a range of approaches, including existing frameworks such as those cited earlier. We also acknowledge the value of trying to gain a deeper understanding of the assumptions, explicit and implicit, that underpin much practice – 'theories in use' as it were (Argyris and Schön, 1974). However, our framework here is intended not simply to replicate existing frameworks but to develop our own, reflecting our own experience, research and understandings. To that end the dimensions we identify in our framework are those summarized above: the continuum from individual to organization along a horizontal axis, and rational-objectivist to reflective-pluralist on the vertical.

As we have noted, the individual–organization dimension is not difficult to explain. Standard texts on management and organizational behaviour (e.g. Mullins, 2007) often note that the study of organizations is a combination of levels of analysis and is variously focused on individuals, teams and groups, and the organization in its environment. The horizontal dimension, however, is less straightforward; this is because of the different (very different in some respects) assumptions that are made about the world, about reality and about how we know them both. Subsequent chapters will discuss each quadrant in greater depth with the intention of provoking readers to reflect further on the assumptions currently influencing thinking and practice, both their own and those underpinning management and leadership in the social work organizations in which they work.

3 The individual manager and leader through a rational-objectivist lens

In this chapter we look particularly at management and leadership approaches that focus on the individual, rather than on the organization more broadly, and that take a detached and 'rational' view, that is, an objective and scientific perspective. We also consider leadership and management developments within the social work context – most notably a framework for leadership in social work. There is a very considerable literature on management in general and a large and increasing literature on leadership. Here we consider briefly the development of thinking about management specifically before examining that of leadership, summarizing the main themes. We do not set out to provide a detailed chronology of management and leadership thinking and to that extent some significant contributors might not be mentioned by name. There are good texts which present such chronologies to which the reader is referred if a more detailed examination is required (e.g. Cole, 2004; Mullins, 2007; Gill, 2006; Northouse, 2007).

In this chapter, as is the case throughout the book, we deal at times with managers and management and at other times with leaders and leadership. We make the point that in some literature there is a conflation of the two. It is relatively easy to clarify whom we mean when we refer to managers, in that the term is used to identify people who are appointed to particular positions in an organization's hierarchy where they have management responsibilities, for people and other resources. The role of leader is less clear in that it is interpreted differently at different times and in different contexts. It might refer to a manager who is expected to exercise some influence beyond that of his or her position. In some cases it refers to people who act as, or are seen as, figureheads for their organizations, professions or communities. In some cases they might have been appointed to such positions but in others, for example in press interviews where a senior professional is approached to comment and is seen to represent the views of profession, they might not. In other cases again, the word 'leader' might be used in relation to someone who might hold a relatively lowly organizational position but might exert considerable influence due to factors other than organizational position. We use both terms, 'manager' and 'leader', throughout this chapter and book. Rather than use both these words continuously, or some composite of manager-leader, we have chosen to use whichever word is predominantly used in the literature on the topic under discussion at that time. Where there is a need to make a clearer distinction, we do so. We should also note here that, despite the number of contributions in the literature, there is still no enduring and universally accepted definition of leadership. We will discuss this later in the chapter.

Leadership and Management Framework in social care

Within the social care context in England and Wales, the General Social Care Council (GSCC) recently produced a Leadership and Management Framework (GSCC, 2005). This has an individual, objective view of leadership and management. This is to say that management and leadership, particularly, are seen as being individual functions whose qualities are derived from detached and objective research. This is evident when we consider the main aspects in guidance issued by GSCC (ibid.) Whereas more broadly we might see management as representing a level in an organizational hierarchy (e.g. 'the management all agree that . . .'), or as a term we use to refer to a set of organizational processes (e.g. the management of a service), or as a particular role (a management post), here we see it as closely allied to leadership and being focused at the individual level – individual managers with particular roles and functions. The guidance particularly focuses on 'distinctive things that social care managers do' (GSCC, 2005: 4) and particularly what 'good' social care managers do and thus actions that should be emulated by others. To this extent the framework provides a set of expectations, a prescription almost, of how good social work managers should behave.

Box 3.1 is an interesting list of what managers/leaders are expected or should aspire to do. Interestingly this list forms the principles that underpin the post-qualifying award in Social Work for management and leadership in England and Wales, to which we refer in the concluding chapter. It is therefore proposed that these activities should provide the foundation for education and training in social work management. As can be seen, the list of tasks and aims for the social care manager/leader represents to some extent generalities, such as valuing people (how is that done, specifically?) and in other respects summarizing a complicated set of contributory behaviours (e.g. developing joint working partnership; challenging discrimination). There are several issues to highlight in relation to using this list as a basis for social work management and leadership.

First, it is establishing a prescription for effective management and leadership across social care, regardless of the different contexts within social service. To that extent it represents a universal and prescribed approach. Second, as with other approaches, it conflates management and leadership (though in doing so it implies that both are necessary for effective social care organisation and delivery). Third, it locates leadership (and management) at the level of the individual – this is a list of what *individual* managers/leaders do. Fourth,

Box 3.1 What leaders and managers in social care do

- inspire staff;
- promote and meet service aims, objectives and goals;
- develop joint working/partnerships that are purposeful;
- ensure equality for staff and service users driven from the top down;
- challenge discrimination and harassment in employment practice and service delivery;
- empower staff and service users to develop services people want;
- value people, recognise and actively develop potential;
- develop and maintain awareness and keep in touch with service users and staff;
- provide an environment and time in which to develop reflective practice, professional skills and the ability to make judgments in complex situations; and
- take responsibility for the continuing professional development of self and others.

(What leaders and managers in social care do – TOPPS Leadership and Management: a strategy for the social care workforce, 2004; cited in GSCC, 2005: 4)

it focuses on conditions or goals – ensuring quality . . . ; promoting aims . . . ; providing an environment . . . – but not on the processes which bring these conditions about.

Lists such as these occur across professions and jobs more generally, in the shape of competency frameworks. They attempt to consider such positions from an objective viewpoint and to identify the component elements of a particular role. One difficulty in relation to this approach is the wide range of qualities and skills any one individual is expected to possess in order to be effective in the post under consideration. If we view this approach in social care as conflating management and leadership we already have one problem. Organizations are seen to need both leadership and management, and theorists (e.g. Kotter, 1990) accept that it is unrealistic for any one individual to embody all the characteristics of both effective managers and leaders, yet such a conflation implies this. The role holder is also expected to demonstrate strong individual qualities: inspiring staff; ensuring equality; challenging discrimination; valuing people; empowering staff. This 'almost iconographic notion of the leader, as a multi-talented individual with diverse skills, personal qualities and a large social conscience' (Bolden, 2004: 16) does present difficulties, not least that we are in danger, almost from the outset, of undermining people in such positions because of the over-ambitious, aspirational quality of such lists. No one individual is likely to be able to achieve all the desired aims. Bolden's critique of such frameworks concludes:

whilst the development of frameworks and standards can be a valuable way of encouraging individuals and organisations to consider their approach to management and leadership development, it is in the application of these standards and frameworks that difficulties often occur. When working with frameworks and standards there is frequently a temptation to apply them deductively to assess, select and measure leaders rather than inductively to describe effective leadership practice and stimulate debate. With an increasing awareness of the emergent and relational nature of leadership it is our opinion that the standards approach should not be used to define a comprehensive set of attributes of effective leaders, but rather to offer a 'lexicon' with which individuals, organisations, consultants and other agents can debate the nature of leadership and the associated values and relationships within their organisations.

(Bolden, 2004: 16)

We return to emergent and relational aspects of leadership in later chapters. The debate about the relationship between management and leadership, between managers and leaders, has a long history and continues, without reconciliation or common agreement as to what the differences are. There are more detailed discussions and debates about the respective roles of managers and leaders elsewhere, for example Bennis and Nanus (1985), Kotter (1990), Zaleznik (1977) and Kouzes and Posner (2002), which we will discuss in due course. To this point much of the discussion of both management and leadership is treated as gender neutral. It is only relatively recently that attention has been given to gender in management and leadership. This has come about largely for two reasons: first, in relation to equal opportunities and the representation of women in higher management posts; second in relation to different styles of leadership. This issue is discussed in Chapter 7, where we look at specific issues for management and leadership in social work.

Developments in management thinking; scientific management and human relations

It is not possible to isolate developments in management thinking from the social context in which they occur. This is an important point now in the age of globalization, electronic technologies etc. as it was a century ago with the rise of mass production and mass consumption. The late nineteenth and early twentieth centuries saw a move in western economies away from an agricultural basis towards an industrialized economy. This was accompanied by the growth in cities as people moved away from the countryside to take up more regular, less seasonal and potentially more remunerative employment in the new factories. This brought with it a focus on efficiency in the new factories, with the introduction of large-scale machinery, constituting a shift away from the previous small-scale, craft technologies. This period up to the middle of the twentieth century is characterized by the development of management techniques to promote efficient working in manufacture. The 'scientific management' approach of F. W. Taylor was popular throughout this time. Among the principles of his approach, as we detail in Chapter 5, was that the design and supervision of work should be separated from its execution, managers and supervisors being responsible for the former, employees for the latter. Ideas of innovation were the remit of managers, who were seen as the technical work experts, through the employment of scientific methods to study work. The application of such methods involved detailed analysis of any particular job or work routine, breaking down any task into its component parts and redesigning it to promote maximum efficiency. Employees were seen to be motivated by the prospect of greater financial remuneration because of their ability to work more productively when work was designed to be more efficient. These methods formed an important feature in the development of mass production as they could be applied on a larger-scale basis than the previous craft technologies; indeed there were considerable economies of scale to be gained.

Whereas the development of large-scale production requires a large investment in the plant and machinery necessary for various processes, the effect of scientific management was to simplify jobs, which became increasingly unskilled and therefore required little investment in training of staff to carry out their particular tasks. At this time there was a particular emphasis on regulation and stability and the belief in and search for universally applicable solutions to work or organization problems. This era also saw prescriptions of what management should involve, as indicated in Fayol's (1916) elements of management or tasks of managers (forecasting and planning; organizing the enterprise; commanding; coordination; control). Within the area of organization more generally (including organizations other than manufacturing) Weber's theories of administration, which we also discuss in Chapter 5, focusing on bureaucracy in particular, became popular again, emphasizing universal principles of organization and management.

Over time and through further research projects, most famously the series of projects that became known as the Hawthorne experiments (Roethlisberger and Dickson, 1964), the limitations of the mechanistic approach to management became more evident. Amongst other factors, including the work of Mary Parker Follett (1934 – a social worker and management theorist!) on coordination in work groups, this led to the development of the 'Human Relations' approach within management, which recognized the importance of social relationships at work, the varied nature of work motivation and opened the exploration of relationships between job design, work motivation and job satisfaction, thus providing an alternative to the notion that economic benefit was the sole motivator for employees. Other developments in this period included aspects of team and group dynamics and the inter-relation of technical and social systems (Trist and Bamforth, 1951).

In many respects in this period we still see attempts to develop generalized theories, that is, theories of management that can be applied regardless of context. It is only over time that approaches begin to emerge that take more notice of particular contextual variables, so-called contingency approaches (see Morgan, 2006). These approaches allow that some management techniques depend for their applicability on the environment within which a particular organisation operates or the particular technology that an organization utilises (see Pugh and Hickson, 2007). The distinction between mechanistic and 'organismic' organization is made by Burns and Stalker (1961), who highlight the stability or instability of the organization's environment as a key factor in determining how it should operate. Mechanistic organizations, with an emphasis on internal efficiency and regular routine, are appropriate in a highly stable, predictable environment. In a more uncertain or turbulent environment, an organic organization is more suited as it can adapt more readily to external changes – both by planning for these in advance and by being able to react positively when faced with unpredicted change. This notion of the more flexible organization is one we will return to in Chapter 6. In this chapter it is the mechanistic approaches that are more our concern. It is only through such and later developments that the importance of contingency approaches has gained fuller understanding and recognition. We can identify, throughout this time, the focus of each different approach. Thus approaches such as those of Burns and Stalker, and earlier of Weber, look at the organization fairly broadly, indeed very broadly if we are to take the organization's environment into account. Other approaches, though, are clearly focused in the individual – what the individual managers should do; or what factors motivate individuals; or *how* they are motivated, that is, the process through which they are motivated. In addition to the universal or generalized nature of much theory exemplified above, a great deal of this is prescriptive: details are given of how managers *should* operate; what they are prescribed to use as management techniques including techniques for managing people. There is a continuing quest for certainty and predictability in organizations; the assumption behind the prescribed approaches to management is that these will result in predictable outcomes, both in terms of the result of people's efforts and in terms of how effectively and efficiently the organization will achieve its objectives. Thus we are focusing specifically here on approaches that focus on the individual from the objective viewpoint and are underpinned by a concern with certainty and predictability. The universal view of management encouraged managers to take certain theories into consideration with the view not that some particular outcomes were possible but that they were (reasonably) certain to have the desired result, in other words they were 'scientifically' based. Whilst other less universal approaches develop, such as contingency theories, this does not mean that universal and prescribed approaches have been superseded. Unlike some natural and physical sciences, in which theoretical developments might render previous theories obsolete, the development of management theory, as in other social sciences, has a more 'layered' aspect, that is, one approach is laid down on top of another but other approaches continue and occasionally see a renaissance in popularity. So scientific management has not become outmoded and is alive and well in the process of delivering certain products such as fast food, and services such as those offered through call centres.

Defining leadership and management

As a later development within management thinking, various attempts began to be made to define leadership but extended research attempts have failed to provide a comprehensive or commonly accepted definition and we are beginning to learn that no such comprehensive definition will now result from further efforts. Some years ago Stogdill (1974: 7) remarked 'There are almost as many definitions of leadership as there are persons who have attempted to define the concept' but no enduring definition is agreed. Later, Senge (1999: 81) commented there is now 'a snowball's chance in hell of redefining leadership in this day and age', and debates about the relationship between leadership and management continue with recent recognition that a universally accepted definition is now unlikely and that, unlike management, in which the debate over definition is less extensive, leadership remains an 'eternally contested concept' (Grint, 2005). Gill (2006) reviews current thinking in leadership and usefully identifies a number of strands. What he too highlights is this lack of a comprehensive definition, let alone a universally applicable model of leadership, despite some claims to the contrary (e.g. Bass, 1997):

> No theory or model of leadership so far has provided a satisfactory explanation of leadership; indeed there is no consensus on the meaning of leadership in the first place. Many theories are partisan or partial, reflecting particular philosophical or ideological points of view. Many are based on limited or even biased research: the answers one gets depend on the questions one asks. As a result, the theories that emerge are often self-fulfilling prophecies and at best explain only some aspects of leadership.
>
> (Gill, 2006: 60)

Despite the debate over the impossibility of a definition of leadership, various authors have sought to differentiate management from leadership (Kotter, 1990; Bennis and Nanus, 1985). Usually, though sometimes unstated, the presumption is made that we have a common understanding of leadership even if it is difficult to define precisely. Some of the arguments about differences between management and leadership are more convincing than others. For example, Kotter (1990: 104) notes that 'management is about coping with complexity' whereas 'leadership, by contrast, is about coping with change'. Whatever such differences might be, there is general agreement that successful organizations need both leadership and management (Kotter, 1990). There are dissenting voices, however. Mintzberg (1975) represents the view that leadership and management are so closely intertwined that leadership can be viewed as a subset of management; in other words a leadership role is inherent in management positions.

Although in some respects the effect of the lack of commonly accepted definitions creates difficulties in using the concepts, there are those who argue that such a situation is beneficial in that a common definition would prove to be too restrictive and limit the potential that leadership seeks to develop (e.g. Alvesson and Svenningsson, 2003). If leadership is to be regarded as being principally focused on change and instability, as noted by Kotter above, this argument has some merit. However, this leaves us without an adequate answer to Barker's (1997) question: how can we develop leadership when we don't know what it is?

There is a growing consensus that leadership is related to a number of themes: being focused on the future; dealing with uncertainty and instability and therefore prospectively considering the ways in which organisational operations need to change; initiating, sustaining and helping maintain a certain amount of momentum through the change process. Some authors (e.g. Pettigrew *et al.*, 2001) have drawn attention to the need for leadership to balance stability and change, particularly at a time when organizational change in itself appears to be lionized. Management on the other hand is seen as being focused on efficiency, regulation, planning and performance. Both management and leadership, though, are increasingly seen as essential for effective organization.

Within social work in England, Skills for Care (the employer-led authority on the training standards and development needs of social care staff in England) has developed a Strategy for Leadership and Management (Skills for Care, 2008), which suggests that there is a continuum from leadership to management with an overlap of common activities (see Figure 3.1). The view of this strategy is that:

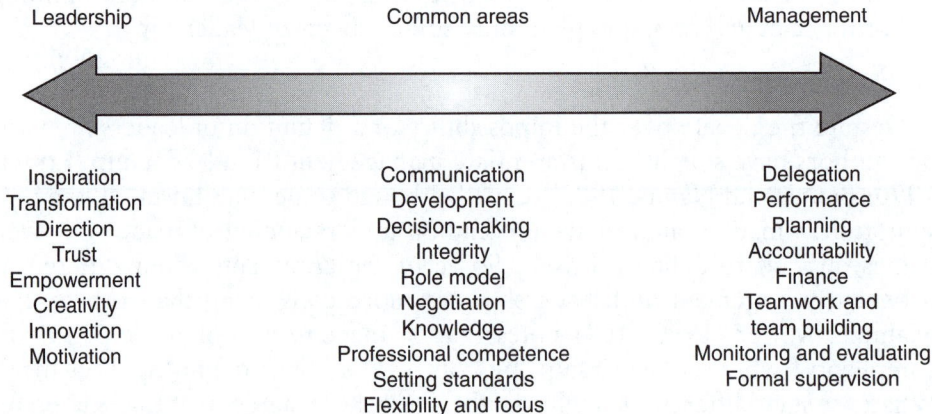

Leadership	Common areas	Management
Inspiration	Communication	Delegation
Transformation	Development	Performance
Direction	Decision-making	Planning
Trust	Integrity	Accountability
Empowerment	Role model	Finance
Creativity	Negotiation	Teamwork and
Innovation	Knowledge	team building
Motivation	Professional competence	Monitoring and evaluating
	Setting standards	Formal supervision
	Flexibility and focus	

Figure 3.1 Continuum of leadership and management. Based on Skills for Care (2008: 4).

Most leaders need management skills and most managers are more effective if they develop leadership behaviours and skills. Leaders need to help define management in their own organisation. Management could be seen as how people behave in relation to managing resources and the tensions between controlling, rationing and providing services that people want.

(Skills for Care, 2008: 5)

In pulling the two concepts of leadership and management together in this way this document continues to focus on the idea that management and leadership reside within individuals. The document goes on to recommend a whole systems model for management and leadership development. Whole systems approaches will be discussed further in Chapter 7, where the implications of their linear rational approach, which has a very limited use of organizational systems theory will be considered.

Whilst the debates on differences between management and leadership continue, much of the literature does not distinguish managers from leaders; rather it refers to leaders as people being appointed to leading roles, usually management roles. As long as these concepts are seen to reside with individuals, and as long as leaders are conflated with managers, the traditional mode of thinking around heroic leaders continues. We thus create the mental picture of leaders as individuals with particular charm or charisma who independently drive other individuals, groups or communities to successful undertakings.

Key theories of leadership

We will now leave behind the debates about the roles of managers and leaders and move on to consider a number of key aspects of leadership theory that are covered in the organizational literature (Figure 3.2). These will include:

- strategic vision;
- Theories X and Y and Theory W;
- 'Great Man', trait theories and further developments;
- transactional and transformational leadership;
- emotional intelligence.

Strategic vision

One aspect of leadership that merits acknowledgement is that of strategic vision, which is seen as fundamental to leadership (Gill, 2006). Leaders are seen as important figureheads in developing, articulating and communicating a vision for the organization (Kouzes and Posner, 2002). What is required is a view of how the organization will be at some future point: what its standing will be; how it will be viewed by others. It forms a goal for the organization to work collectively towards and sets the direction for the development of the

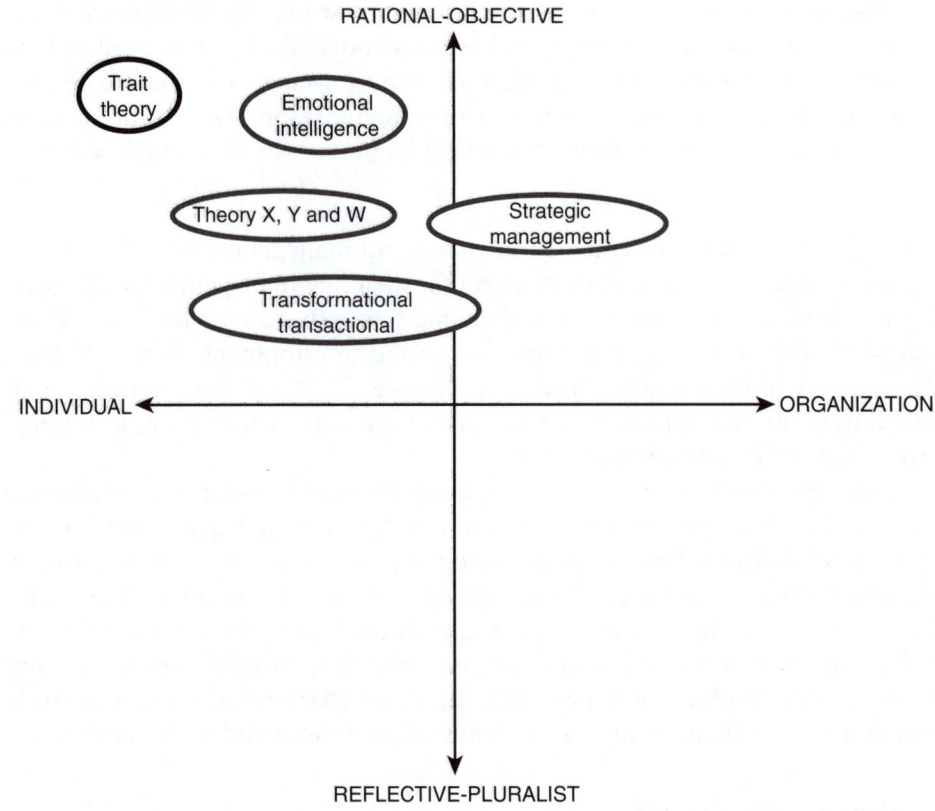

Figure 3.2 The rational-objectivist and individual quadrant.

organizational strategy – the plan to bring the vision about. To the extent that such 'vision' has an organizational focus, for our purposes it belongs more closely with the rational and objective approaches discussed in Chapter 7 where we discuss strategy. It merits comment here because it is often implied that the individual leader is the source of the vision, which is then used to inspire organizational members to action. A strategic vision is seen to appeal to organizational members because it presents pictures of how current difficulties might be resolved through a rational and persuasive solution, even if that solution presents as challenging (Kanungo and Conger, 1992).

Theories X and Y and Theory W

McGregor (1960) argued that managers held different sets of assumptions about their employees, which he described as two polarities X and Y, and that those assumptions directly affected the ways in which managers behaved towards their staff. What he called 'Theory X' managers, in his view, believe that employees are fundamentally lacking in any motivation, dislike work, are intrinsically lazy and need close supervision. In addition, such employees avoid responsibility and lack creativity. Managers who believe this are likely to manage and supervise in a very directive and autocratic way. On the other hand, 'Theory Y' managers believe employees enjoy challenge and responsibility and have the capacity for self-regulation and self-motivation. Managers who assume this are more likely to take a participatory and empowering approach to how they manage staff. Theory Y assumptions can be seen in the later approach of transformation leadership, which we discuss below. Both approaches take a rationalist view of the individual: they have different rationalities, on which their respective styles of management are therefore based. Shiba (1998) added a further perspective in developing what he called Theory W, following McGregor's lead. We noted above how both management and leadership are argued as being necessary in that successful organizations appear to deal directly with the tension between stability and continuity on the one hand, and change and uncertainty on the other. Shiba's 'Theory W' accommodates this in recognizing the duality of individuals, namely that they want both some security and predictability in the contexts in which they operate, together with the opportunity to act creatively and to contribute to future improvement in their organizations.

Trait theories and further developments

In relation to leadership specifically, initial texts used great national and international leaders going back through history as their source. Such work is characterized by the focus on the analysis and description of notable characters of wide renown: famous politicians, military figures and royalty; leaders recognized on a national scale at least. Efforts were made to identify which particular innate qualities such leaders possessed that separated them from the majority of the population. This focus on great leaders in national contexts is echoed in early work on leadership in organizations. This approach, known initially as the 'Great Man' approach (for the focus was almost always on a man), is founded on the concept of identifying someone seen as being outstandingly influential and effective – often heroic. This person's character was then analysed with the purpose of identifying the characteristics or traits that set 'him' apart from his contemporaries. The belief was that these people possessed some relatively rare and innate qualities that equipped them for leadership. They were largely seen as 'born leaders'. Although leadership might have become considerably more sophisticated in many respects, there is still a strong feeling in some camps that it is innate qualities of an individual, rather than any qualities or skills that have been learned or developed over time, that suit them for leadership. It was also felt that nations, communities and organizations needed such heroic leaders to inspire and enthuse their constituents in order for their respective communities to prosper. Such thinking is characterized as the trait approach, through its search for the essential traits of leadership. This approach received much attention in the first half of the last century and in some respects has seen a revival more recently. Over time different lists of traits, with some degree of commonality, have been developed but still no universal set of traits is agreed.

This notion of born leaders led to more thorough analysis of significant leaders in order to specify the particular behaviours of leaders and to develop these, rather than assume that leadership was simply an accident of birth. Behavioural approaches initially challenged trait theories directly and sought to identify crucial leadership behaviours – what effective leaders *do* and therefore how leaders should behave. At the same time there was the increasing recognition that the challenges faced by leaders varied according to the context in which they operated and thus a focus developed on the appropriate leadership *style* or behaviour for that context. Situational leadership, however, stressed that there was no single effective style of leadership but that different styles were more or less effective and appropriate to different situations. Contextual differences included differences in the staff in that situation, that is, different levels of skill and motivation in different individuals and groups of 'followers'.

Transactional and transformational leadership

Transactional leadership (Burns, 1978) concentrates on the exchanges between leaders and their staff, for example offering particular rewards (such as a pay bonus) in exchange for meeting a particular standard of performance. It includes a focus on issues such as contingent reward for a certain standard of performance, or taking action only when performance falls below expected standards. In sum this approach tends to lead at best to performance up to but not beyond a desired and expected standard. Transformational leadership (Bass, 1985) on the other hand, highlights the importance of leaders demonstrating such behaviours as idealized influence, inspirational motivation, intellectual stimulation and individualized consideration, with the aim of stimulating performance beyond standard expectations (Northouse, 2007). In terms of the management versus leadership debate above, transactional leadership might be seen as another term for management, with transformational leadership constituting leadership. As with other discussions on the relative values of management and leadership, there are some authors (e.g. Kotter, 1990) who argue that both transformational and transactional leadership are essential in effective organizations. Models of transformational leadership attracting particular attention can be found in the US in the works of Bass (1985) and in the UK – in a public service context – in the work of Alimo-Metcalfe and Alban-Metcalfe (2001). These approaches identify important dimensions of leadership (qualities and behaviours) on the basis of empirical work. Both have developed 360-degree feedback instruments. This form of feedback collects information on a range of identified leadership dimensions, usually in the form of anonymized questionnaires, from a group of people. This is around six people in total, including the person's manager, two or three peer colleagues on the same organizational level and two or three staff who report to the individual concerned, thus providing a rounded, or 360-degree, perspective. Both current and aspiring leaders can use sets of characteristics or personal qualities and behaviours, such as those noted in the above, in this feedback process. In this way they can gain an idea of how they are perceived and how they are progressing, and can identify areas for their own further personal development. This feedback process is an increasingly important factor in the development of current and potential leaders (Alimo-Metcalfe *et al.*, 2000).

The approaches of works such as this reflect the important distinction made by Shamir (1995) between distant and nearby leaders. As noted, earlier 'Great Man' approaches set the trend by focusing on particular figureheads with whom the majority of individuals had no inter-personal contact or relationship. Such figures represent 'distant' leaders as opposed to 'nearby' leaders, with whom we interact on an inter-personal level. Shamir notes that descriptions of distant leadership are characterized by a focus on vision and charisma and extraordinary qualities of communication. Studies of nearby leaders, on the other hand, are more focused on everyday behaviours and their effect on, for example, levels of motivation and commitment and of job satisfaction. The idea of a nearby leader gives more attention to the effect of leaders on others and to the needs of those others. In addition it brings the quality of the relationship between leaders and their staff into greater focus. This leader–follower relationship is an important aspect of the transformational model of leadership and is reflected in the models used in the 360-degree feedback approaches noted above. Northouse's (2007: 176) definition of transformation leadership is: 'a process whereby a person engages with others and creates a connection that raises the level of motivation and morality in both leader and follower' and 'treats people as full human beings' (2007: 175). As such it has a clear moral element within it. This is not the only approach to leadership that has a strong moral theme; for example the concept of Servant Leadership (Greenleaf, 1970) similarly emphasizes a moral dimension and the drive to serve others first and to lead next, rather than the reverse.

The role of charisma in leadership has attracted attention over time. Weber (1947) makes note of the importance of charisma as part of his schema of authority. Other, later theorists developed theories of leadership based on charisma that were seen as being particularly appropriate where there was a great need for morale building and a challenging vision. In some respects charisma has been subsumed by transformational leadership. As an approach to leadership in its own right, it has become less popular not least because of the recent disasters in organizations seen as being headed by charismatic leaders (Bolden, 2004). However, charisma remains an important dimension within transformational approaches to leadership.

Emotional intelligence

A relatively recent and popular development within leadership thinking particularly has been the emergence of interest in the concept of 'emotional intelligence', developing earlier notions of 'social intelligences' (Thorndike, 1920; later Salovey and Meyer, 1990). Its popularization in the management and leadership literature owes much to the work of Goleman (1996, 2001), who defines emotional intelligence (2001: 317) as 'the capacity for recognising our own feelings and those of others, for motivating ourselves, and for managing emotions well in ourselves and our relationships'. Martinez (1997: 72) argues that emotional intelligence can be viewed as a competence: 'an array of non-cognitive skills, capabilities and competencies that influence a person's ability to cope with environmental demands and pressures'. This follows a tradition going back to trait approaches and continuing in some ways in the development of competence approaches to management and leadership.

Goleman (1996) develops this concept in his Emotional Competence Framework, which comprises self-awareness, self-regulation, motivation, empathy and social skills. There are similarities with the notion of IQ (Intelligence Quotient) reflected in the label 'EQ' (Emotional Quotient). In a similar way this is seen to be measurable by breaking down the above factors into specific 'competencies' such as self-confidence, self-assessment, adaptability, achievements drive, understanding others, political awareness, influence, collaboration and competence.

EQ is concerned with recognizing our own emotional states and those of others and dealing with – managing – feelings and expression appropriately. Unlike the related concept of IQ, which is seen as being established at a fairly early stage in life, EQ is regarded as a range of competencies which can develop and be developed over time (Dulewicz and Higgs, 2000). This approach, then, demonstrates that an aspect of ourselves that may be seen as quite intangible can be made more manageable by objectifying it, that is, developing a framework and developing quantitative measures (e.g. questionnaires), which can present a score for an individual across a range of items that are seen to make up each component. It adds to the approach of objectivizing leadership qualities.

Summary of approaches to management and leadership

Grint (1997) summarizes the development of leadership thinking and the limitations of the major strands of theory over time. The focus was initially on the person and neglected context. Whereas other models took some account of this, often there was inadequate accounting for sufficient individual and other contextual differences. According to Grint, at different times leadership is seen as being focused on four elements: the *person* or individual as leader; the *results* of leadership; the leadership *process* and relationships; and the organizational *position* of the leader. This different focus has been part of the reason for the lack of an enduring definition. This difficulty is added to as there is no consensus within each of these four areas on what leadership represents. Gill (2006) notes that leadership research has taken different routes to examining the phenomenon: 'cognitive, spiritual, emotional and behavioural' (p. 60); but the spiritual aspects of leadership are less often the focus than the other three. He cites Greenleaf (1970) as giving this attention. One might also suggest Block (1996) as following a similar theme although, interestingly, not naming the phenomenon 'leadership' in as direct a way, referring instead to 'stewardship'.

The focus on the person and on position in leadership studies, as noted by Grint above, includes trait approaches to leadership, which we have already noted. This approach itself is seen largely as inadequate to analyse and describe leadership in its entirety. The general focus of this approach, though, continues with some credibility. Thus the focus on the individual can be seen in approaches such as the Multi-Factor Leadership Questionnaire (Avolio, 1995) and Alimo-Metcalfe and Alban-Metcalfe's (2001) Transformational Leadership Questionnaire. In both cases, certain characteristics are seen to be essential characteristics of effective leadership. In relation to leadership and position, Grint (1997) refers to people who have been appointed to specific posts that are seen as having leadership responsibilities, perhaps a Chief Executive or someone with less seniority, such as a team manager who might still have some leadership responsibility. The individual is seen as having some capacity to influence other people due to one or more of a range of factors: their personal charisma; the strength of their relationships with people around them; their specialist knowledge, expertise or reputation; their personal integrity or trustworthiness. This is different from the manager working from a basis of positional authority, someone who operates on the basis of their position in the organizational hierarchy. In Weber's terms this person operates on the basis of legal-rational authority: others are prepared to defer because of the authority delegated to the position and thus the position holder.

This constant search for an all empirically based, encompassing theory of leadership is eloquently described by Connor and MacKenzie-Smith (2003: 60):

> We can best describe the way 'leadership' has been tackled as butterfly catching. Researchers, management theorists and practitioners have brandished their nets in an effort to find the genuine article. After netting a wide variety of species, some of which were truly attractive, they turned their attention to finding the rarest of specimens in particularly demanding or exotic ecosystems. Once caught, the interesting butterflies were pinned and labelled. The differences with lesser varieties were noted. However, having pinned, labelled and classified, the essence of leadership remained as elusive as ever. All of these approaches share a similar frame of reference. They have taken leadership as an objective 'reality' and worked to identify common aspects such as behaviours or competence. Even those approaches seeking to identify less tangible aspects, such as values, personality traits or even emotional intelligence, have tried to establish leadership facts.

Leadership and power

It is important to note here one aspect of leadership and management that is explicit in some related literature and less so in others, namely that of power. Power is inextricably linked with management and with leadership, however defined. Approaches that belong in this chapter typically make the assumption that power resides in individuals and is exercised, consciously, by those individuals. This is evidenced by Gill (2006: 245):

> Managers get things done through using authority, manipulation ('politicking') or influence. They motivate people by using various forms of power. Power is the ability to influence the thoughts and actions of another person or group of people.

A very commonly used framework for examining power used within the management and leadership literature, is that developed by French and Raven (1986) in which they distinguish five sources of power (Box 3.2).

This approach is based on the assumption that power resides in particular individuals – is it something they *have* and can exercise through choice. It is to some extent attributed to them by others with whom they interact: one cannot individually claim, for example, referent power as one might claim role power. Nevertheless the exercise of power is largely seen as a singular, linear process: the direct influence of one person on another.

The issue of power is important in organizational life and, as such, merits attention in any text on management and leadership. Early work on power and authority is based on the work of Weber (1947), who identified different sources of authority or legitimate power: traditional – that which was obtained typically through inheritance – literally being born into a position; charismatic – which resided in the personality of the individual; and rational-legal – that which came with the position within the hierarchy to which a person is appointed. His work on charisma in particular influenced later writers on leadership. His comments on rational-legal authority still resonate in relation to the authority that managers have within organizations because of their position. His comments on traditional authority perhaps ring less true now than they did at one time when, for example, the mill owner's offspring inherited the mill on the owner's retirement or demise, but within some areas of industry and politics references are still made to 'dynasties' prolonged through inherited power. Within the context of social work, itself the context for varied discussions on power (e.g. Hugman, 1991; Webb, 2000) the topic is dealt with in varied ways. However the predominant way in which power is dealt with in many standard management texts (e.g. Buchanan and Huczynski, 2007) is also reflected in social work management texts. Here power is seen in a rather uni-dimensional way: power emanates from particular sources for use by the individual manager in influencing staff. Thus more complex, dynamic and less explicit ways of considering power (e.g. Lukes, 2005) often go unregarded.

Box 3.2 Sources of power

Legitimate power: which stems from the position someone is given by a legitimate authority. For example, we may respond to a request from our manager because s/he has been given authority by the organization to make decisions and to take certain actions.

Coercive power: the ability to influence someone through the threat or actuality of delivering negative consequences (including withholding positive consequences) if a certain line of action is not adhered to.

Reward power: the reverse of coercive power in that the enticement to certain action is the knowledge that positive consequences will result from compliance with someone's suggestions or direction. The positive outcomes include both material gains (e.g. direct payment or promotion) and less tangible gains (such as respect or acknowledgement and thanks).

Referent power: this indicates a source of power based on the individual and the general acknowledgement of their personal influence. It may be based on their individual experience or reputation or their general charisma. People will concur with a suggestion from a person exercising this form of power when they agree on the basis of who makes the suggestion – their view or judgement is trusted because of who they are.

Expert power: this is seen when we agree with a certain direction because of the person's technical or professional knowledge. We may not like this person but we agree to their suggestions because of our trust of what they know.

Adapted from French and Raven (1986).

Texts dealing with management issues in social work that follow a similar line include Hafford-Letchfield (2006a: 28), for example, who sees power as part of a process exercised 'to ensure people act according to the rules' and cites the French and Raven typology of power as above. Coulshed and Mullender (2006) take a similar managerial and restricted view in citing Weber's work on power and authority as noted above. Later, in their discussions on taking a systems view of organisations, they do note that it is important not to overlook the 'bigger questions of power and powerlessness' (p. 48) but these are not discussed in any detail. They too cite French and Raven's typology and point to the 'responsible use' (p. 112) of power and note the situations where power might be abused in the organizational context. Martin and Henderson (2001) make similar points and also highlight the need to empower service users in making decisions about their care, but the concept of power itself is not discussed in detail. The relatively powerless position of users, especially in the residential care context, and the possibilities for abuses of power here are also discussed by Skye *et al.* (2003). In each of these applications in the context of social work organization, power is dealt with in a linear rational fashion.

Communication in management and leadership

The issue of communication is an important process within management and leadership, which is analysed and theorized in different ways. Here we focus on how communication is interpreted at the individual level. When viewed from the individual and objective perspective, communication is generally seen as an unproblematic concept in itself (though it is seen as potentially complicated), largely a linear process whereby information, about a range of issues, is 'transmitted' from one party to another, received and understood (or not as the case may be) and information is likewise transmitted back. The focus of concern is with modes of communication and ensuring that the message being transmitted is received, understood and accepted. This might involve, for example, 'communicating the vision' (Kotter and Heskett, 1992) that leaders and managers have developed, so that members of the organization are clear what the aim of the organization is. Indeed communicating the vision of the organization is seen as a prime constituent of many leadership theories (Antonakis *et al.*, 2004). In addition to communicating the content of any strategic vision, which would be a relatively simple transaction, it is argued that the vision should be communicated in such a way as to inspire others who receive the communication, so that they are committed to achieving the vision through their work activities (Gill, 2006). Thus there is the implication that communication is concerned not solely with *what* is being communicated but with the process – the *how* of communication and particularly the role of this in influencing people.

The means of effective communication in management and leadership are detailed by some; for example, Kakabadse and Kakabadse (1999) note the different channels of communication used by effective managers and leaders. They argue that communication has two purposes in relation to leadership: to provide direction (as in communicating the strategic direction of the organisation) and to provide example, that is, how the leader behaves is seen as a strong indication of the leader's integrity. They highlight the different means of communication from face-to-face discussion and personal emails to meetings, communication cascades etc. that are available for leaders and managers to communicate with different parts of their organizational networks. According to this theory, how they are seen to behave will have a significant impact on how the recipients respond to the communication. The notion of communication as a necessary skill in management and leadership is highlighted in different ways. For example, studies of the daily activities of managers (see Buchanan and Huczynski, 2007) indicate that a substantial part of the manager's time is taken up in inter-personal communication; by implication, managers need to be skilful communicators. Management competencies similarly highlight communication as being a set of key skills for managers and leaders (Bolden *et al.*, 2003).

Communication is key within social work practice, most notably between social worker and the user of services. Exploration of communication within that relationship is beyond our scope here but the issue of communication within social work organizations and between organizations involved in social work has always been most important and receives increasing attention today. Repeated inquiries into child protection tragedies have highlighted inter-organizational communication and its failures as being significant factors in certain child fatalities. Similarly the importance of communication is recognized in inter-professional, inter-organizational partnership in delivering services for older people.

In the context of dementia teams, Manthorpe and Iliffe (2005) note the importance of communication in diagnosis and in promoting a disability model of dementia in inter-agency working and also in the therapeutic process in service delivery. In child protection, Reder and Duncan (2003) note that communication is often used as a synonym for coordination or partnership or collaboration: meaning the ways messages that (should) impact on service delivery are transmitted and received between organizations. They note how often this is cited in investigations of failures in child protection. For their purposes, they distinguish communication from these other terms, as they argue that communication refers to interpersonal transactions rather than (inter-) organizational activity, which is better described by the other terms used. Reder and Duncan also cite the factors that interfere with effective communication between agencies, based on the evidence of other research. Such factors include lack of clear definition of responsibilities, the protection of organizational/professional boundaries, the quality of existing relationships between agencies, competition between agencies over resources and resource allocation, professional and organizational priorities, different value systems and different levels of respect of organizational and professional reputations and expertise. Overall they argue that calls for restructuring child support services miss the point about communication and that supervisors and managers may have a more important role than is currently acknowledged. Supervision, they argue:

> is also an ideal opportunity for practitioners to review how they communicate with others and to rehearse, for example, giving messages clearly, reporting to a child protection conference and keeping accurate but succinct records. If supervision is used as a reflective learning process (Reder and Duncan, 1999; Munro, 2002), the practitioner could be encouraged to think systemically and to hold in mind other professionals who are relevant to the case.
>
> (Reder and Duncan, 2003: 97)

White and Featherstone (2005) also note the call for restructuring in child protection to facilitate better inter-organizational communication. Managers become responsible for restructuring and themselves are located in the same site rather than being geographically dispersed. The aim of better communication is not necessarily achieved by this as professional boundaries, in particular professional identities, remain largely intact and present real barriers to communication. They argue the need for reflective practice, which we would argue can be extended to reflective management, in order that the cultures within which professionals operate can be reviewed and developed as a direct aid to communication. The role of social work managers and leaders is key in this. The issue of culture goes beyond an individual perspective to organizations and is discussed further in Chapter 7.

In some of our work on leadership within social work we have noted the different themes pursued by writers in this area (Lawler 2007), one of which is that of social work leadership, referring to the leadership and coordination of inter-professional activities, something that is noted as necessary by other writers but largely not in evidence; in other words, other professions appear more strongly represented in this area of work. Bisman (2004) notes the strong moral basis of social work as being a good foundation for leadership and cross-agency communication in social work. Mohan (2002), however, argues that the profession overall lacks the credibility to take on such a role on a systematic basis. On that basis we might see occasions when individual social work leaders are sufficiently notable as individuals to take on this role but the profession as a whole is significantly less so. There is a significant challenge then for social work managers and leaders to take on what appears to be a neglected role in leading and enabling effective communication across and coordination between agencies.

The underlying theme throughout the approaches that we classify in this quadrant is that of means and ends: management and leadership are seen as the means through which to achieve organizational results in the shape of more effective and/or more efficient organizational performance. The attributes, qualities and skills of the individual leader or manager are seen as being the means, when applied to others (i.e. employees), to achieve organizational ends. The *process* through which ends might be achieved receives far less attention and is an issue to which we shall return in later chapters.

4 The reflective individual in management and leadership

> Having been facilitated to explore the negative and controlling aspects of the work they undertake as managers, and the ways in which the organization controls and dominates them, some may find instigated in themselves a form of rebellion against or resistance towards the organization. Rather than return to their daily work determined to lead employees to greater productivity and higher conformity, they may do the opposite and return determined to bring about changes of a different kind. What those are cannot be predicted. We can surmise only that there are possibilities that the leadership style evoked may just as likely be that of a quiet revolutionary as that of the more effective manager.
>
> (Ford and Harding, 2007: 488)

Introduction

This chapter will now consider theories and approaches to leadership that focus on the individual's participation in leadership and management rather than the individual as leader or manager (Figure 4.1). Despite the dominance of the views of leadership we saw in the last chapter, approaches covered here are gaining significance on account of the restricted perspectives offered by traditional approaches to leadership and management. Major changes, including globalization and the increased use of information technology, render old models of direction and supervision inadequate. Also with the demise of traditional organizational authority and as organizations continue to 'delayer' – to remove layers of management – other methods of motivation and influence that draw on all the human resources of the organization or team become necessary. Similarly as we move increasingly to a knowledge economy, knowledge management has assumed a priority and again, given its intangible and invisible nature, other models of leadership are now required. Sbarcea (2003) notes the need to reconsider management and leadership in an era of complexity and change. *Direction* of staff is no longer adequate: the role of the manager and leader is now to notice and support emergent process in organizations, to encourage autonomy and to create opportunities for staff to inter-connect in ways that traditional organizational structures do not enable. Although these are general trends with regard to organizational leadership and management,

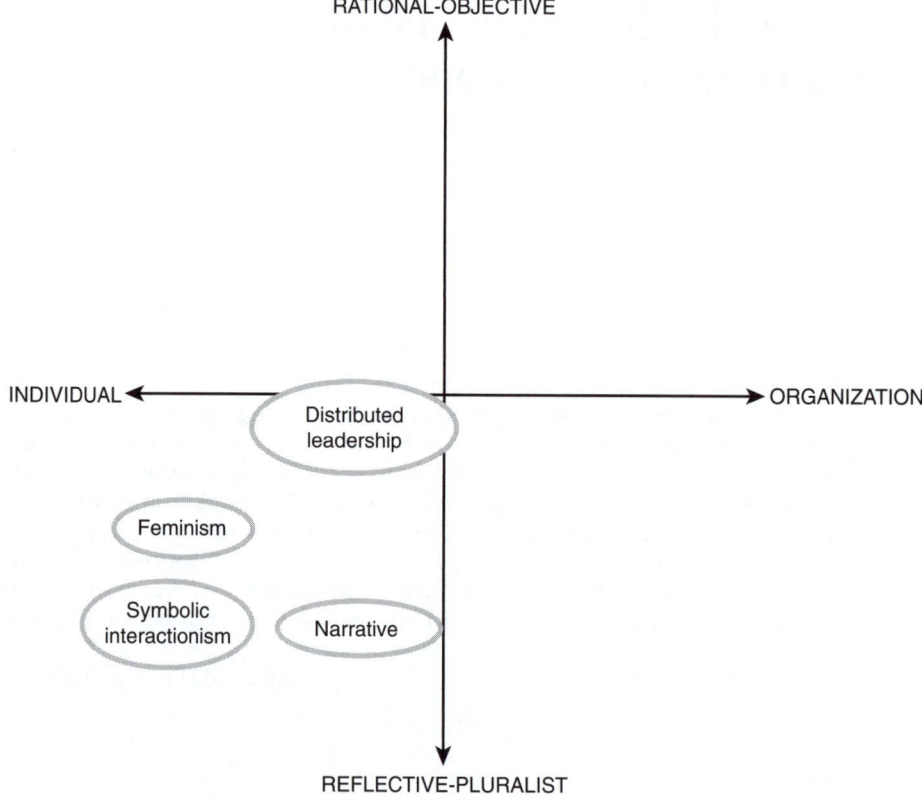

Figure 4.1 The reflective-pluralist and individual quadrant.

similar trends and influences are visible in social work. Parton (2004), for example, highlights increased complexity in children's services due to changes in each of the following areas: globalization and identity; systematic care, responsibility and accountability; managerialization; trust and uncertainty; and the rapidly changing nature and complexity of legislative contexts.

There are a wide range of approaches to leadership that can be seen to fall within this section of our classification (Figure 4.1). These tend to have different philosophical or sociological underpinnings which reject a naïve realist view of the world. Because of the importance of this grounding we will start by discussing some of the philosophical underpinnings of theories and approaches in this sector. We will discuss social constructionism and existentialism and their implications for views of organization as two representatives of this range of underpinning philosophies. We will then go on to discuss some specific theories and approaches. These include the work of Weick and colleagues on sense-making in organizations; its relationship with a narrative approach to leadership is particularly concerned with dialogue between colleagues in the work context. Following this we will look at the development of distributed approach to leadership, which includes both individual and organizational elements. We also discuss feminist approaches to leadership with a particular emphasis on the individual's view of the organizational world from this perspective.

Philosophical underpinnings

The approach to management and leadership that we explored in Chapter 3 takes an objective, rational approach to the study and practice of management and leadership. However, in social work, situations are frequently messy and have significant moral and emotional depth. Thus Olive Stevenson in her minority report on the inquiry into the death of Maria Colwell said the following, which we see as equally true several decades later:

> There are few, if any, situations of the kind in which Maria was involved which are 'black and white' . . . there are very few situations in which choices are clear cut and outcomes predictable. Unhappiness in children is something which the ordinary humane person finds very difficult to bear and, in consequence of this, frequently seeks simple solutions or suggests that they are attainable.
>
> Olive Stevenson (Maria Colwell Report, Secretary of State for
> Social Services, 1974: para. 316)

We believe that one of the things that lead to the belief in simple solutions, which we see time and again in criticisms of social work activities, is the rational and objective viewpoint towards organization. In contrast, approaches required to deal with this increasing complexity can be described as interpretivist and/ or constructionist. Thorpe provides a helpful distinction of the rational and constructionist approaches:

> Rational–analytic approaches seek to explain social experiences by isolating and classifying elementary parts or variables and understanding how these function within mapped, causal chains of influence. Constructionist–synthesis approaches understand explanation as materializing from description, where description involves appreciating and recounting social experience through forms of involvement within that experience, whether participating in real time or second hand, through the study of narrative accounts.
>
> (Thorpe, 2008: 116)

He is keen to point out that this is not necessarily an ideological difference, though it is treated as such in some quarters. Allowing for a variety of approaches helps us understand better the phenomena we are exploring and assists in the development of more effective practice. Thus it is not limited to an intellectual exercise but provides us, as practitioners, with a set of different analytic tools to examine our own management and leadership practice and that of others. The category of reflective-pluralist we see as broadly parallel with Thorpe's constructionist–synthesis category of approaches. Taking this view, we see an organization not as an external and concrete reality that can be clearly defined and identified but as something that will be interpreted and experienced subjectively in many different ways by the people who interact within the boundaries of organizational life. To that extent then we are not relying on one external reality of management and leadership but regarding them as being socially constituted (Grint, 1997). In considering management and leadership from this perspective, 'emphasis shifts from a belief in a scientific and observable reality, to a socially constructed reality, with emphasis on meanings and symbolism' (Rickards and Clark, 2006: 103).

The approach favoured by much traditional writing on leadership and management regards the manager/leader as the active person in the relationship whereas others are seen in a much more passive way, as the label of 'followers' implies (e.g. Kellerman, 2008). In this chapter, we move from this passivity to a view of management and leadership, particularly the latter, as dynamic processes that are not constrained by universal and generalist descriptions of the respective roles. This focus on individual and reflective aspects of leadership and management also enables us to look beyond regarding leadership as occurring only where people are formally appointed to roles with 'leadership' responsibilities, an approach by which only leaders are seen to exercise leadership. It is much easier to see management in this way because of the management responsibilities that are inherent in many positions. However, conflating management and leadership positions restricts our understanding of leadership and the leadership process. It does not allow for people taking leadership roles regardless of their organizational status. The interest in alternatives such as that of 'leaderful' organizations (Raelin, 2003) helps us appreciate leadership from a much more rounded perspective. Leadership can happen outside and beyond the formal organizational relationship. In most if not all organizations of any size, each position is acknowledged to have a specific relationship with other positions, as is usually demonstrated on the organizational chart. One generally knows who one's manager is: such lines of responsibility and accountability are laid out from the onset. (We also acknowledge that it is possible in some situations, especially in professional organizations, for one individual to be responsible to more than one more senior colleague or manager.) Leadership might rely on a different quality of relationship, different sources of influence, from the more organizational-based authority associated with management. It is this relational aspect of leadership together with viewing leadership as emerging within organizational relationship and activities that form the main themes of approaches in this chapter.

This echoes the thinking of other writers (e.g. Gold *et al.*, 2003; Barker 2002) who consider leadership as an emergent process, rather than something captured by universal definitions that determine what it is and how it operates from the outset. Despite the important aspects of leadership provided by traditional and objectivist research and models, such objectivist approaches to social relations have particular limitations. For example, Cooper (1999) argues that the traditional disengaged, disinterested research approach leads to 'standard accounts' of the world, useful in some respects in considering social relations but only up to a point. They present generalizations and do not capture the complexity and variety of social interactions, or the different individual perceptions of those involved. The individual and objective models of leadership that abound in the approaches covered in the last chapter provide evidence of such 'standard accounts' of leadership, described in different leadership models or competences. These do not, though, reflect in any depth the 'lived experience' of leadership in its various settings and at its various times. Leadership is not always carried out by designated leaders, does not necessarily take the 'heroic' form of the rational-objectivist approaches and is not necessarily concentrated in the same individuals over time. At the same time, leading involves not only leaders but followers. The perspective of others involved in leader relations, particularly their subjective experience, is notably absent from such accounts. Such people are clearly crucial to the effectiveness of leadership in practice. It is this perspective that writers such as Pye (2005) note as needing further exploration for a fuller understanding of leadership and a more effective means of separating leadership from and linking it with other important aspects of organization, such as organizational culture and other forms of social influence. She sees a lack of emphasis on social relationships and the changing contexts within which they operate within much organizational literature. The uncertainties and the interpersonal dynamics in organizational life are acknowledged in her comment: 'What remains key to this conception (of organizing) is the emphasis on relationships between actors and developing context over time which ensures leadership is situated and seen through the improvisational dynamics of moving *to* the future' (2005: 32, original emphasis).

From the reflective-pluralist viewpoint many aspects of organizations, including communication, power, vision and culture, are seen in a different light. If we begin to look at management and leadership as being less about an individual and more about dynamic and creative roles and processes, we begin to see different possibilities. We can, for example, begin to allow for people creating their own roles as managers and leaders, creating meaning for themselves in their own contexts and creating meaning in their interactions with other people. This makes it possible to see other people with whom we interact in a different light. We would begin to see roles, relationships and interactions in a much more dynamic and uncertain way. When we move away from universal, objective ways of seeing management and leadership, to consider the relational aspects of these roles, that is, the personal and interpersonal elements involved in these roles, there may be far more interpretations and appreciations of effective leadership than we allow for currently.

Relationship in management and leadership: alternative perspectives

The approaches we considered in Chapter 3 take an essentialist approach. Their main premise, as expressed by Thorpe in the quote above, is that through research we can identify the different components of leadership, the different traits or characteristics crucial for effectiveness. The approaches we consider here start from a different premise. We draw here on themes from existentialist thinking and social constructionism (seeing recent application in the context of leadership, e.g. Lawler, 2007; Ashman, 2007; Tourish and Jackson, 2008) to give insights into relational aspects of management and leadership.

Existentialism has as a core theme, the notion that we as individuals have no essence that determines our being and whom we become. In simplified form, this is contrary to many preceding ideas that the essence of something exists before that something is brought into existence, which is the premise of the approaches in the preceding chapter. This approach questions ideas of human 'nature' that predetermine our lives. In relation to management and leadership, this line of thinking challenges the idea that leadership is an entity in its own right and that the characteristics of leadership can be identified and inculcated in others. Rather it sees leadership as the label that can be attached to a particular relationship by those involved in the relationship once it develops and not at the outset. It is here that this approach concurs with that of social constructionism. Constructionist thinking is interested in how concepts develop in their social contexts (Berger and Luckmann, 1966). Thus in some contexts certain concepts might not apply or indeed be recognized by those from another context. So, in this line of thinking, we might expect a concept such as leadership to mean different things in different contexts and for its definition to vary according to culture.

Unlike a managerial relationship, a leadership relationship is not necessarily recognized from the beginning of the relationship; it might be possible to designate a fruitful leadership relationship or to identify a good leader only during or after the process. We might see that someone has the skill and ability and motivation to be seen to lead or to influence others but, until they do so, we have no guarantee. Furthermore, although someone might prove their leadership ability in some contexts and certain times, this too is no guarantee that they will be regarded as effective leaders in another context or at another time. The history books indicate that public figures seen as being effective at certain times are deemed to be less so at other times or in other contexts. Thus the leadership role may be more situationally defined than the management role, which might endure as long as the post holder is in position.

The notion of *becoming*, of the lack of a static *being*, is a core issue within existential thinking. Our own self is viewed as not a static and complete being but a self that is continually developing or 'becoming'. We make choices of varying degrees of importance constantly throughout our lives. These choices are seen as the action we take in the world. This is the core of the existentialist view of 'being in the world': we can never see ourselves as separate from the world; we constantly are affected by it and affect it in turn. The concept of the self here is as a being situated in the world and constantly interacting with it. This is not a view of the self with inner and outer aspects, a 'real' self and an external projection of that onto the world. We are what we choose to do, how we act and interact constantly in the world. The existential concept of the self is one of a conscious and aware being, able to act and live 'in the moment' and with constant freedom to choose whom to become, despite the objective physical, social and temporal constraints under which we operate.

The constructionist view is different again in that it acknowledges a variety of 'selves' as the notion of 'self' is seen as a construction. We take up and resist various selves as a result of the contexts in which we live and work. Constructionism, in particular, places the emphasis on 'reality' as that which is experienced by the individual her- or himself: it does exist as an outside, objective entity.

Both approaches look at the 'self' in a dynamic way, one that is significantly influenced by the different physical, temporal and social spaces we inhabit. To that extent we are conscious beings 'who participate(s) in the construction of reality' (Yablon, 1980: 24, cited in Klugman, 1997: 303). So existential-ism provides the perspective of consciousness of the present situation and of future intention to act, whereas constructionism enables reflection and aware-ness of influential factors both past and present. In this way we have more than one means of including the subjective perspective in our understanding of management and leadership, which provides further opportunity for a fuller understanding. One might argue that such approaches could be included under the 'organization' rather than the 'individual' heading. However, we argue for the value of these approaches at the individual level to allow for individual reflection, prior to a more collective approach using these perspectives.

This theoretical approach informs our understanding in a number of ways. First, it accepts that definitions and interpretations of leadership vary, con-trary to the approaches that list essential characteristics of effective leaders and managers. The difficulty presented by this latter approach is that it can be restricting, because it confines leadership to a particular set of dimensions and does not necessarily allow for what might be needed in particular, differ-ent contexts. It can also be disheartening in that it presents an ideal that few if any individuals can live up to. Second, the reflective-pluralist perspective accepts that an understanding of the local culture and context is of great value in managing and leading effectively and that someone who does not necessarily possess the 'heroic' characteristics included in leadership models discussed in the last chapter may be a very effective leader. Thus people can still oper-ate as effective managers and leaders in their local situations even if they are quite idiosyncratic in some respect, provided they have a detailed and sensitive understanding of the local context and the agreement of people with whom they work about what actions and behaviours are appropriate. Third, it stresses the importance of language and communication and so encourages discussion and dialogue. This can lead to consensual local constructions of leadership as a reciprocal process (Lambert *et al.*, 2002), an aspect that will form part of the discussion of dialogue, which will be developed next.

Dialogue in management and leadership

What we mean by dialogue in this context is the open interaction, largely through language, of one person with another. The constructionist approach views language not as representational in itself, that is, not just as directly reflecting 'reality', but as a way of constructing that reality. A word such as 'chair' is not a simple reflection of an item we use to sit on. It is a generic description of such, but not everything we sit on is a chair (e.g. a stone, a sofa, a bench). Nor might a chair be interpreted in exactly that same way in all contexts (e.g. what does 'chair' mean in the context of the US penal system?). Through language we, intentionally or otherwise, create common understanding, which can change over time, through the developing use of language. Our dialogue brings things into existence. For further examples, consider how concepts such as 'child protection' have come into the language and are used to signify particular phenomena. In this case, the constituent parts (e.g. 'child abuse') may not themselves be new phenomena, though elements of them are: such concepts are interpreted, construed, constructed in different ways over time through the development of the language that is used to describe it and its associated processes. Furthermore, in addition to transmitting information and aiding the construction and articulation of concepts, language has the power to influence us personally, what is termed by some as 'social poetics' (e.g. Katz and Shotter, 1996; Cunliffe, 2002). This means that language can transmit feeling as well as more concrete information and that the process of dialogue itself, because of the interpersonal exchange, creates something new, new individual understandings that can affect people emotionally and intellectually. We know we can be 'moved' in an emotional manner by a particular experience, personal or artistic; similarly our dialogue with others can be 'moving' in the sense that it alters some aspects of our being. This might affect the quality of relationship with the person with whom we are speaking; or produce a change in our understanding; or lead to the development of a new perspective or idea. Cunliffe (2002) argues that dialogue is a creative process that itself aids the construction of reality, that is, it helps us form and make sense of our social experience. Thus dialogue both examines and clarifies unique, individual experiences in contrast with generalized or universal understandings or prescriptions. Shotter and Katz (1998) take a similar view that the process of discussion does more than explain these experiences and, as with Cunliffe, is more than representational. Dialogue is a form of action by which all participants can be affected, a process through which understandings of organizational life develop, beyond the predictable and ordinary. As we noted above, such conversations go beyond the simple transmission of information but are part of a formative, constructive process, affecting, as they do, relationships, interpretations, understandings and meaning and in some respects, as Shotter and Katz refer to it, effecting a 'change of being'.

Dialogue, then, is not merely a process of disclosing information or impressions, though that is an element, but it is the creation of new interpretations and understandings occurring in the 'conversational space' between people where meaning is clarified. Taking this approach and jointly constructing shared meanings releases individuals from the restrictions of prescribed roles. This in turn presents the opportunity to examine what might be created individually and in relationship with others. As Shotter (2005: 122) explains:

> It is in such living moments between people, in practice, that utterly new possibilities are created, and people 'live out' solutions to their problems they cannot hope to 'find' solely in theory, in intellectual reflection on them'.

He refers to 'knowing' from this process as 'knowing of a third kind', that is, not developing knowledge by adding to facts – knowing *that* – or skills – knowing *how* – but 'knowing from within'.

From the existential perspective, Buber (2002) sees dialogue as the key to creating 'inter-subjective' understanding, that is, that individual understanding is used as the basis for fuller understanding rather than being an end in itself. Both existential and constructionist approaches point to *potential*: both of individuals and of relationships. It is largely because of this that these emergent approaches go beyond the static, objectivist approach, which seeks to define and prescribe as the end point. These approaches allow for a variety of definitions and then take that as a starting point rather than a goal: to consider what can be developed from that point.

Management and leadership: sense-making and meaning

> An approach premised on rationality and logic misses the power of the symbolic: to assume that symbolic processes are irrational and perhaps resistant to rational investigation or deliberate application, is to place symbolic leadership alongside discarded superstitions of the inspired charismatic leader.
> (Rickards and Clark, 2006: 112)

The issues of the management of meaning and sense-making in organizations are important concepts that contrast sharply with approaches founded on an external rationality such as those we have considered as being presented by objectivist views. Smircich and Morgan (1982) were interested to explore some of the complexities of organizational life in terms of the meaning people developed and attached to certain people, roles and events in organizations. They focused particularly on emergent aspects of leadership: behaviours, beliefs and understandings that developed in their organizational context – which emerged, rather than following a particular prescription of how things ought to be. They argue that leaders emerge in unstructured situations, through the social process of leadership relations and through helping others make sense of the situation they are in and of their actions within that situation. This helping to make sense grows to the extent that others look to these individuals more and more to interpret the situation, to define 'reality' and in doing so interpret the situation less for themselves, thus surrendering authority to leaders to make sense for them, to *manage meaning*, in that respect. 'Individuals in groups that evolve this way attribute leadership to those members who structure experience in meaningful ways. Certain individuals . . . take a leadership role by virtue of the part they play in the definition of the situation' (Smircich and Morgan, 1982: 258). In more structured settings, in formal organizations with appointed managers and leaders, the leadership process, they argue, becomes depersonalized and the reality as defined by senior figures is often accepted without much questioning. From Smircich and Morgan's perspective, the leader continues to have great influence in providing meaning in the organizational context – s/he becomes the symbol for what the organization stands for and how it operates. The leader in this context makes sense of the situation facing the employee, makes sense of operational strategy and actions in the sense of creating a particular logic or rationality for sets of actions. There is, however, a need for engagement with staff whereby interpretations and meanings emerge. There are other possibilities, as we shall go on to discuss, for developing shared meaning in a more productive, less instrumental way.

Muldoon (2004) notes a key aspect of leadership as: 'the effectiveness of a leader lies in his ability to make activity meaningful for those in his role set (Pondy, 1978: 94)' (Muldoon, 2004: 9). Muldoon also points to a range of approaches within leadership that are not covered by orthodox leadership models. These he refers to as the 'Fifth Paradigm' in leadership thinking (the others being trait theory; leadership style; contingency theory; and transformational–transactional theory), which includes a range of approaches in which making sense and managing meaning are crucial aspects. Muldoon summarizes sense-making as 'a psychosocial creation, not some objective reality awaiting discovery' (2004: 9). In addition to sense-making occurring at the individual level, meaning is something that can only attributed by individuals to a particular event or set of behaviours. Thus effective leadership, in this perspective, is something that can only be defined by individuals on a subjective basis. They may seek other evidence to support their view, or to refute the views of others, but the subjective perspective take precedence over any other objective data.

> Theories and models in this paradigm stress uniquely human abilities to create and interpret meaning in leadership events, to examine differential meanings of the same leadership event, and to analyse and comment upon leadership events through the veil of culturally impregnated language.

No other approach to leadership takes meaningfulness as its predominant *raison d'être*. Yet meaningfulness is arguably among the chief distinctive features of being human, and even more so of the phenomenon of leadership.

(Muldoon, 2004: 23)

Closely related to the meaning-making process on leadership is that of sense-making in organizations. An important figure in the literature on this is Weick (1995). His approach to sense-making has certain crucial components including:

- That it is *retrospective* – we make sense of things in relation to other things that have already happened and it is continuous as we reframe certain issues and make a different sense on occasion with hindsight. We also project our sense into the future to frame our future actions.
- That it is related to the *construction of our own identity* in that we judge situations and make sense of them in relation to our sense of self, what in the situation might challenge that or how we can use the situation to enhance particular aspects of our selves.
- That it takes place in a *social context*: the interpretations and sense that others make of situations and events influence the sense we make ourselves.
- That *coherence* is an important future: consistency of events and the sense we gain from them need to make a coherent 'story' as it were. We acknowledge that this might be plausible rather than comprehensively convincing but we need to be sufficiently sure of its coherence for our actions and understandings in the current context.

Weick *et al.* (2005) note that, among other things, sense-making is a social process and a central component of that process is communication. Weick pays particular attention to the ways in which communication between people creates shared understandings of relationship between different parts of the process or organization and that collaborative sense-making creates far wider understanding than could be achieved for any one manager or leader. He uses a quotation from the work about air traffic control, to illustrate this:

If one looks to see what constitutes this reliability, it cannot be found in any single element of the system. It is certainly not to be found in the equipment . . . for a period of several months during our field work it was failing regularly . . . Nor is it to be found in the rules and procedures, which are a resource for safe operation but which can never cover every circumstance and condition. Nor is it to be found in the personnel who, though very highly skilled, motivated and dedicated, are as prone as people everywhere to human error. Rather we believe it is to be found in the cooperative activities of controllers across the 'totality' of the system, and in particular in the way that it enforces the active engagement of controllers, chiefs, and assistants with the material they are using and with each other (Hughes *et al.*, 1992).

(cited in Weick *et al.*, 2005: 418)

This is a particularly important when applied in the social work context with its attendant complexities and uncertainties and when considering the succession of initiatives to improve rules and procedures or to focus the cause of failure on single individuals.

The elements above of retrospection, identity, social context and coherence all help make sense of difficult and at times chaotic circumstances. These aspects are particularly important in the narrative approach to leadership, which we discuss in the next section. Grint (2005) notes that in a non-essentialist approach, which is that taken here, there are many interpretations from the many different individuals involved in management and leadership relations and so there can be no comprehensive objective account or profile of the manager or leader. There are many subjective realities of management and leadership rather than one objective reality.

Gaining access to these different realities and interpretations requires different levels of engagement and communication from what is referred to in standard management approaches, which tend to view communication as the transfer of information, as we have already discussed. As Lambert (2002: 65) puts it, 'It is in the conversation that we find shared meaning'. Thus meaning is not created, dictated or managed by those in senior positions but is created jointly in the conversation, establishing a common understanding of the dialogue in a spirit of reciprocity, not one that is based on covert agendas or is founded in influence through organizational power. It has a common purpose and is not pursuing a predominantly private agenda.

> It is the genuine pursuit of understanding as it exists in the moment and within the context of the conversation, the relationship, the community. This means, of course, that this understanding will be context influenced and developmental; therefore it will change with time.
>
> (ibid.)

Her view of conversations is that they are characterized by 'shared intention of genuine "truth-seeking", remembrances and reflections of the past, a search for meaning in the present, a mutual revelation of ideas and information, and respectful listening' (p. 65). This does not mean to say that every exchange involves all these, but that continuing conversations are characterized by those elements. Counter to prescriptive approaches, here conversations are regarded as 'verbal improvisation' (Schön, 1987: 30–1), not following a preordained script or structure but the means of creating something with its own meaning. In this respect such conversations are very different from other means of communication – directives, instructions, speeches, information transmission, persuasion – which lack this interactive meaning-making capacity.

Lambert *et al.* (2002) identify four categories of conversation: sustaining, personal, inquiring, partnering. Each category has a slightly different focus but all have elements in common. Cooper sums up the difference between dialogue and other more superficial communication in that she argues dialogue and the stories that we tell each other convey emotion as well as fact and are both more memorable than facts and more likely to 'move' us. Dialogue and the narrative that it helps create, as we noted above, have three particular virtues: first they create connections across difference; second they help provide a structure for how we think, perceive and imagine and therefore ultimately choose our actions; and third they 'elicit and clarify tacit knowledge' (Cooper, 2002: 116). In the next section we go on to discuss approaches to leadership that explore these issues of meaning, interpretation and dialogue. Prior to doing so we need to note the increasing attention given to the notion of *authentic leadership*, as our interpretation of that concept relates closely to dialogue and narrative leadership. There is undoubtedly a rise in the attention given in leadership studies to *authentic leadership* (Sparrowe, 2005). We have concerns about the promotion of this concept in the form of an individualized and static morality that is being promoted as the new advance in leadership to address contemporary problems. A further concern is in bringing together leadership and authentic as a single construct, which arguably over-simplifies both.

The literature on authenticity appears to treat the term as a synonym for honesty, integrity or genuineness and to that extent few would argue against it. But if it is no more than a synonym we must doubt its value as a new concept. It is also seen to represent an inner, 'real' self as opposed to the self who operates in the outer world and interacts with others in that context. So the developing orthodoxy on authenticity assumes a 'true' self that might not always (or ever?) be evident to others. As such it represents a contrary position to that taken in this chapter. Additionally, it is difficult to differential authentic from transformational leadership as it may be seen as a component part or closely related concept (Bass and Steidlmeier, 1999) and is based on personal character and qualities, as in trait approaches to leadership. Despite the developing attention given to this concept there appears as yet to be little criticism of the approach in general. The work on authenticity appears to pay little attention to the part played by individual choice: whom we choose to 'follow'; how we choose to 'lead'; how we choose our values. If authenticity is seen as a trait then it rather predetermines these other elements; that is, choice plays little part. This is not, though, to dismiss the concept of authenticity but to suggest it has other interpretations. Also there are some contributions to discussions on authentic leadership that feed into our discussions here on conversations and dialogue.

In other work, we have examined authenticity from an existentialist perspective (Ashman and Lawler, 2009), which provides an alternative interpretation. From this view authenticity is seen as emerging from interactions with others:

not as a precondition for interaction but as its product. Thus inter-personal dialogue forms a key part of authenticity, which relates closely to the issues of sense-making and dialogue, as discussed above, and narrative leadership, which we go on to discuss next.

> If leadership is to be authentic, in acknowledging our condition of freedom and choice, we need to be able to make sense of that with others in the leadership process – not relying on leaders to impose sense or to make sense *for* others but to engage in narrative or dialogue, to make sense *with* others. Such dialogue is needed to promote authentic leadership.
>
> (Ashman and Lawler, 2009: 15)

Narrative leadership

Muldoon makes the following comment concerning narrative and leadership: 'Followers and leaders together create the story of organizational life, the mechanisms of which are illuminated by theories in the symbol/meaning literature' (Muldoon, 2004: 24). The narrative approach recognises the centrality of relationships and inter-relationships to our understandings of leadership. It uses inter-personal dialogue to explore the sense we make of leadership; in a manner of speaking, the 'story' of leadership from our perspective. Ochberg argues that:

> Lives, like stories, are the way we fashion ourselves: encountering and temporarily surmounting the projected demons that would diminish us. This is what a narrative perspective allows us to notice: not only about the way we talk, but also about the way we live.
>
> (Ochberg, 1994: 143)

We have been involved for some time in developing a narrative approach to leadership development (Ford and Lawler, 2007; Lawler and Ford, forthcoming), which has been successful in developing new insights for participants and which we draw on in this section.

> Feedback from some of the leadership development workshops that we have facilitated indicates that participants find the storied nature of the workshop sessions of considerable benefit in generating new insights into shared and inter-subjective understandings of their role as leaders and participants in the leadership process. This has led to participants generating a range of creative plans for their personal development but, as importantly, has established an enhanced dialogue with a range of colleagues. In this way . . . leadership development, can be viewed as continuous and integrated activity, not sectioned off into a formalised process, separated from the everyday work environment
>
> (Lawler and Ford, forthcoming)

Inter-personal discussions and the recognition of the narrative we are creating, and of which we are a part, present the opportunity for reflection. Dialogue is a crucial element in forming our narrative, dialogue being the largely unfettered interaction with other individuals that helps us to develop our own individual narrative or narratives. This approach to leadership thus emphasizes the importance of dialogue and structured conversations with others in the leadership process. So, although we initially construct individual narratives, we do so through dialogue, in relationships with others. We may then contribute to the development of collective narratives around leadership in our own organizational context. This involves discussing with significant others, past achievements and failures as well as present activities, plans and aspirations for the future. In this way the narrative goes beyond the 'standard accounts' of leadership. The individuals who choose to be part of this process have opportunities to discuss what their roles mean to them rather than work to prescribed competencies or dimensions of leadership and management. The process thus presents the opportunity to explore locally constructed and locally interpreted meanings. 'Concepts and things will have the meanings they do only through membership of an immense network which, however many of its elements we care to articulate, will remain as a whole *unsurveyable*' (Cooper, 1999: 52, italics in original). So this constitutes a narrative exploration of leadership activity 'in the world', 'unsurveyed' in more general approaches, rather than a conversation in relation to a framework abstracted from its context.

We noted our concern with the developing consensus around authentic leadership in the section above. We do note, though, that there are some inter-personal elements within that literature that apply in relation to leadership relations. Mazutis and Slawinski (2008) refer to the four capabilities that are increasingly seen as crucial parts of authentic leadership as being *self-awareness, balanced processing, self-regulation* and *relational transparency*. We have concerns with the notion of authentic leadership as an objective concept, as we have noted, in that it is a further essentialist approach to leadership: looking at what the leader has and does to demonstrate his or her own authenticity. The narrative approach to leadership moves away from this essential basis of what a leader *has* or *is*, to consider the possibilities of authentic futures: future actions, relationships etc. informed directly by individual and collective values. The capabilities referred to by Mazutis and Slawinski are of value in relation to narrative. *Self-awareness* refers to knowledge of our own skills, abilities, values, ambivalences, contradictions etc. and also to our capacity to develop. *Balanced processing* refers to the ability, in reflecting on feedback about oneself, to see this in an unbiased and undistorted way, that is, not simply to confirm views one had already formed. *Self-regulation* refers to transparency of the individual's values and motives in the eyes of others and to the coherence of actions with those values. *Relational transparency* refers to the ability to disclose clearly one's aspirations, values and intentions to colleagues. This 'builds trust and intimacy, foster(s) teamwork and cooperation' (Mazutis and

Slawinski, 2008: 445). We feel this is the most important of these capabilities for narrative leadership.

The practical process of this approach uses a framework of conversations and reflections. Conversations take place between the individual concerned and a number of 'significant others'. These conversations form the basis for reflection. These in turn are used by the individual to consider implications for their own practice and development. The process is similar to the 360-degree process we referred to in Chapter 3 but without the preordained dimensions on which such feedback is based. So this narrative process asks individuals to focus on the meaning of their work and role and how leadership practice and relationships are co-constructed within their own organizations. As such this approach deliberately avoids rigid definitions or frameworks of leadership and management. It pays attention instead, to the constructed meanings and experiences of organizational life in general and leadership in particular. Leadership is thus seen predominantly as a social process, in which meaning is made through inter-relationships within the individual's own network.

> The adoption of this approach to leadership within an organization requires the creation of opportunities for ongoing dialogue between those in explicit leadership roles and those in other roles. Power and structural relationships will continue to define the dominant discourses, but continuing conversation and dialogic communication can facilitate the development of perspectives beyond these restrictive regimes of 'truth'. Such an approach would form a response to those within some of the critical management writings which call for a strong ingredient of management of meaning (Alvesson 2002, Smircich and Morgan 1982), in which greater attention to the above factors is given.
>
> (Ford and Lawler, 2007: 420)

From the discussions in this approach it is intended that participants have a heightened awareness of the different interpretations of leadership and the influences on those interpretations and that they have begun a continuing process of development of leadership within their own context. This notion of sharing of understandings and continuous development of leadership is also a theme within approaches to distributed leadership, which we consider next.

Narrative leadership is seen by some as having both a prescriptive and an iconoclastic role – the latter to challenge current practices, behaviours and interpretations and the former to give direction to new understandings (Fleming, 2001). Fleming argues that narrative leadership can be used effectively in applying Weiss's (1999) elements of sense-making: diagnosing, communicating and adapting. Diagnosing involves using the narrative in operation currently to highlight particular points – to support the desired culture or to challenge existing practice, to draw out a particular development point. Communicating involves developing further stories and interpreting narratives in relation to other organizational issues. Adapting means using the concept and language of flexibility in narratives, to illustrate the need for constant adaptation. These elements appear closely linked with the capacities of Mazutis and Slawinski (2008) outlined above but with less of an emphasis on the value base of the individual concerned. Fleming's approach is focused on those in formal leadership positions but the same points can be made in relation to people who are in less overtly powerful positions: they can identify current narratives, produce reinterpretations and support change through their own developing narratives.

Sparrowe (2005) argues for a 'narrative self', that is, a self we constitute through the dialogue we have with others, not a self abstracted from the world and relationships. The self in this way is seen not just as a continuous entity but as one with contradictions and paradoxes:

> Rather than treating the self as identical through time and events, narrative portrays the self as the subject of a myriad of experiences in the form of a story-like account. The narrative self is not a constant self, identical through time, but the subject that experiences change, reversal, and surprise. Narrative discloses the self not as consistency or continuity, but – to use Ricoeur's (1992, pp. 141–142) logically awkward term – as 'discordant concordance'.
>
> (Sparrowe, 2005: 426)

Sparrowe explains further that narrative helps to develop connections or relationships between events that are not immediately obvious, replacing 'one thing after another' with 'one thing because of another' (Sparrowe, 2005: 425). In this way those individuals involved in leadership relations begin to develop an understanding of a logic of events. This collaborative facet of leader relationship, of making sense with others, is applicable on a broader collaborative basis in considering distributed leadership, which we go on now to consider.

Distributed leadership

We are focusing on the individual here but we need to expand that to consider how individuals relate and interact with other individuals. This has two dimensions to it. The first is how the individual relates to other individuals on a one-to-one basis, through individual dialogue as we have described above. The second is the inter-relation of a number of individuals, and the most appropriate means of examining this in practice is to acknowledge the contribution of distributed leadership. In this approach, leadership is seen as a function distributed between or dispersed among the individual members of the work community rather than being concentrated in one manager or leader. To that extent one might argue that this belongs at the collective rather than the individual side of line of distinction. That would be a fair point but we include it in this quadrant because of its foundations of individual subjectivity building to shared understandings and meanings. These approaches most definitely belong in the emergent rather than prescribed category of management and leadership.

Gronn (2000: 323) discusses social cognition in distributed leadership and the relationship of the individual to the wider social context: 'Central to the view of socially distributed cognition is the idea that mind and mindfulness are not solely features of the interior mental life of individuals, but are manifest in jointly performed activities and social relations', and it is this manifestation that presents our primary reason for including this approach in this quadrant. The second justification is also provided by Gronn (2000: 325) in that '(distributed) leadership is more appropriately understood as a fluid and emergent, rather than as a fixed, phenomenon' and it is *meaning* particularly that is negotiated, discussed and agreed. From this perspective, leadership can be viewed as being distributed both horizontally, that is, between organizations, and vertically, that is, throughout the organizational levels within each organization (Brookes, 2008).

The particular shift in this approach is from focusing on *leaders* to thinking about *leadership*. Influence does not reside only in organizational position but occurs throughout the work community. Leadership occurs through different people at different times and on occasions through several people at the same time. Thus distributed leadership presents a very different model from the heroic, prescribed approach. The focus is on the process of interaction and how leadership is enabled throughout the work community. As it gives high regard to the particular context and the individuals within that, it is inevitably an emergent and varying phenomenon rather than a universal prescription.

The need to go beyond the individual model of leadership is also highlighted by Ancona *et al.* (2007: 94), who note the impossibility for single individuals to possess all the qualities for effective leadership in organizations, and they similarly argue for the development of others through a dispersed leadership. The key elements needed are:

> four capabilities: *sensemaking* (understanding the context in which a company and its people operate, as we have already discussed), *relating* (building relationships within and across organizations), *visioning* (creating a compelling picture of the future), and *inventing* (developing new ways to achieve the vision).

With the possible exception of visioning, all these elements can be seen as relevant in relation to the constructionist and existentialist approaches discussed above. Ancona *et al.* argue that individual managers need to examine their own capabilities in each of these areas and suggest different means of engaging other individuals to develop each of these capacities more widely in the work organization. All of these involve dialogue with others and the development of respectful relations that encourage further development on all sides. As an emergent and interpretive phenomenon there can be no prescriptions for how distributed leadership is conducted:

Distributed leadership in theoretical terms means multiple sources of guidance and direction, following the contours of expertise in an organization, made coherent through a common culture. 'It is the "glue" of a common task or goal – improvement of instruction – and a common frame of values for how to approach that task.'

(Elmore, 2000: 15)

The distributed perspective focuses on *how* leadership practice is distributed among formal and informal leaders. As Bennett *et al.* (2003: 3) note, 'distributed leadership is not something "done" by an individual "to others"'. Distributed leadership is then clearly based on establishing firm relationships and is seen as a set of practices, such as those noted above, rather than specific traits, characteristics or behaviours. Rather it is 'an emergent property of a group or network of individuals in which group members pool their expertise' (Gronn 2000: 325).

Spillane (2006) notes that distributed leadership practice has three dimensions: collaborative, in which people are working together largely within the same space and at the same time; collective, in which separate individuals work independently yet inter-dependently also; and coordinated – a recognition of interdependency and the need for sequencing or organization. There is a similarity here to components in Raelin's (2003) approach to distributed leadership. He places particular emphasis on what he refers to as leader relationships in *leaderful* organizations. The four 'traditions' of leaderful practice for Raelin are:

- *concurrent* practice, in which the manager deals with the specifics of particular situations and the flexibility to adapt to different situations; the role of team facilitator is important here also;
- *collective* practice, in which the manager/leader acts as steward, is learner her/himself and facilitates meaning-making and clear interpretation;
- *collaborative* practice, in which dialogue is valued and promoted, individuals act as change agents and mutual influence is exercised; and
- *compassionate* practice, which relies on trust and strong inter-personal relationships, in which individual and collective conscience is respected and social and individual wellbeing is a legitimate concern.

Johnson and Johnson (2003) detail the particular elements involved in distributed leadership, drawing on the considerable work in the area of group and inter-personal relations. The basic assumption is that goals can be accomplished most effectively and continuously if attention is given both to achievement of the tasks and to the maintenance of positive social relationships. Thus the distinction is made between two categories of behaviours necessary to maintain group relations and activity: actions that are orientated towards *goals* (task focus) and those orientated to towards *relationships* (maintenance). As leadership is distributed, any individual within the work group can take on these functions at any time. Although this distinction between task and maintenance is made in the context of distributed leadership, the dimensions and the distinction between them are very similar to style models of individual leadership, such as Blake and Mouton (1978), in which people orientation and task orientation are seen as the main factors. However, in the distributed leadership context, various aspects of each dimension are presented in greater detail and the attendant behaviours are not restricted to us by one individual or in relation to one organizational role (Box 4.1).

This approach demonstrates the different and necessary functions of distributed leadership. This occurs in an emergent way, that is, functions are not allocated to specific individuals but are adopted by different individuals at different times when each is seen to be appropriate by members.

In one respect one might suggest that this latter approach to leadership belongs in the objective rather than subjective category of leadership theorizing. We could choose to regard it as a prescriptive list of required behaviours for distributed leadership and, if we restricted its use to that of a formula, it would indeed belong in that objective category. However, if we regard this set of functions as a means towards an end of developing leadership relations, increasing meaningfulness and sense-making in communities, it can be seen as sitting more appropriately as a reflective-pluralist approach – it promotes the development of pluralist understandings. It is with the view of plural understandings that we move on to consider feminism in relation to management and leadership. We include feminism within this section as we believe the individual interpretation of the role of gender within work is important. With that in mind we discuss feminism as individual experience rather than as imposed or defined from the external world.

Box 4.1 Distributed leadership functions

Task functions	*Maintenance functions*
Information and opinion giver	Participation encourager
Information and opinion seeker	Harmonizer and compromiser
Starter	Tension reliever
Direction giver	Communication facilitator
Summarizer	Process observer
Energizer	Inter-personal problem solver
Reality tester	Evaluator of emotional climate
Evaluator	Standard setter
Diagnoser	Active listener
Coordinator	Trust builder

Feminism

> Our point is that the predominant values and ideas in our society, embraced not just by many men but also by many women (in particular those occupying or who are candidates for managerial positions), need to be thought through in a deeper way than is encouraged by what may be referred to as a 'narrow' gender vocabulary. Such profound rethinking goes far beyond issues of sex ratios or the employment of feminine leadership. Such values and ideas, like growth, exploitation of nature, hedonism, affluent consumption, careerism – firmly anchored in the material operations of capitalism and market economy – seem to be the major constraints to radical transformations.
>
> (Billing and Alvesson, 2000: 144–5)

Feminist critiques of the patriarchal nature of much management theory and practice add much to the approaches to leadership in this chapter. Thus Alimo-Metcalfe (2004: 161) says:

> Leadership research like most, if not all, of the research in management, has been gendered. Studies from the days of 'The Great Man/Trait Theories' to the emergence of the 'new paradigm' charismatic and transformational models, have been the studies of men, by men, and the findings have been extrapolated to humanity in general.

In Chapter 7 we will look in detail at the specific issues for women managers within the current managerialist framework of much social work management. Here we will focus on how feminism provides a powerful perspective for considering management and leadership for men and women. This is not to say that the implications will be identical for men and women. Thus Yoder points out that:

> both definitions of leadership and the context in which leadership is enacted put gender front and centre in our discussion, and we must never lose sight of the facts that the leaders we are discussing are women, that doing leadership may differ for women and men, and that leadership does not take place in a genderless vacuum.
>
> (Yoder, 2001: 815)

Our intention in including feminist approaches within this chapter is not to write solely for or about women but to consider its implications for management and leadership as a whole.

We also recognise that feminism does not have a singular voice but is multivocal and offers a range of perspectives. Thus Parker (2004: 9) states:

> Feminist perspectives critique the persistence of male dominance in social arrangements and advocate some form of change to the status quo . . . However, despite the common focus on critique and change, there are a range of feminist approaches – Liberal, radical, psychoanalytic, Marxist, socialist, poststructuralist and postmodern and postcolonial – that vary in their ontology, epistemological positions and degree of political critique, and therefore vary in the type of influence on leadership theory.

So our aim here will be to introduce some key ideas that we find relevant and useful to the individual perspective on leadership and management and we will leave it to others to give a fuller overview of both the theoretical perspectives and their implications more widely.

Feminism sits within our reflective-pluralist framework for a number of reasons. First, much of feminist theory challenges the rational-objectivist position and values a range of voices of those who are oppressed. It has also made a range of contributions to pluralism in organizational studies (for example see Marshall, 2000).

In her influential text *The Female Advantage,* Helgeson (1990) described what she called the 'feminine principles of management'. These are characterized as caring, making intuitive decisions, and viewing leadership from a non-hierarchical perspective. Helgesen argues that women tend to think of organization in terms of a network or web of relationships, with leadership at the centre rather than the traditional masculine hierarchical thinking. In a similar vein Fletcher's (2001) model of 'relational practice' provides evidence of a practice based on the feminized qualities of connectedness, empathy, emotional sensitivity and vulnerability. According to Binns (2008: 601) 'the 'relational ideal' defines leading as a practice of caring for colleagues, enabling others to act, acknowledging and learning from one's mistakes and being emotionally authentic.' It will be seen that these characterizations of female leadership challenge the dominant masculine discourse of the 'heroic leader'. Fletcher's work in particular creates a description of how women do leadership differently building on a reconceptualization of leading as social practice. In her research she identified four types of relational practice which, although they were found in her study of women engineers, seem very apposite for social work. These were:

- *Preserving*: Preserving the project through task accomplishment;
- *Mutual Empowering*: Empowering others to enhance project effectiveness;
- *Self-Achieving*: Empowering self to achieve project goals; and
- *Creating Team*: Creating and sustaining group life in the service of project goals.

(Fletcher, 2001: 48)

According to Fletcher *preserving* included activities aimed at promoting the life and well-being of the job and doing them with an attitude of 'doing whatever it takes' (2001: 49) even where this means surrendering some status or putting aside personal agendas. Her interviews revealed that this included a range of relational activities including minimizing power and status differences, being inconvenienced, and even doing unpaid work where the project required it.

Mutual empowering activities enable others to 'produce, achieve, and accomplish work-related goals and objectives' (Fletcher, 2001: 63). They are characterized by a willingness to put effort into outcomes that support and develop other people such as increased competence, increased self-confidence, or increased knowledge. Thus they have a focus on empowering another person. This relational activity is characterized by fluid power relations and a focus on interdependence. Mutual empowering behaviour is based in the belief that it is worth working for the support and development of others and that everyone needs and should be able to expect this kind of help. Thus there is an implicit belief that others should adopt this orientation and be willing to give and receive help. It also requires 'an ability to operate in an environment of "fluid expertise," where power and expertise shifts from one party to the other, not only over time but in the course of one interaction' (Fletcher, 2001: 64). Thus this area of activity requires nominated leaders not only to share their expertise in ways that are accessible to those they work with, but also to be willing to be influenced by and learn from others by stepping out of the expert role.

The third form of relational activity, *self-achieving*, revolves around maintaining relationships and using relational skills to enhance one's own effectiveness. It is different from other relational activities because of its focus on the self and the use of relational activities to promote strategies for enhancing personal efficacy. It involves urgency in mending relationships and preventing disruption in them. Within this activity there is a particular focus on emotions. Thus:

> Spending time and effort reflecting on the emotional complexity of situations indicates a belief that emotions are an important source of information, both about oneself and about situations. Using these emotional data to understand ambiguous or confusing circumstances helped the engineers develop what they perceived as more effective strategies in dealing with situations. It allowed them to choose their battles and to avoid unintentionally creating obstacles to their own effectiveness and ability to achieve results.
>
> (Fletcher, 2001: 73)

The research found that women needed an ability to live with contradictions in feelings and motives. For example, women in the study lived with the contradiction of feeling good about getting recognized and feeling bad about how it was done, and through recognizing this contradiction a new strategy was able to evolve. Thus, this activity requires an ability to blend thinking, feeling and action, and engage in holistic thinking. In this sense it is seen to bridge the emotional/rational divide.

The final form of relational activity, *creating team*, involves fostering group life. The focus is on creating a general experience of team rather than the more usual management approach of team building, which focuses on creating team identity. Fletcher (2001: 81) sums this up as follows:

> the activities that characterize this fourth category of relational activity are a blend of attending to the individual – creating growth fostering conditions *within* people – and concern for the collective – creating growth-fostering conditions *between* people. Implicit in these efforts is the belief that individuals have a right to be acknowledged or noticed as unique and that part of what it means to be a good coworker is to do the noticing. In practice, this meant listening to others even when they did not feel like listening and taking others' preferences, situations, and pressures into account when making decisions. Rather than action motivated by strong affect, this behavior appeared to be a strategy based on a belief about the potential benefits of working this way – a belief that being conscious of others' feelings creates team spirit.

Despite the success of these relational practices Fletcher also suggests that such practices are frequently devalued or dismissed; she uses the term 'disappeared'. This occurs even in organizations that have a rhetoric that acknowledges the importance of collaboration and supportive teamwork; at the same time behaviours that reflect more masculine values such as individual achievement, autonomy and specialization continue to be prized and rewarded. This is frequently because relational work comes to be seen as 'women's work'. It is often characterized as a personal idiosyncrasy or trait, often with negative connotations such as naïveté, powerlessness, weakness or emotional need.

Fletcher (2004) suggests that many women have become quite adept at challenging the dominant norms, often in small but persistent ways, without being disappeared, exploited or dismissed. From this she lays out four strategies for 'pushing back' on the disappearing dynamic. These are naming, norming, negotiating, and networking.

* *Naming* is a strategy of drawing attention to relational practice and framing it positively, by recognizing it as a competency rather than a personal characteristic. This can take several forms. Thus she says (2004: 32): 'One simple approach is to substitute the word "effective" when someone else notes the "nice" or "sensitive" attributes of a relational practitioner. Another is to name the skills and intended outcomes of your own, or others', relational practice and, in this way, focus organizational attention on invisible work.'

- *Norming* is a strategy of drawing attention to organizational norms of effectiveness and pointing out their potential costs or unintended negative consequences, and putting forward relationally based alternatives. For example, this might involve in a management presentation drawing attention to a dysfunctional norm in a workplace of taking sole credit for group effort and instead publicly demonstrating an alternative model of credit sharing.
- *Negotiating*: this strategy suggests that, rather than simply take on assignments that entail relational work, which are often then disappeared or not properly valued, greater visibility for them should be negotiated.
- *Networking*: the fourth strategy is to form a network to support and foster relational practice.

Thus in these works Fletcher not only highlights alternative approaches to leadership in the form of relational practices but also shows how such alternatives can be 'disappeared' and offers us ways of using those relational practices to challenge dominant norms through the processes of naming, norming, negotiating and networking. This need to avoid disappearance and to challenge dominant norms is not needed simply within a feminist management and leadership framework but can be used in the other approaches in this chapter when disappearance is also a risk. This approach forms an important element in recognizing aspects of organizational life and relationships from a perspective other than a detached, objectivist one, which, as we have already noted, itself forms the dominant approach in management and leadership studies.

Summary

The approaches discussed in this chapter constitute a very different conceptualization of leadership from those in earlier chapters: they are much more indeterminate and dynamic and a reflection and product of the context in which they occur. We have already highlighted the difficulties of trying to define leadership. We can note, though, that the earlier definition of leadership by Northouse – leadership is 'a process whereby an individual influences a group of individuals to achieve a common goal' (2007: 3) – (which we cited in Chapter 3) would not apply here. A more appropriate summary definition is provided by Szabo and Lambert (2002: 204): 'Leadership is described as the reciprocal processes shared by many rather than as a set of behaviours invested in one person. It is not role-specific but derives from a mutuality of purpose, shared values and communities'.

Even this definition, though, is not entirely adequate here, as we are really arguing that leadership is primarily a self-defining process. We as individuals create meaning for ourselves in and through our interactions with others and define aspects of the relationships we form with others as 'leadership' for ourselves. Thus we ascribe relationships with the label of leadership, either as those relationships develop or even in some cases after they cease, rather than impose the label from the outset. This approach sees leadership as a process of growth, reflection and development.

As we noted in Chapter 3, individual and objective accounts of management and leadership tend to consider management and leadership and organizational performance as part of a means–end relationship, with little attention being given to the process through which results can be achieved. Gold *et al.* (2003: 5) argue that:

> An alternative view might suggest that the behaviour of leaders is contingent on the situation faced and dependent and interdependent on the behaviour and response of others. Thus leadership (or better, leading) should be regarded as a dynamic and living activity, an ongoing process of interaction with emergent properties. Here there is shift in emphasis from leaders with skills who achieve results to a world of movement, emergent processes and relationships with others. Leading makes no sense without others who follow (or otherwise) and also the context of enactment. A process view understands leading as an activity that occurs in a time and place, involving more than one person and subject to a variety of contextual factors including structures and procedures, the state of relationships and cultural/social/historical factors.

Our focus in this chapter here has been on those relationships and individual meanings and understandings rather than with inputs and outputs or ends and means. We have also considered the theoretical bases for taking this view and processes which seek to explore these issues in practice.

These approaches question the extent to which we can view leadership as existing 'out there', free from subjective interpretation and open to objective examination This approach applied at the individual level highlights context as an important factor influencing how we view leadership. The result is the proposal of a counter to the view of universal characteristics and understandings of leadership, by accepting that it can be locally constructed and interpreted. These approaches allow for emergent rather than prescriptive leadership practices. From this perspective the responsibility for the effectiveness of the relationship is shared between those involved in management and leadership processes.

5 Rational planning and control
Rational-objectivist approaches to organizations

We take 'bureaucracy' to be, in common parlance, a broad synonym for poor management of the system and of provider organizations and believe that this prompts a fruitful
approach to reducing the level of bureaucracy. The way forward is not to adopt the
narrower approach of shortening forms and streamlining administrative processes but to
modernise management to the highest standards. Bureaucracy in the narrow sense will
naturally drop away as a by-product of managing well.

Sir Andrew Foster, Chair, Bureaucracy Review Group (Foster, 2004)

Introduction

This chapter will now consider theories of management that focus on the
organization as a whole and are also rational and objective in their approach.
Theories of management in this chapter focus less on managers as individuals, instead focusing on organizations as systems operating in a larger context.
Likewise, in this chapter organizations are generally seen as unitary collec-
tives, with an assumption of shared interests and values, common goals for the
organization and one dominant organizational culture. As we discussed earlier
there is a tendency for new management theories not to replace their older
counterparts but to layer new concepts and ideas on top of a firmament laid
down by earlier theories. The management and organizational theories in this
chapter provide many of the early concepts, which are important because they
underpin later theories and approaches. Thus, in social work, concepts based
on a range of older theories such as span of control, line management, specialization, payment by performance and incentives sit happily alongside newer and
sometimes contradictory concepts such as key performance indicators, critical
success factors, benchmarking, learning organizations, strategic objectives and
mission statements.

As shown in Figure 5.1 we will look at three groups of theories and
approaches in this chapter. These are:

1 classical management;
2 strategic management;
3 humanistic psychology and technical systems.

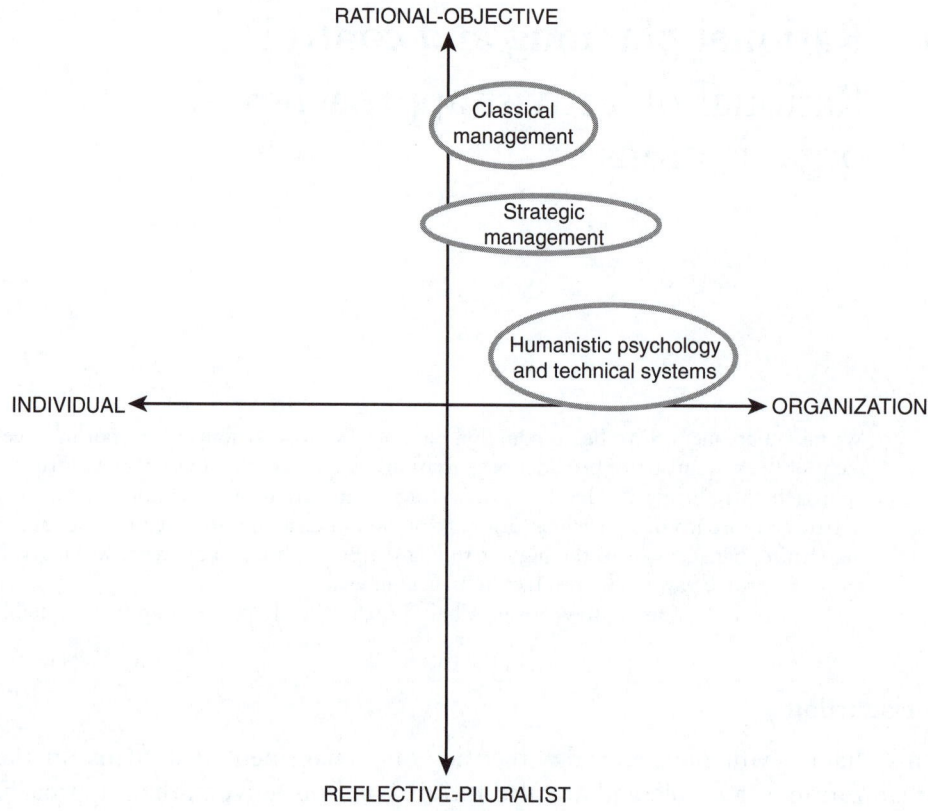

Figure 5.1 The rational-objectivist and organization quadrant.

The first covers a major group of management theories that we earlier (Chapter 3) called classical management theory, which developed in the early part of the twentieth century as a rational, scientific approach to management. In this chapter we take the organization as the centre of attention rather than the individual as we did earlier. These theories have developed from mechanistic and militaristic metaphors for organizations and lead to approaches that stress rational planning and see the manager as being in command or a representative of central control. These approaches tend to have a mechanistic view of organizations founded on the ability to predict the future, follow a plan with minimal deviation and design out difficult (or irrational) process variations. They deal with difficulties through command and control or as a problem for rational control. We thus see here a focus on organizations having clear goals and mechanistic, assembly-line approaches to service production, whereby individuals within organizations are part of the machinery that produces the desired outcome. Similarly, service users are seen as relatively passive consumers who are part of the continuing process, whose needs and demands are relatively easy to predict.

The second group of theories and approaches we address in this chapter have developed further the idea of management as a strategic activity. These ideas focus on strategic and operational objectives and organizational vision. They come from a series of linked but essentially similar approaches to management that have shaped the structure and management approaches of human services organizations in both the statutory and voluntary sectors.

The third group of theories covered in this chapter take more account of the non-rational forces that shape organizational life than those above. They have a basis in humanistic psychology and often draw on early ideas from systems theory, seeing the organization as an organism surviving within its ecosystem. They thus take a different approach to the staff of organizations, seeing them as a resource for achieving organizational goals. Although they have more of a view of the needs of employees and other aspects of organizational health, they still tend to see the goal of the organization as being unproblematic and its managers take action through steering the organization. They thus fall closer to the far less certain approaches based on complexity theory and models of self-organization, which are the subject of the next chapter, but are predominantly rational and objective in their orientation.

The final section of this chapter will then discuss the strengths and weaknesses of these three overlapping sets of approaches. Throughout the chapter we will give brief overviews of different management theories. The aim in doing this is not to give a comprehensive review of all these approaches but to provide a summary and outline key concepts, many of which have persisted, even when the theory from which it emerged is no longer in the mainstream of management thinking. In this way we will show how managers and policy makers in human services use concepts and tools drawn from a range of theories, often without knowledge of the limitations or strengths of the theoretical framework on which they draw. Where possible we will indicate key texts and research that will allow the reader to further explore a topic if you so desire.

Classical management theories and advances in bureaucracy

Classical management approaches initially developed out of military theory, and later during industrialization further developments, variously called scientific management and Fordism as well as the development of bureaucracies, have had major influence. These early theories were essentially inward looking, focusing on what was happening within the organization, its structure and operation. Although there is recognition of human aspects of organization, this revolves around factors seen to influence motivation such as leadership, equity, and *esprit de corps*. Essentially, although there is recognition of the need for harmony between the human and technical aspects of the organization, the problem is essentially seen as a technical one of making humans fit the requirements of the organization.

Scientific management

As we discussed in Chapter 3, key amongst these developments is scientific management, which was developed by F. W. Taylor and has been widely influential on management theory. Whereas he gained a reputation as 'an enemy of the working man' (Morgan, 1986: 30), his principles of scientific management formed the basis of work design for much of the first half of the twentieth century. We will now look again at these theories and how they apply to the organization as a whole. Taylor advocated five basic principles for his approach:

1 *give responsibility for the organization of work to managers*: this was a shift from previous approaches in which workers were craftsmen controlling all aspects of their work;
2 *use scientific methods to assess the most efficient ways of doing work*: this involved studies of tasks (here we see the introduction of time and motion studies) and specifying in detail how work should be undertaken (for example how different types of coal should be shovelled);
3 *the scientific selection and training of workers*: this involved selecting the best person to fit the job as designed and training aimed at ensuring efficiency;
4 *monitoring work performance*: work was monitored against the detailed specification for the job and measured in terms of efficiency and specific outcomes;
5 *management by exception*: this suggests that routine decision making should be handled by lower-level managers who report only exceptional cases to higher management.

This approach suggests organizations are arranged in a hierarchy with systems of abstract rules and impersonal relationships between staff. It works by having a clear delineation of authority and responsibility; separating planning from operations; and promoting task specialization. In order to get employees to do this work there are specific incentives linked to performance. At the same time management by exception should lead to greater responsibility being taken at all levels of management.

It is interesting that radical social work theorists in the 1980s (Simpkin, 1983; Bolger *et al.*, 1981; Jones, 1983; Joyce *et al.*, 1988) suggested that social work was increasingly becoming the subject of scientific management, though this view has been challenged by Harris (1998: 843), who suggests that the role was rather that of a 'bureau-professional' according to which social workers are seen to oversee the rational administration of bureaucratic systems, and use professional expertise to control the content of services. We will explore such notions through looking at the founding of the concept of bureaucracy and its role in social work management.

Administration and bureaucracy

At the turn of the century Weber first wrote about what he saw as a new trend in organizations, namely bureaucracy, and his ideas were developed much further in his later studies on economy and society (an English translation by Talcott Parsons was published in 1947). Weber studied the developments of administration in a diverse range of organizations in Germany including the civil service, the army and the introduction of American approaches to industrial production. From this study he saw a new type of administration had developed that was different from before. He suggested that the most important and pervasive characteristic of what he termed bureaucracy, and one that to some extent explains all the others, is the existence of a system of control based on rational rules. According to Weber (1947: 339) 'Bureaucratic administration means fundamentally the exercise of control on the basis of knowledge. This is the feature of it which makes it specifically rational'. By this Weber means that rules to design and regulate the whole organization are based on technical knowledge with the aim of achieving maximum efficiency.

Weber drew out the essential features of bureaucracy. These features are now pervasive in many types of organizations and include: (1) functional specialization, (2) clear lines of hierarchical authority, (3) expert training of managers, and (4) decision making based on rules and tactics developed to guarantee consistent and effective pursuit of organizational goals. He outlined further factors stemming from these basic features, which included that the appointment of staff and promotion were based on merit rather than favouritism or nepotism, and those appointed were to full-time positions that were the person's primary career. He also suggested that, in order to promote effective decision making, business is conducted on the basis of written rules, and records are kept of relevant communications. Other issues that stem from this form of organization are those of line management and a chain of command; that is, people give orders only to their own subordinates and receive orders only from their own immediate superior. Thus Weber's bureaucracy leads to the type of organization represented in an organizational chart with defined jobs organized in a hierarchical fashion.

Bureaucracy has become seen as a term of derision implying ponderousness and, as the *Collins Essential English Dictionary* (2006) states, 'any administration in which action is impeded by unnecessary official procedures.' This was not Weber's view of bureaucracy. He saw it as a powerful new force replacing older forms of administration. He saw these new forms of administration having many benefits, particularly the way they were designed to ensure accountability and transparency; promote equality (i.e. everyone receives the same treatment rather than the previous favouritism); standardize processes to aid the above; and prevent nepotism by assuring promotion on the basis of technical merit. However, he was particularly worried about the way that bureaucracies might intrude their rational processes into ever wider areas of society. Morgan (1986: 25) thus says that Weber 'saw the bureaucratic approach had the potential to routinize and mechanize almost every aspect of human life, eroding the human spirit and capacity for spontaneous action.' It is evident that much of the structure of modern social work organizations is still essentially bureaucratic.

Despite this negative view of bureaucracy, which is powerfully stated in Andrew Foster's quote at the head of this chapter, it is interesting that many calls for change in the management of social work, such as those by Lord Laming in the Climbié Inquiry, call for clear lines of accountability, clear roles and responsibility, and more effective procedures, which are the essential elements of a bureaucratic system.

McDonaldization

More recently writers have stressed the way that recent developments have continued this rationalizing process of society. It is claimed that, in area after area, the introduction of a linear rationalistic approach to management can be seen and its hallmark is the stifling of creativity under the weight of procedures and guidelines. Those identifying this trend say it is not limited to social work management. It has been analysed by George Ritzer (1992), who has persuasively argued that it represents an approach to management epitomized by the McDonald's food chain, which he calls 'McDonaldization'. According to Ritzer, McDonaldization is a modern extension of Weber's theory of rationality to modern capitalist practices. For Weber, as we discussed above, formal rationality

> means that the search by people for the optimum means to a given end is shaped by rules, regulations, and larger social structures. Thus, individuals are not left to their own devices in searching for the best means of achieving a given objective. Rather, there exist rules, regulations and structures that either predetermine or help them discover the optimum methods.
>
> (Ritzer, 1992: 17)

McDonaldization has a number of precursors, namely bureaucracy, scientific management and the assembly line. It is based on the valuing of efficiency, calculability, predictability and control through the substitution of non-human for human technology. Although McDonaldization can have many of the benefits which Weber saw in bureaucracy, it is essentially dehumanizing and leads to the irrationality that can be seen in queues for 'fast' food that is eaten in an environment in which even the chairs are designed to be uncomfortable enough to make customers eat quickly and move on. Ritzer suggests that western culture has embraced this increasing 'rationalism' in most spheres.

When Ritzer talks about efficiency he means that there is seen to be an optimum method for carrying out a task. McDonald's, for example, offers a highly mobile society the drive-in takeaway in which we can satisfy our need for food without even having to get out of our cars. In many social work agencies the call centre efficiently collects social work referrals. For example, in our research into referrals in one organization where a call centre was used, the administrators answering the calls, who were very junior and relatively low paid staff, took the referrals for children referred by the public and other agencies. They would answer the calls swiftly and type the referral into a computer as the person spoke to them or soon after. The referrals were then passed electronically to the social work team responsible for dealing with the referrals. This system was efficient in the sense of McDonaldization in that it was an optimum way to get the referrals onto the computer system and could guarantee that a written record of all referrals was made and that calls were answered quickly. Efficiency in this sense does not necessarily mean that the quality of the response is correct or even helpful. Our research showed that, prior to the reforms that we helped to create, this referral system led to high levels of referrals being classified as child protection cases and dealt with through an investigation, with very few of the people referred receiving the help that the person referring wanted for them (Bilson and Thorpe, 2007).

The second dimension of McDonaldization is calculability. This implies that the services can be easily quantified and calculated. In McDonald's this is epitomized by the size of the food – the Big Mac, Large Fries, the Quarter Pounder. In these ways McDonald's gives the impression that we are getting a lot of food for our money yet the portion sizes are very precise and consistent. Another aspect of calculability raised by Ritzer involves time. Hence McDonald's offers fast food with precise times for food preparation and delivery. This issue of calculability is often an element of referral systems such as the call centre discussed above, where it is often the case that performance is measured in terms of targets for the speed with which calls will be answered.

The third dimension of McDonaldization is predictability. We all know that the burger we buy in the UK will be the same as the one in Moscow and the same as the next one we buy next year or the year after. Similarly McDonald's seeks to produce predictable responses from its staff by giving them detailed scripts for how they should greet a customer or persuade them to go large. We see a similar approach in social work aiming to rid ourselves of 'postcode lotteries' and to ensure that a similar service is available wherever it is sought. Thus in England there are targets for how quickly an initial assessment should be completed. Regardless of the complexity of the case the timescale for the initial assessment is the same. In the UK we have also seen increasing levels of procedures aimed at increasing the predictability of social work. This includes detailed outlines and targets for carrying out assessments, and computer forms that reduce the social worker's ability to tell a story that might give complex descriptions. This is replaced with tick box selections and specific questions on computerized forms.

The fourth and final dimension of McDonaldization is control. This is achieved through training, rigid rules and the substitution of non-human technology for human judgement. The way the performance of each member of staff is assessed is precisely detailed (Morgan, 1986: 21, reproduces a section of the management observation handbook, which even provides a check for when someone should smile). Thus in McDonald's the number of fries served to a diner is controlled by the use of a scoop that accurately collects the specified number of fries to place them in the pack. The increasing regulation of all areas of social work is an example of the increasing control of social work practice through an attempt to constrain the scope of human judgement through ever more rigid procedures. The use of computerized assessment schemes in areas such as youth offending also controls social workers and constrains their judgement.

Thus it is possible to see that, rather than reducing bureaucracy, current trends can be seen to create the hyper-bureaucracy that is McDonaldization. Although the processes of McDonaldization are rational the outcomes are frequently irrational. Whereas it can be seen the process of McDonaldization can lead to the opposite of its intention – inefficiency, unpredictability, incalculability and loss of control – the fundamental problem is that the proliferation of nominally rational systems leads to unreasonable systems (Ritzer, 1992: 121). These are systems that deny the basic humanity of the people who participate in them. In the extreme, rational systems are effectively dehumanizing. In the social work agency where referrals were taken by a call centre discussed above, the pressure on intake teams became greater as referrals requiring child protection assessments led to ever greater strains on workers. It was only when the irrational rational system was reversed and social workers were reintroduced into the referral process that levels of referrals requiring child protection responses fell and a vicious spiral became virtuous (Bilson and Thorpe, 2007), leading to reductions in a whole range of measures; child protection registrations, numbers of children entering care and even levels of referral fell significantly.

Scientific bureaucracy

Another view on the development of bureaucratic forms in social work is linked to trends in the development of 'scientific' approaches in health and social care. This approach has been seen across many of the English-speaking countries, starting in medicine (for example see Harrison *et al.*, 2002 for accounts of its development in the United States and in the United Kingdom). Harrison has noted that one particular dominant form of rationality underpins contemporary policy in the United Kingdom's modernization programme. This form of rationality Harrison terms the 'scientific-bureaucratic' model, which he defines as follows:

> Scientific-bureaucratic [rationality] . . . centres on the assumption that valid and reliable knowledge is mainly to be obtained from the accumulation of research conducted by experts according to strict scientific criteria . . . It

further assumes that working clinicians are likely to be both too busy and insufficiently skilled to interpret and apply such knowledge for themselves, and therefore holds that professional practice should be influenced through the systematic aggregation by academic experts of research findings on a particular topic, and the distillation of such findings into protocols and guidelines which may then be communicated to practitioners with the expectation that practice will be improved . . . The logic, though not always the overt form, of guidelines is essentially algorithmic.

(Harrison, 2002: 470)

So, this model is 'scientific' in the sense that it promises a secure knowledge base that can provide rational foundations for clinical decisions. It is bureaucratic in the sense that this knowledge is codified and manualized through the use of protocols, guidelines and targets such as time-scales for assessments, which are monitored by managers, sometimes using computer systems or through internal and external audit. This internal auditing activity has been augmented by the establishment in the United Kingdom of three bodies: the SCIE; the Commission for Social Care Inspection (CSCI); and the new OfSTED – the Office for Standards in Education, Children's Services and Skills. SCIE aims to promote the use of evidence-informed practice by providing knowledge reviews and best practice guidelines. Every year CSCI and OfSTED give each council a star rating that shows how well the council is performing and its ability to improve in the future. These star ratings are part of the Audit Commission's yearly Comprehensive Performance Assessment (CPA). A low rating in social care may result in a low overall CPA score, and that leads to the government placing restrictions on how a council can spend its money.

Thus, governance in its current incarnation relies on a view of professional practice as rational-technical and linear. The guidelines and protocols depict the processes of assessment and intervention as consecutive and straightforward. The social worker and his or her manager make a decision about the nature of the problem and then can consult the evidence base to find out 'what works'. Although this does not fit with the realities of professional decision making, managers are left to handle the consequences of either non-compliance or making practice fit the constraints of procedures and guidance. An example of the issues raised by this approach to governance can be seen in the time-scales for carrying out assessments in children's services. Managers and social workers in many cases face the dilemma of having to undertake an assessment when there is insufficient time to collect the necessary information. In a number of children's services departments where we have undertaken research this has resulted in many assessments being 'completed' but without any real plans or even a thorough discovery of the situation of the family.

Management by strategy and objectives

In addition to the general and universalist approaches to management discussed above – management philosophies almost – there is a range of narrower management approaches and techniques that have been and remain influential across organizations. We will now consider those management theories, which still have a major influence on managerial practices in a number of areas of social work. This group of theories is concerned with strategy and objectives. Initially it was built on a militaristic metaphor in which an 'officer class' of leaders create a strategy to be undertaken by those lower in the hierarchy. In this group of theories the main approach is the development of strategy and objectives to achieve a vision for the organization which comes from the senior staff. We will look at three methods/approaches: (1) management by objectives; (2) strategic management theory; and (3) the Balanced Scorecard. This is not meant to be a comprehensive overview of these approaches but rather focuses on those commonly and increasingly used in human services and representing typical rational management approaches.

Management by objectives

The first of these is management by objectives. The term 'management by objectives' (MBO) was first popularized by the economist Peter Drucker in his 1954 book *The Practice of Management*. In this book Drucker suggested that the objectives for an organization should be defined for each individual working in the organization, both managerial and other staff, and that these objectives should be the basis for assessing performance throughout the organization. In this way the approach aims to align goals and sub-objectives throughout the organization. MBO thus sets out to be a systematic and organized approach that allows management to focus on achievable goals and to get the best possible results from available resources.

One of the aims of MBO is to help managers to keep in sight their main purpose and objectives. In this way MBO aims to avoid managers getting into the 'activity trap' where they are so caught up in day-to-day activities that they lose direction. MBO is also intended to promote the idea that strategic planning should not just be the job of a few individuals within an organization but should be a part of the job of all managers.

This focus on objectives and clear statements of purpose can be seen as part of the foundations for the idea of having an organizational mission statement. In fact in the 1970s Drucker (1974) himself proposed the need for an organization to have a mission statement and is famously quoted as saying it 'should fit on a tee-shirt' (Hesselbein, 1996: 7). Although having a mission statement has been argued to lead to better performance through aiding strategy formulation and implementation, there is little empirical evidence to support this argument (Sidhu, 2003: 439). Perhaps this is because the statements do not reflect the organization, as in Wright's (2002) study of middle and senior-level managers, which found that, although most firms had a mission statement (82 per cent), fewer than half of the managers (40 per cent) felt that the mission statement accurately reflected the organization.

Another common management tool used in human services, SMART objectives, is also associated with MBO. Although it is often attributed to Drucker the acronym SMART for objectives is not specifically mentioned in *The Practice of Management*, though the emphasis on specificity in SMART terms is clearly part of the approach. The acronym suggests that objectives should be:

- Specific: the objectives should specify in detail what they need to achieve;
- Measurable: it should be possible to measure whether you are meeting the objectives or not;
- Achievable: the objectives should have aims that are achievable and attainable;
- Realistic: the objectives should be attainable within the resources (material, financial and staff) available (sometimes the R in SMART stands for resourced and others have it standing for relevant);
- Time-bound: the objectives should set timescales within which they should be achieved.

Many human services organizations use SMART objectives; for example, the Scottish Executive's guidance on Corporate Action Plans on Alcohol Abuse (Scottish Executive, 2007) lays down a framework for basing the strategy on sets of SMART objectives.

However, mission statements, SMART objectives and the other aspects of MBO rely on an uncomplicated notion of organizational direction. A frequently cited quotation from Drucker himself suggests the limitations of this approach: 'It's just another tool. It's not the cure for management inefficiency ... Management by objective works if you know the objectives. Ninety percent of the time you don't' (Jeston and Nelis, 2008: 171). MBO, as in other fields, is now infrequently used directly as a management theory to inform human services organizational practice. However, the underlying notion of rational planning, mission statements and clear objectives is ubiquitous. As will be seen later, many other forms of management theory are built on this framework.

Strategic management theory

Strategic management has been developing considerably over the last thirty years. During this period a range of competing theoretical positions have evolved. At one end of this range are approaches that have essentially a rational linear approach to planning. For example, Hill and Jones (1995: 7) identify five components of a model for strategic management:

(1) selection of the corporate mission and major corporate goals; (2) analysis of the organization's external competitive environment to identify

opportunities and threats; (3) analysis of the organization's internal operating environment to identify the organization's strengths and weaknesses; (4) the selection of strategies that build on the organization's strengths and correct its weaknesses in order to take advantage of external opportunities and counter external threats; and (5) strategy implementation.

In this model, the first four steps are normally referred to as strategy formulation. Thus this approach to strategic management is the source of SWOT analysis (Strengths, Weaknesses, Opportunities, Threats), which is so often used in exercises within human services teams and organizations. According to Hill and Jones (1995: 8) the fifth step, strategy implementation, typically involves 'designing appropriate organizational structures and control systems' to put the chosen strategy into action.

The existence of multiple theories for strategic management has given rise to a confusing use of terminology in the field, with different authors and managers using the same terms or definitions to mean different things, or using different terms and definitions to mean the same thing. Mintzberg and Quinn comment on this wide and confusing use of terminology particularly regarding the central concept of a strategy:

> a good deal of confusion in this field stems from contradictory and ill defined use of the term strategy. By explicating and using various definitions, we may be able to avoid some of this confusion, and thereby enrich our ability to understand and manage the processes by which strategies form.
>
> (Mintzberg and Quinn, 1996: 21)

Mintzberg (1978) suggests that rational design is often an inaccurate account of how strategies are formulated. He identifies three forms of strategies: (1) *intended strategy*, which is the strategy conceived by the senior management team – even these are not simply a result of a rational process but arrived at through bargaining, negotiation and compromise; (2) *realized strategy*, which is the strategy that is actually undertaken; and (3) *emergent strategy*, which is the pattern of actions that emerge as managers respond to changing external conditions. The realized strategy may follow from an intended strategy or an emergent one. The rational approach above thus tends to focus on intended strategies rather than emergent strategies. The difference between emergent and intended strategies is often exemplified using Richard Pascale's description of Honda Motor Company's introduction into the United States (1984). An original analysis funded by the UK government presented the story as if the winning of the American market was a direct result of a strategic intent. Pascale's description is based on meeting the executive team who worked in the US. He suggests that they were struggling with their strategic aim to introduce the 250cc and 300cc models but that their personal use of 50cc models drew attention to this product and they later built on this interest with a deal with

Sears Roebuck and distribution through the, then, non-standard use of general rather than specialist suppliers. In this way a strategy emerged that was far from the intent of the company when it sent its team to the United States. Pascale explains the difference between his story and that of others as follows:

> Western consultants, academics, and executives express a preference for oversimplifications of reality and cognitively linear explanations of events . . . [there is] a tendency to overlook the process through which organizations experiment, adapt, and learn . . . How an organization deals with miscalculation, mistakes, and serendipitous events outside its field of vision is often crucial to success over time.
>
> (Pascale, 1984: 57)

It is in this vein that Mintzberg suggests that strategy development is done through a process of crafting rather than planning. Thus he states (Mintzberg, 1987: 65):

> Crafting strategy . . . is not so much thinking and reason as involvement, a feeling of intimacy and harmony with the materials at hand, developed through long experience and commitment. Formulation and implementation merge into a fluid process of learning through which creative strategies emerge.

In taking this approach Mintzberg moves us nearer to the approaches that will be described in the next chapter. However this less 'certain' approach is not espoused by all those using strategic management theory. For many writers there is a strong desire to cling to the rational approach to strategic management even where there is an acceptance of issues such as the emergent nature of many successful strategies; the limited and contradictory nature of the evidence for the success of formal planning systems (Hill and Jones, 1995: 15); and the role of culture, power and other non-rational processes in shaping strategies and their implementation. Thus Grant (2002: 27), after acknowledging many of these points, goes on to say:

> The danger of the Mintzberg approach is that by down-playing the role of systematic analysis and emphasising the role of intuition and vision, we move into a world of new-age mysticism in which there is no clear basis for reasoned choices and in which disorder threatens the progressive accumulation of knowledge.

Thus, like many writers on strategic management, Grant asserts the rational, objective basis of strategic management theory. In fact he ridicules any use of intuition as a threat to the ordered logical approach that underpins strategic management theories, clearly seeing even the approach of strategic management as craft, rather than logic, as a threat to the whole edifice of strategic planning.

The Balanced Scorecard

The Balanced Scorecard is an approach being given increasing emphasis in public services in the UK – for example in health, higher education and local government. Again it demonstrates a fairly narrow and rational approach to management. In the early 1990s Robert Kaplan and David Norton (1992) developed the Balanced Scorecard, which builds on approaches such as MBO and strategic management. Its development was in the context of commercial organizations, at a time when financial measures alone were seen as being inadequate measures of an organization's overall performance. This is now used in many human services organizations because it is seen as a step beyond the unidirectional focus of finance as a measure of organizational purpose and success. It builds on the recognition that 'What you measure is what you get' (Kaplan and Norton, 1992: 71). In other words the targets that are set for people and the rewards for achieving them will shape what is achieved, often with unintended and sometimes disastrous consequences. One problem with targets is that it is much easier to measure financial results than it is to measure progress in other essential areas (such as staff or user satisfaction). This leads to an over-reliance on financial measurement. A second issue is that staff and managers will focus their activities to meet key targets, possibly at the expense of other important areas of work that are not directly targeted.

In keeping with other approaches in this chapter, the Balanced Scorecard is seen as a tool for improving the performance of a whole organization, a large department or a small team. Its aim is to help to measure and improve performance in an integrated way and on a wide set of issues. Its intentions are to set goals that give appropriate weight to financial and non-financial measures. Like MBO it starts with the organization's vision and strategy, seeing this as being set from the top by senior managers and then communicated down to other levels of the organization. From this analysis of the mission of the organization, it suggests a need to identify the drivers of success for that vision, and then develop targets that measure progress towards that success. To prevent organizations getting overwhelmed with performance measurements, it limits measurement to what are proposed as four critical areas: financial performance, customer service improvement, internal business processes, and innovation and learning. The approach suggests the need to identify the key factors, known as *Critical Success Factors,* in each of these areas that contribute to organizational success.

An important element of the Balanced Scorecard is the emphasis on establishing a balance between four types of measures:

- Short-term and Long-term;
- External (for customers and shareholders) and Internal (for critical business processes, innovation, and learning);

- Leading indicators (outcomes desired and performance measures) and Lagging indicators (outcomes);
- Objective measures (e.g. financial) and Subjective measures (e.g., customer satisfaction, organizational climate).

There are claims that the Balanced Scorecard empowers staff at all levels: Kaplan and Norton are clear that it should be used as a communication, informing and learning system, not a controlling system. However, like MBO, the Balanced Scorecard is normally seen to work from the top down. The entire framework hinges on aligning performance with intended strategy, which is mostly seen to come from the top of the organization. So, although lower-ranked employees might be ostensibly empowered, there is a danger that this remains within the tightly delineated boundaries of a strategy driven from the top.

This section has dealt with a set of theories and approaches that have as their basis a view of management as mission control, developing strategies or occasionally taking charge of emergent strategies and then rationally planning, designing organizational structures and objectives. Managers have the role of providing strategic leadership to articulate the organization's strategic vision and to motivate staff. Although issues such as organizational politics are sometimes acknowledged, these messy organizational issues tend to be seen as problems to be managed by a 'strong chief executive or a well designed structure' (Hill and Jones, 1995: 434).

Humanistic psychology and systems

We will now discuss developments in management theories that, though in some respects they have some aspects in common with theories in the next chapter, still fall into the rational-objectivist sector of our categorization as this is their predominant orientation. This section includes those approaches to management, which we see using the metaphor of the organization as an organism alongside those drawing on humanistic psychology. These theories developed from biological metaphors and understandings, particularly those of open systems theory inspired by the work of Ludwig von Bertalanffy (1950).

Morgan (1986) sees this change from mechanical to biologically based metaphors for organizations as one that led to some of the most important developments in management theory in the latter half of the twentieth century. He says that the move from mechanical science to biology as a source for metaphors and ideas about management means that:

> We find ourselves thinking about them as living systems, existing in a wider environment on which they depend for the satisfaction of various needs . . . we begin to see that it is possible to identify different species of organization in different kinds of environment.
>
> (Morgan, 1986: 39)

Whereas the metaphor of growth and development implies flexibility, the ways in which these management approaches interpret this tend to be within a framework of organizational effectiveness. Just as different animals have their niche in which they are well adapted for survival, this biological view of organizations sees that different 'species' of organizations are better adapted to different environments. For example, bureaucracies thrive best in relatively stable environments whereas turbulent environments such as those found in new technology industries have different 'species' of organization able to adapt quickly to change. The move from mechanical to biological metaphors for organizations thus meant a move in our attention to consider more biological issues such as survival, organizational health, fitness and learning, and, later, relationships between organizations and their environment, often thought of in terms of ecology. These biological approaches developed alongside recognition that the human workforce had needs and the suggestion that organizing work so that it might meet those needs could lead to better productivity.

This has led to a wide range of theories and approaches. We will now discuss some of the key ones that have impacted on human services management. These are socio-technical systems, human resource management and the learning organization.

Socio-technical systems

In the early to middle twentieth century the optimism concerning the application of classical management and scientific management was confounded by failures of mechanization to provide the desired outcomes. There were many examples of the introduction of technology being associated with problems often linked to resistance by the workforce such as in the English coal-mining industry, where mechanization had decreased productivity.

Eric Trist and other researchers, notably at the Tavistock Institute in London, with a background in behavioural science disciplines such as sociology, psychology and anthropology, suggested a new approach. They proposed that in manufacturing and a wide range of other organizations it is necessary to consider both technical systems and human/social aspects and that these two are tightly inter-connected. Attempts at bringing about change thus need to address and 'optimise' both these systems.

The technical system was seen to comprise the devices, tools and techniques and their physical arrangements (thus we often think of car factories in terms of their production lines). The social system comprises the staff (at all levels) and the knowledge, skills, attitudes, values and needs they bring to the work environment as well as the reward system and authority structures (both formal, as seen in organizational charts, and informal power structures) that exist in the organization.

Later this view of the organization was broadened to encompass what became known as the environmental system. This included the organization's customers, suppliers, and the relationships between the organization and society including formal and informal rules and regulations.

At the centre of the socio-technical approach is the intention to develop a design process aiming at the joint optimization of the social, technical and (later) environmental systems. In this approach it is considered that organizations will maximize performance only if the interdependency of these subsystems (social, technical and environmental) is explicitly addressed. Attempts to bring about change must seek out the impact each system has on the others and attempt to ensure that all the systems are working in harmony.

Land (2000) suggests that two sometimes conflicting set of values underlie much socio-technical thinking. The first of these is a belief in the importance of humanistic principles. The main task of the manager as designer (the term 'design' or 'redesign' is often applied to change strategies in this literature) is to enhance the quality of working life and the job satisfaction of employees. The second set of values reflects a more managerial position. The achievement of changes, for example, to job satisfaction is to enhance productivity and yield added value to the organization. In this way socio-technical principles can be seen as primarily instruments for achieving economic objectives. Humanistic objectives have little value in themselves but rather their achievement is to produce better performance from employees leading to the fulfilment of the economic objectives of the organization.

The idea that, in designing or managing an organization, there is interdependence between the technology used in the organization and the social systems is now widely recognized in organizational theories that followed the ground-breaking work on socio-technical theory. The socio-technical approach has much synergy with social work and its organization. It stresses a more democratic, empowering approach to organizational life, which sits well with social work values. It also stresses the importance of autonomous teamwork. Uncertainty has become a theme of socio-technical systems theory since Emery and Trist (1965) discussed the 'turbulent environment'. Much of the recent use of socio-technical theory has focused on the implementation and design of information systems in which the stressing of the interaction between human and technical systems is plainly visible.

Human resource management

Human resource management (HRM) operates on the slogan that an organization's greatest asset is its staff. It is a development from personnel management that occurred in the UK in the 1980s. Karen Legge (1989: 27–8) suggested that the major differences between personnel management and HRM were that the latter gave greater emphasis to work with the management team; it was more coordinated into the work of line managers and had a more bottom-line (meeting strategic goals etc.) emphasis; and it emphasized the management of corporate culture. More recently it has been recognized that the distinctions were slim, though it is seen as having a more central and strategic focus (Legge, 2005: 221). However, what falls within the remit of human resource management is open to debate. Human resource management can be seen as a further development of the concern for having an effective workforce found in socio-technical systems approaches. Thus Schuler and Jackson (1999: xiv) state that human resource management:

> is based upon the recognition that organizations can be more effective if their human resources are managed with human resource policies and practices that deliver the right number of people with the appropriate behaviours, the needed competencies and the feasible levels of motivation to the organization.

The core elements of human resource management are debateable but are often seen to include:

- recruitment and selection of staff;
- training and staff development;
- managing staff performance;
- teamwork and involvement in decision making;
- compensating and rewarding staff;
- developing effective corporate culture.

The approach to human resource management is in the main linked to a strategic management approach, and recent literature often refers to strategic human resource management. Legge (2005: 223–4) suggests there are two models, initially called the hard and soft models; the latter is often now referred to in both the UK and the US as high-performance work system (HPWS). The hard model stresses that human resources systems, policies and practices should be closely integrated with business strategy, with employees to be 'managed in exactly the same rational, impersonal way as any other resource, i.e. to be exploited for maximal economic return' (2005: 224). In contrast, whilst still stressing the need to integrate human resource practices with business objectives, the second model has more humanist foundations aiming to promote better performance through gaining commitment and development of the workforce. This second model is now seen as an exemplar of best practice though both models are still seen to be in use.

Like socio-technical systems, human resource management also focuses on the social systems and on the environment. Thus the UK Department of Health's document 'HR High Impact Changes: An Evidence Based Resource' (DH Workforce Directorate/NHS Partners/Manchester University, 2006) stresses the importance of context to human resources approaches to change strategies in health and social care. This highlights ten human resources practices that it is suggested have an evidence base demonstrating how they can contribute to improving services and improving productivity and efficiency. The ten practices are: support and lead effective change management; develop effective recruitment, good induction and supportive management; develop shared service models and effective use of IT; manage temporary staffing costs; promote staff health and manage sickness absence; promote job and service re-design; develop and implement appraisal; involve staff and work in partnership to develop good employee relations; champion good people management practices; provide effective training and development (ibid.: 5–6). Although the focus of this document is on health care, the areas are equally relevant to social work. The review concludes that there is no 'one size fits all' solution and the context of a change must be taken into account during implementation. Further human resource practices need to be aligned with business strategy. It goes on to suggest that the amount and quality of evidence on these issues is variable and there is no evidence that any one of them is superior to any other with regard to its effect on performance. It also acknowledges that their scope is beyond that traditionally associated with the human resource function and many will need the involvement of many other areas of the organization if they are to be successfully implemented.

Thus human resource management still mainly works within the framework of management approaches discussed above. Whereas much of the mainstream of theory and research in this field has a unitarist and positivist framework, placing it clearly alongside the other approaches in this chapter, there is a literature that draws on a more critical approach using, for example, discourse analysis, but this forms a minor part of the predominantly rationalist and instrumental approach overall. Managerial approaches incorporating this critical approach are discussed in the next chapter.

Learning organizations

The idea that an organization as a whole learns is clearly based on a biological metaphor and can be traced back to the 1930s (Visser, 2007: 659). Although the concept of the learning organization is widely promoted, especially to deal with developing an organization's capacity to change and adapt to unstable environments, it is less a model than a school of thought and there has been a proliferation of concepts and interpretations. Senge (1990) suggests that a Learning Organization is one in which it is impossible not to learn because learning is so much a part of everything the organization does. Early concepts of organizational learning were developed by Chris Argyris and Donald Schön (1978), who in turn drew on the work of the biologist, ethnographer and systems theorist Gregory Bateson (for a discussion of Bateson's work and its application to social work see Bilson and Ross, 1999) for their model of what it means for an organization to learn. Argyris and Schon defined organizational learning as 'the detection and correction of error' (1978: 2), a concept that draws on Bateson's early cybernetic and systems ideas. Later Fiol and Lyles define learning as 'the process of improving actions through better knowledge and understanding' (1985: 803) and Dodgson describes organizational learning as 'the way firms build, supplement, and organize knowledge and routines around their activities and within their cultures and adapt and develop organizational efficiency by improving the use of the broad skills of their workforces' (1993: 377).

From the early days it was recognized that organizational learning was not a simple concept and, echoing Bateson's model of learning (see Bilson and Ross, 1999: 157), Argyris and Schön (1978) describe three levels of learning:

- *Single-loop learning*: This is where errors are detected by the organization and corrected and the organization carries on with its present policies and goals. In Bateson's terms this level of learning means nothing new is learnt, the organization uses current models to deal with any problem or error; in other words it repeats what it has done in the past.
- *Double-loop learning*: This occurs when, in addition to detection and correction of errors, the organization uses its response to errors as a basis for questioning and modifying existing norms, procedures, policies and objectives. At this level of learning the organization can be seen to learn as it changes its capacity to respond to errors and problems.
- *Deutero-learning*: This occurs when organizations learn how to learn; in other words they learn to better carry out single-loop and double-loop learning. At this level the organization not only learns from the way it deals with errors and problems but also develops structures and mechanisms to improve future double-loop learning.

In this model single-loop learning is the ability of organizations to respond to problems without adaptation whereas in double-loop learning the organization itself adapts and changes. Deutero-learning thus goes beyond this and the organization is reflexively learning to learn. Senge (1990) refers to adaptive learning, which is equivalent to double-loop learning, and generative learning, which is deutero-learning, saying that, in the current highly competitive world, organizations need to develop generative learning if they are to survive. Similarly it is this third level of learning that writers such as Argyris and Schön suggest should be the aspiration of a learning organization.

In the field of human services a simplistic model of a learning organization is being promoted in the United Kingdom by the SCIE. This model suggests that a learning organization is 'an organization that uses evidence-based practice and informed decision-making' (SCIE, 2004: 1). This attempt to equate evidence based-practice with organizational learning clearly has little to do with the literature on learning organizations but a lot more to do with SCIE's remit of promoting the effective use of evidence.

The SCIE model builds on the five characteristics of a learning organization identified by Iles and Sutherland (2001): structure; information systems;

human resource practices; organizational culture; and leadership. In suggesting this framework, Iles and Sutherland claim (2001: 17) that there is growing consensus about these features characterizing the learning organization and SCIE have slightly adapted this model to include service user views.

Although it is welcome that this model promoted by SCIE seeks to develop a culture in which it is possible to 'nurture innovation and provide the freedom to try new things, to risk failure and to learn from mistakes' (SCIE, 2004: 7), this does not fit with the very top-down management that comes from the target-setting and scientific bureaucratic approach outlined above. The thinking behind this approach still focuses on similar issues to those in the management approaches above; for example, interventions are aimed at the organization as a whole and structures are important (e.g. flat managerial hierarchy). Staff are seen to be motivated by appraisal and reward systems, although these do now focus on rewarding learning, and learning itself has some intrinsic value to staff. Leadership is still seen to be vested in nominated leaders who model risk taking and reflection. Also we see the idea that there is a single culture within an organization that is easily manipulable. This issue about manipulating culture is also reflected in the broader management literature on organizational learning:

> most of the writers and practitioners . . . throw around the concept of 'Culture' . . . as if we understood well what that concept means. I am especially struck by the glibness of those who call for the creation of 'learning cultures' or 'cultures of openness and trust,' as if culture could be ordered up like an item on a restaurant menu.
>
> Schein (1999: 1)

Learning organization approaches do have a focus on the wellbeing of staff, which differs from the approaches above in which staff needs are subordinated to the needs of the organization. There is also a recognition that organizations need to adapt to an environment that is possibly turbulent and will require changes to the organization's direction. However, the approach is still in most cases certain, with a view that there is an agreed direction for the organization set from the top.

Within the management literature there is a view that many approaches to developing a learning organization are over-simplistic. Thus Schein states (1999):

> the [Learning Organization] is a complex beast consisting of many systems whose separate learning and change efforts must be coordinated and integrated. It is time to accept the reality of this complexity and stop oversimplifying systemic learning processes by touting particular remedies like leadership, vision, re-engineering, total quality, customer focus, systems thinking and the like.

He poses the question, why does change in a subsystem rarely diffuse to the whole organization?, and goes on to propose that stable organizations are stable because they have a tendency to respond to such changes without fundamentally changing themselves.

Thus the theory of organizational learning has much to be said for it. It does have humanistic values that recognize the worth of staff working in the organization. It also has a conception that organizations have to be reflective and may have to change their own fundamental character to respond to changes in their environment.

Strengths and weaknesses of rational planning and control in human services

The approaches discussed so far in this chapter have developed on the basis of a framework of rational planning and control. These approaches use a machine metaphor to build a picture in which organizations can be steered from the top by having a clear statement of shared mission; their culture and structure can be designed and adapted to remove irrational or poor performance; work can be specified and detailed using written procedures and rules; risks can be anticipated and procedures to remove them put in place; and the workplace can contain staff who fit in their place because they have clear roles and responsibilities.

The assumptions that shape approaches based on rational planning and control, and which most of the theories discussed so far in this chapter hold in common, are surprisingly deeply ingrained in our thinking, even in the field of human services. They often become evident in statements made by those who are critical, sometimes rightly, of the operation of human services organizations. Thus Lord Laming, in his report on the inquiry into the death of Victoria Climbié (DH, 2003a), says that 'the single most important change in the future must be the drawing of clear lines of accountability.' This call for clear lines of accountability will be familiar to those who have read the many reports of inquiries into child deaths in which it is made time after time. In a similar vein we see those trying to shape a new approach to human services management, such as Simmons (2007: 13) in her workbook on social care governance published by the SCIE, saying:

> Leaders need to have a strategic vision and an understanding of social care governance. They will determine the culture, structures and resources required to take this agenda forward. Corporate leadership is about ensuring there is a competent workforce, clarity about roles and responsibilities, clear structures which address current and future service needs and accountability regarding relevant legislative requirements. Controls and assurances should be in place to manage anticipated risks linked to achieving strategic and operational objectives.

The strengths of mechanistic approaches to organizations are those in the underlying metaphor of a machine. Mechanistic approaches work well in the conditions in which a machine works well. This is: (a) when the tasks to be performed or the services and products to be produced are straightforward, simple and limited in variety; (b) when it is important to produce the same product or standard of service time and again; (c) when the environment is stable enough to ensure that the products produced or services provided will be appropriate to the requirements of those needing them; (d) when precision, rather than discretion and judgement, is at a premium; and (e) when the humans who make up the machine can routinely follow the rules and conform to the organizational design.

From this description of their strengths it is understandable how a range of organizations from fast food chains through to aircraft maintenance departments have applied mechanistic approaches to their work with varying degrees of success. In certain aspects of surgical wards where safety, precision, and clear accountability are at a premium, the application of mechanistic approaches has clear strengths.

A key weakness of mechanistic models for organizations is that they create difficulty in adapting to changing circumstances because their rule-based structures make them rigid and inflexible and restrain creativity and innovation. They can create mindless conformity to rules and regulations, producing at worst a 'jobsworth' approach in which anything out of the ordinary cannot be done as 'It's more than my job's worth'; or a simple blindness to those aspects that fall outside the standard, routinized responses to problems. This latter type of approach was seen in a local authority social care department in which one of us carried out research (Bilson and Thorpe, 2007). The organization had developed a mechanistic approach in which standardized packages of care were provided to older people. In many cases this meant that the recipient got an effective if somewhat depersonalized package of support. However, the lack of vision this created is illustrated by the comments from a case file at the point of closure of a case leaving an old couple with little support. The case concerned a bedfast woman whose husband was worried about his continuing ability to care for his spouse, exacerbated by living in a third floor apartment with restricted access:

> Mrs. Y is a very poorly lady all of her needs are met by her husband (he will not accept help) . . . issues raised were around housing issues. Mr. and Mrs. Y have been waiting for ground floor accommodation for a long time. I have liaised with housing re my concerns.

The extract shows what we saw as the assumption of the worker, and the manager who closed the case, that their role was to provide packages of physical care and that social aspects of the problems such as inappropriate housing were not part of the team's responsibility. Note the bold statement is made that 'he will not accept help' despite the file making it clear that the husband would have valued emotional support and advocacy to help secure rehousing. The help that Mr Y turned down consisted of packages of home care and he made it clear that this was not the support he needed. The statement that 'the issues raised were around housing' shows how social problems such as inappropriate accommodation were not seen to be the responsibility of this social work team. The research showed that Mrs Y and her husband were not alone in suffering from what appeared to be a rigid mechanistic approach to social work that was unable to meet the needs of anyone who did not require the support available from the range of standardized packages of care that the organization produced. The approach used to help the organization to reflect on and change these rigid practices is written about elsewhere (Bilson and Thorpe, 2007) and will be the subject of the next chapter.

Like Morgan, quoted at the beginning of this chapter, we believe that any image or metaphor that we use to shape our vision of an organization is partial, and will reveal some aspects whilst hiding others. In recognising this it is important to realize that what is revealed and what is hidden is not random but is a function of the metaphor we use. In particular Morgan (1986: 34) suggests that:

> in understanding organization as a rational, technical process, mechanical imagery tends to underplay the human aspects of organization, and to overlook the fact that the tasks facing organizations are often much more complex, uncertain, and difficult than those that can be performed by most machines.

Conclusion

The approaches to management discussed in this chapter continue to be dominant currently. Thus, according to the Chartered Management Institute's survey of 1,500 UK managers (Worral and Cooper, 2007) the most commonly experienced management styles are bureaucratic (experienced by 40 per cent of respondents. Note that managers could select more than one style to represent their experience so percentages given add up to more than 100), reactive (37 per cent) and authoritarian (30 per cent), while just 17 per cent experienced management as innovative, 15 per cent as trusting and 13 per cent as entrepreneurial. Public-sector organizations scored highest on the bureaucratic, reactive and authoritarian measures and lowest on the accessible, empowering, innovative and trusting ones. Also the proportion of managers that reported their organization was bureaucratic, reactive and authoritarian had increased over the levels reported three years earlier. This is despite the evidence that such approaches to management were found to be more associated with declining rather than growing organizations. In this vein the report concludes, 'It is disappointing that bureaucratic, reactive and authoritarian styles prevail in the UK, when entrepreneurial, accessible and empowering styles are associated with far higher levels of motivation, health and productivity' (Worral and Cooper, 2007: 9).

We believe that this proliferation of command and control approaches comes not from the personality traits of managers but rather from the metaphors and beliefs through which we view organizations and hence their management. In particular we fear we are seeing the fruition of Max Weber's (1968) concerns and that we are getting increasingly caught up in what he called an *iron cage of rationality* in which rational processes proliferate within bureaucracies and their outcomes dehumanize the workplace and lead to what Ritzer has called the *McDonaldization* of society. We are concerned that the present trend to standardize and control, through target setting, auditing and viewing services users as consumers, can on occasion lead to irrational outcomes such as poorer-quality, less flexible services that do not meet the needs of those we serve.

The very rational nature of classical management approaches can be seductive. It is attractive to believe that having a clear and well-communicated vision, clear and specific targets, a well thought-out plan, clear lines of accountability, or detailed procedures, along with a planned workforce, will lead to effective services. However, it will be argued in later chapters that, not only can these rational devices lead to a devaluation of the human nature of human services organizations, but they do not provide solutions to some of the most pressing and enduring problems such as failures in child protection or meeting the needs of a growing elderly population. Whereas the worse excesses of classical management approaches can be ameliorated by the humanistic approaches that developed later, they still continue to have a singular view of the nature of organizations, their purpose and goals. The workforce is valued in these later approaches, but only in so far as that improves the performance of the organization; in other words they are not valued in their own right. This frequently singular managerial focus of human resource management and its tendency to rely on organizational design make it, like the classical management and strategic approaches, less able to deal with messy or turbulent environments such as those frequently encountered in social work.

Our view is that human services are particularly complex and uncertain. Not only is there difficulty in matching resources to the particular needs of the individuals requiring our help, but it is also frequently difficult to even know what the nature of the problem of those that we wish to help is. In these circumstances the routinized procedures of rational-objectivist approaches to organizations can stifle the flexibility and creativity that such difficult problems require. We will suggest that, in the unstable environment that typifies human services agencies, a different approach is required: one that can deal with the uncertainty of the environment in which social work operates. We will deal with this issue in the next chapter, in which we will consider the approaches to management that operate on very different assumptions from those based on rational planning and control that have been the subject of this chapter.

6 New metaphors for management
Reflective-pluralist approaches to organizations

> We are reaching the end of a line of development associated with the mechanistic thinking of the industrial age and are in need of an alternative. We need new metaphors that can help us remake ourselves, our society, and our relations with planet Earth.
>
> (Morgan, 1993: 293)

> Some problems are so complex that you have to be highly intelligent and well informed just to be undecided about them.
>
> L. J. Peter (cited by Blockley and Godfrey, 2000: 57)

Introduction

In this chapter we continue to focus on management and organizational theories and approaches that apply to the organization as a whole. However, we will now look at those that take a more reflective-pluralist approach and thus acknowledge the different viewpoints and multiple voices that are heard in organizations. We will thus look at theories and approaches that use a range of metaphors for organizations and which focus on their creative and adaptive capacities. Whereas organisations are often viewed within these theories as holistic their behaviour is essentially unpredictable and seen as emerging from complex interactions within the networks of their components and their environment (departments, teams, people, other organizations etc.). In contrast to the mechanistic approaches of the rational-scientific and the later socio-technical theories seen in the last chapter, approaches here have a major focus on the uncertainty of problem definition and multiplicity of viewpoints through which organizations can be seen. The approaches discussed here include some of the more recent developments in systems theory and complexity theory as well as ideas drawn from postmodern theorizing.

The chapter is intended not to provide a comprehensive view of all the more recent theories that acknowledge the uncertain basis of management but to give an introduction and brief overview to some that the authors think are particularly useful for understanding the social work management task in the twenty-first century. In the last chapter we considered a range of theories that dominate much of the social policy context of social work. These approaches tend to view organizational goals as being, or able to be, widely agreed and, where there are different perspectives, these represent a problem that needs to be solved by better communication of and conformity to the vision or goals for the organization as a whole. We are looking at a number of different approaches here that recognize diversity and pluralism because we believe that when a manager takes action to improve or otherwise change an organization s/he does so based on how s/he sees the world. Each worldview leads to very different actions, which are rational within that viewpoint. The approaches discussed in this chapter offer diverse viewpoints, which lead to different possibilities for action. We believe it is necessary for a manager in social work to have an understanding that includes a range of approaches to organizations that recognize and work with the diversity and sometimes conflicting interests of a wide range of stakeholders.

It will be seen that, in the theories discussed below, management control is replaced by approaches to promote creativity within all levels of the organization (Bilson and Ross, 1999). Such theories highlight the importance of considering the activities of any one organization in relation to that of others. In this respect, joint working and interdependence of organizations is highlighted. These organizational theories generally agree on the importance of flattening hierarchies, facilitating informal networks and celebrating diversity. We will mainly look at ideas that involve some form of systems thinking about the organization as a whole, which in its newer forms has a reflexive quality indicated in the quote below:

> Systems thinking respects complexity . . . [t]his means, among other things, I accept that sometimes my understanding is incomplete. It means when I experience a situation or an issue as complex, I don't always know what's included in the issue and what's not. It means I have to accept my view is partial and provisional and other people will have a different view. It means I resist the temptation to try and simplify the issue by breaking it down. It also means I have to accept there is more than one way of understanding the complexity.
>
> (Open University, 2008)

The approaches in this chapter draw on a diverse set of understandings that have in common a questioning of simple realist beliefs about the nature of the world and the understanding of our experiences of it. They are underpinned by a range of sociological and philosophical theories including social constructionism, critical theory, phenomenology, constructivism, postmodernism and, in the sciences, complexity theory, cybernetics and certain aspects of biology. These are applied to management with a primary focus on the organization as a whole though there are overlaps with approaches to leadership seen in Chapter 4.

Figure 6.1 shows the five main approaches we will consider, starting with soft systems methodology, developed by Checkland and Scholes. This approach to organizations draws on phenomenology and rejects the earlier mechanistic systems thinking. The second approach focuses on complexity theory, which deals with the ideas of complex adaptive systems. Next comes a postmodern perspective with examples of its application drawn from the writing of Gareth Morgan. Following this we will consider critical systems theory, which attempts to apply to action research in organizations ideas that are underpinned by Habermas's sociological theories. This puts forward an approach that pluralistically draws on a range of methodologies whilst attempting to combat oppression. Finally we consider how writings of Gregory Bateson and Humberto Maturana, two of the key systems thinkers whose work was influential in family therapy, have been used in organizational management. Here we will also look at approaches to organizations that view the organization as a network of conversations and that provide a more embodied emotional/rational approach to organizational change.

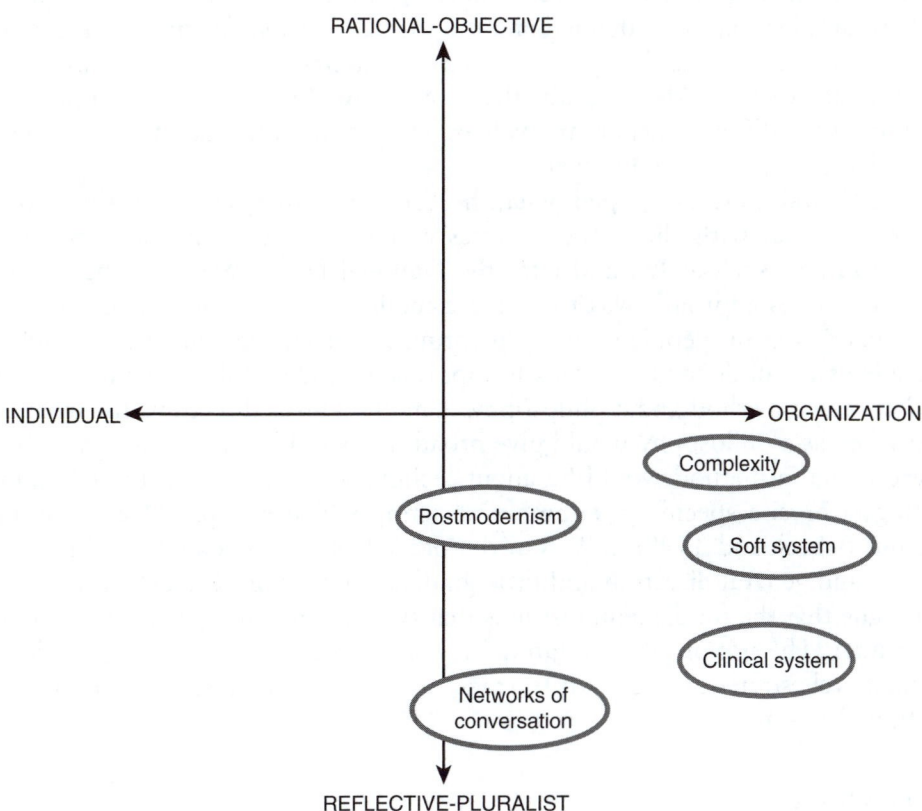

Figure 6.1 The reflective-pluralist and organization quadrant.

Soft systems methodology

The soft systems approach has its roots in phenomenology, with its focus on the mental world of the observer rather than the external world. It has produced a methodology for dealing with organizational problems rather than a framework for organizational design. This framework has been expounded in a number of publications but key texts are Checkland's two books (Checkland, 1999; Checkland and Scholes, 1990). The former lays out the original framework whereas the latter makes some changes to deal with developments and criticisms, and in particular expands the framework for use by managers within organizations. Checkland's approach was developed out of his own failing attempts to apply the systems methodologies of Operational Research (OR), Systems Analysis (SA) and Systems Engineering (SE) to managerial problems. These systems approaches had developed out of efforts in the Second World War to assist the allies through, for example, increasing the efficiency of radar systems and optimizing the results of bombing raids on German cities. They used a mathematical modelling approach mainly based on mechanistic metaphors. Because of this Checkland called them hard systems approaches. However, although these approaches were immensely successful in a number of areas where problems are well defined and the various factors effecting them can be accurately ascertained, they proved less useful in management of organizations where they were unable to handle the complexity of problems or to cope with a plurality of different beliefs and values, and, significantly, had no way to deal with issues of politics and power.

Checkland thus developed what he termed Soft Systems Methodology (SSM) to deal with these uncertainties and complexities in his work with organizations such as ICI and later the National Health System. The aim of a soft systems approach was to create a methodology for action research to be undertaken by people wanting to bring about changes in systems where problems are ill defined. He calls his approach a methodology, which he says is between a method and a philosophy. A method gives directions for what to do whereas a philosophy would give broad non-specific guidelines. The point here is that a method would be about technique, which would be too rigid, being 'a precise specific programme of action which will produce a specific result' (Checkland 1999: 162). On the other hand, a philosophy offers only broad and general direction and little guidance for action. Checkland goes on to argue that the fundamental issue is that the basis for his approach is one of learning: 'The notion of "a solution" . . . is inappropriate in a methodology which orchestrates a process of learning, which, as a process, is never-ending' (1999: 278–9).

Four activities

Initially SSM consisted of a seven step model as shown in Figure 6.2. The methodology has gone on to have a looser framework consisting of four activities

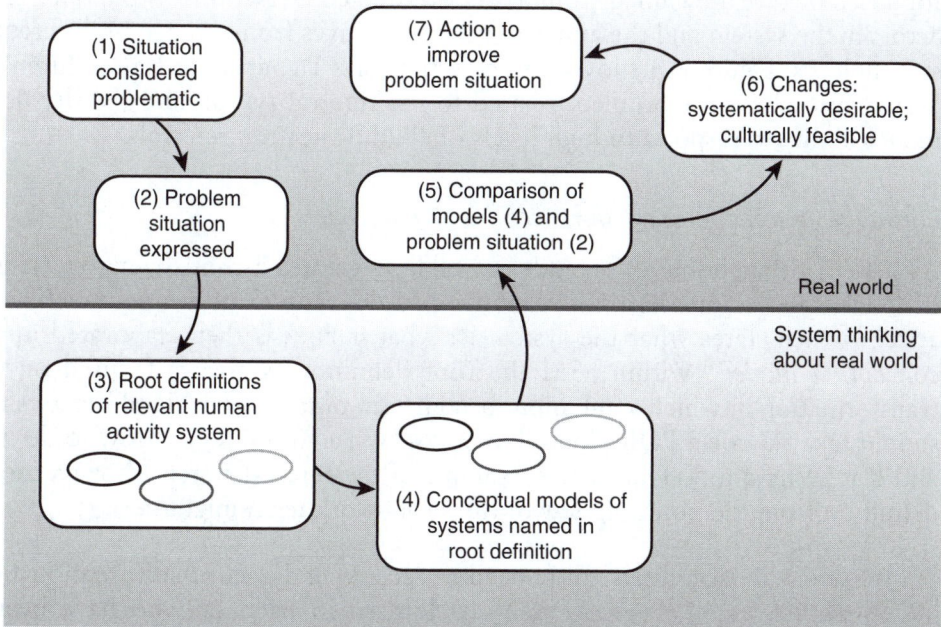

Figure 6.2 SSM seven step model. Based on Checkland (1999: 163).

(Checkland 1999: A15): (1) finding out about a problem situation including its cultural and political environment; (2) formulating some relevant purposeful activity models; (3) comparing the models with the problem situation and using them to debate about 'desirable and feasible changes' and also to debate the accommodation between conflicting interests to identify actions that will improve the situation to be undertaken; (4) taking action based on the previous steps.

Finding out about a problem situation

The first activity involves producing a rich description of the relevant system(s); the method typically used for this is to draw a *rich picture* or pictures. These are usually drawings that represent key features of a problem situation, as perceived by the person drawing the picture. There are no rules for drawing rich pictures and, whereas some are quite formal, others are cartoon-like in nature. Much depends on the skill and purposes of the person(s) doing the drawing. By their nature rich pictures are selective. It is an art to select issues, conflicts and other problematic and interesting aspects to depict. When done well, rich pictures can promote creativity and express the relationships in a problem situation better than prose. They are used in the development of models and in the process of debate, in which they allow the easy sharing of ideas between those involved, catalyse discussion and act as an excellent memory aid. Data for a rich picture are gained from interviews and conversations with a range of actors in the system and the aim is to get perspectives from a range of different stakeholders. Figure 6.3 shows a rich picture of a Department for Children's Services in which the problem related to the referral system and the department's ability to respond to high levels of child protection referrals.

Formulating some relevant purposeful activity models

As part of the building of a model Checkland creates a root definition. This is defined as: 'A concise, tightly constructed description of a *human activity system* which states what the system is; what it does is then elaborated in a *conceptual model*'. Within SSM the root definition is always focused on a transformation in which some input becomes an output. Checkland suggests it should take the form PQR where P denotes 'What to do', Q is 'How to do it' and R is 'Why do it'. Thus in the example of the referral system above a root definition from the point of view of the social work team might be:

> A system to accurately and speedily receive and record information by telephone, email, fax or letter on children in need or who have been significantly harmed or are at risk of significant harm from agencies and individuals by the social work team in order to make decisions on initial actions to be taken to meet the child's needs or provide protection.

When building a conceptual model for the transformation (T for short) it has to be recognized that this is done from a particular weltanschauung, or worldview – which defines the assumptions, belief or point of view that makes the transformation reasonable and worth achieving. Each root definition reflects a different way (W) of conceiving the problem situation. Checkland gives the example of a prison, which might be considered as a punishment system, a system to deter crime, a rehabilitation system, a system to protect society or a 'university of crime'. Together, T and W form the core of CATWOE analysis, which is a mnemonic for an approach to build coherent and comprehensive root definitions. The components of CATWOE are:

- Customers: the victims or beneficiaries of T (in our example the children and families, though other models might see this as those referring);
- Actors: those who do T (the social work team and call centre);
- Transformation: process input into output (referral into initial action);
- Weltanschauung: the worldview that makes the T meaningful in this context (the department's view of their service as offering help and providing protection);
- Owners: those responsible for T (departmental managers and local councillors);
- Environmental constraints (this would include the local political system, public opinion, the media, communities and so on).

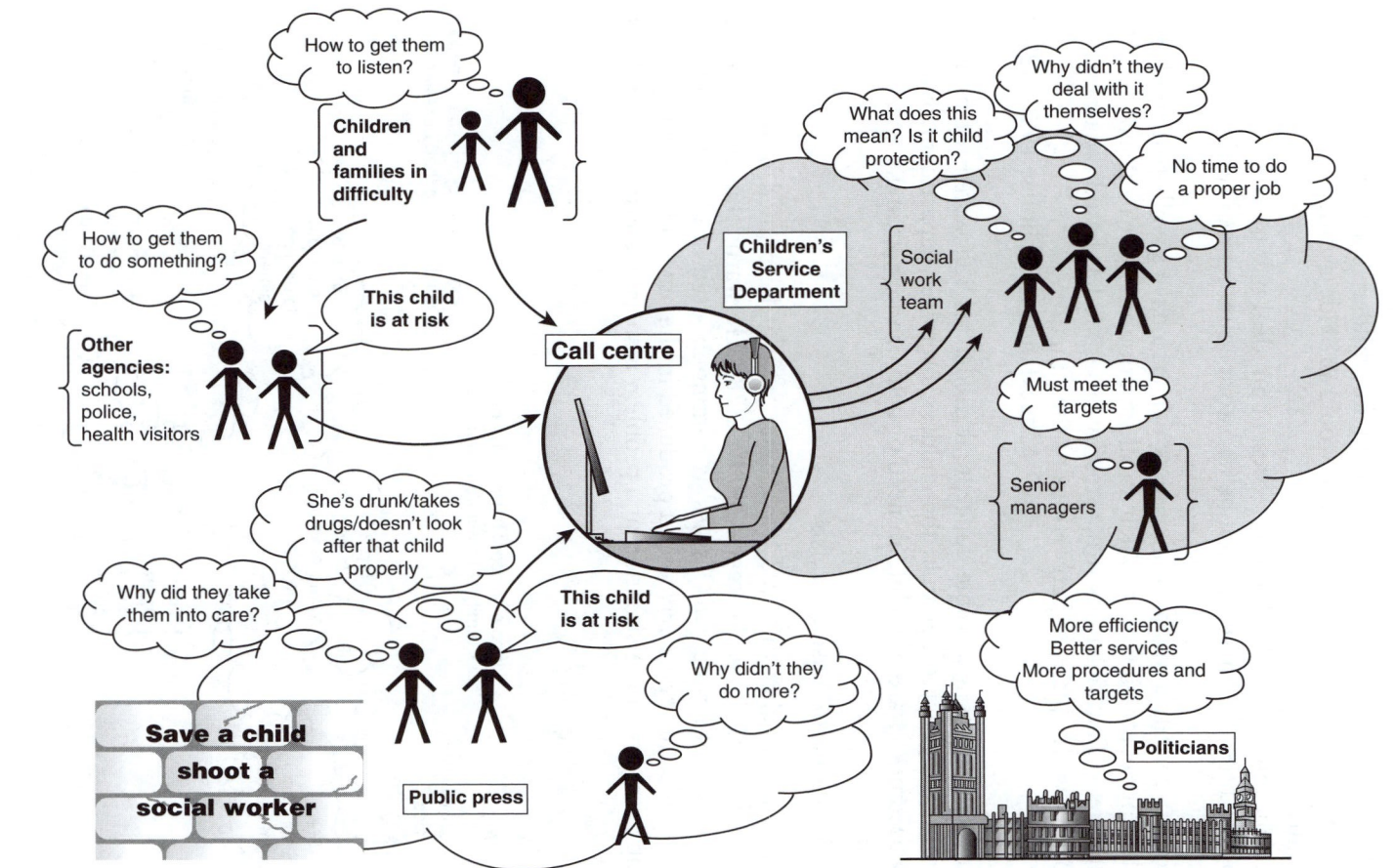

Figure 6.3 Rich pictures of a children's services referral system that uses a central call system.

However, as each W provides a different perspective then this may change the view of who the customers might be, and so on. In our example this is drawn from the point of view of the department for children's services. Interviews with children and families in difficulty would provide a different assessment and picture.

The conceptual model is built to represent an ideal picture of the system. It is recognised that the model cannot be transformed into a reality, thus:

> Models are only a means to an end, which is to have a well-structured and coherent debate about a problematical situation in order to decide how to improve it. That debate is structured by using models based on a range of worldviews to question perceptions of the situation.
>
> (Checkland and Scholes, 1990: 42–3)

Figure 6.4 shows a possible conceptual model for the system of decision making by an agency other than the children's services department once the agency becomes aware of a child in need of help or safeguarding.

Debating the situation using models

Checkland argues that the final two phases 'cannot be pinned down and as sharply defined as the early stages' (1999: A28). He warns that the language of 'problems', 'situations' and 'issues' is commonly used in everyday talk but they are subtle concepts derived and produced in the flux and happenings that make up everyday life. A situation or a problem is socially constructed and not

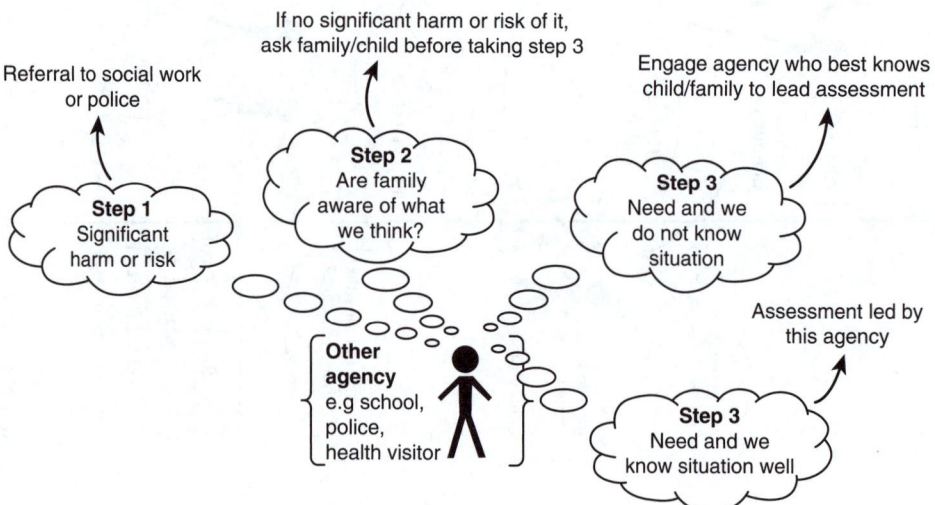

Figure 6.4 Conceptual model for other agency decision making.

a thing in the way that a desk or a chair is. No two people, even if they agree about it, will see it in precisely the same way. He thus says:

> If . . . the senior managers of a company all agree in discussion that they have a problem due to the failure of a new product to build up sales following its launch, no two of them will have precisely the same view of this situation and/or this problem. What is more some of those who 'agree' about the situation/problem may privately be seeking to ensure the failure of the new product in order that more resources can come their way!
>
> (Checkland, 1999: A28)

In the phase of having a structured debate, it takes forms that fit the particular organization. The aim is to debate with 'concerned participants in the problem situation' (1999: 177) based on a comparison between relevant aspects of the rich picture and the ideal models. To think about desirable and feasible changes participants are encouraged to consider the questions shown in Figure 6.5. Checkland warns of a frequent excessive focus on structural changes rather than process or attitudes, saying that this has been a major issue in the UK government's attempts to reform the National Health Service and a similar comment could be made about the frequent changes in social work.

In our example the Department for Children's Services would ideally have liked to have taken referrals on children directly but this was felt not to be feasible as there was substantial political commitment to a single 'front door' represented by the call centre. Instead it was decided to post social workers in the call centre on a rota basis.

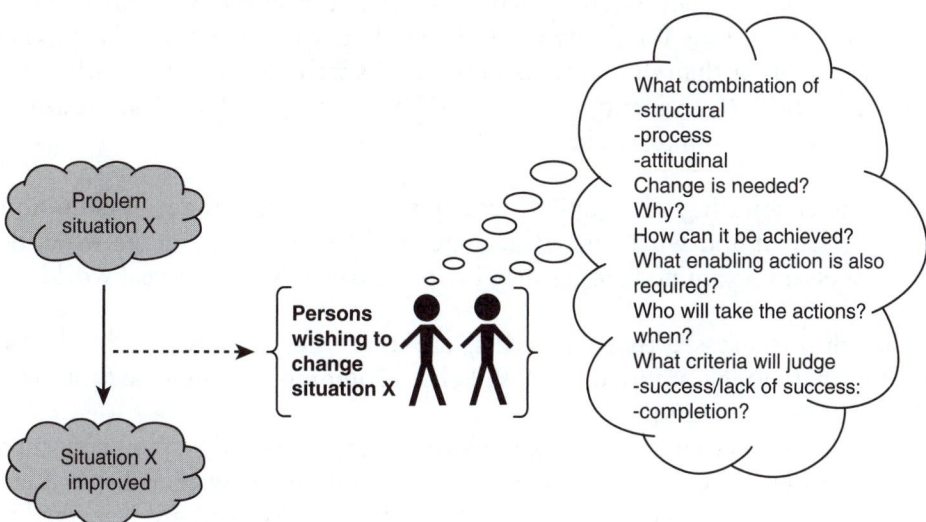

Figure 6.5 Thinking about desirable and feasible change. Based on Checkland (1999: A30).

Taking action to bring about improvement

The final phase is making 'desirable and feasible changes'. It is stressed by the authors that the changes have to take place in a 'human culture' and 'the changes will be implemented only if they are perceived as meaningful within that culture, within its world view' (Checkland and Scholes, 1990: 52).

However, although there are examples given of how this happened in practice there is little specific guidance on this step.

Soft systems methodology is seen as an iterative process that cycles through using the systems models to reflect on and debate different perceptions of the 'real world', and then taking action; the cycle is started again by using systems models to reflect on what has happened, and so on.

Strengths and weaknesses of soft systems methodology

In SSM the nature of the approach is such that there is a considerable focus on analysis and building of models of the problem situation and the 'purposeful activity system', to compare with perceptions of reality. Comparison between these models and the rich pictures of the current situation form the basis for debate. However, there is relatively little discussion on the question of how debate can best be structured to create effective change. Checkland and Scholes suggest that the social sciences literature did not produce a model for the analysis of the 'culture' of the organization and that they had to develop one 'experientially' (1990: 48) but again there is little said about the use to which this form of analysis is to be put.

Also Checkland uses systemic models conceived of as 'ideal types' for comparisons in debates. Although these models are not meant to be normative they do have implications for the type of change that will stem from them. They are seen as 'purer than the complex perspectives we manage to live with in our everyday world' (Checkland, 1999). Thus Checkland (1999: 167) suggests that the 'best systems thinkers' will:

> be quickly testing what kind of model will follow from the root definitions entertained and what kind of changes will be likely to emerge when the models are examined alongside what presently exists in the real world.

Although it is stressed that the models are used only to structure the debate, the fact that models are used at all is likely to communicate an ideal (not in the Weberian sense) solution.

Another issue lies in the development of SSM from a hard systems approach. This has implications for the nature of the definitions of systems in SSM and hence the types of model that are developed from it. Systems are described by looking at inputs and outputs in a relatively linear fashion.

Further, the notion of how changes occur in human systems through an SSM approach is implicit rather than explicitly stated. After a 'structured debate', which focuses on a comparison of the model developed through the preceding stages, changes are defined that are 'systemically desirable' and 'culturally feasible' (Checkland and Scholes, 1990: 52). These changes are then implemented, although implementation may itself be a problem situation to be tackled through a further application of SSM. Thus, despite the comments about the complex nature of human systems and the role of myths and power in organizations, there appears to be a rather linear structure to the approaches to change and to a large extent the interpersonal process involved here is glossed over or taken for granted.

Soft systems methodology has been widely used and helps to move away from the linear rational approaches seen in management theories in the last chapter. The particular use of rich pictures and models of a system to encourage debate ensures that a wide range of viewpoints can be engaged. Similarly the use of a rich picture to consider not only processes but also different perspectives on a problem helps to stimulate reflection on the nature of the problem and people's views about it. Likewise, the focus on understanding and responding to different worldviews allows it to deal with complex problem situations in which problems are understood differently and have different consequences. Soft systems methodology does not require clear goals to be established before problem solving can commence and thus allows a flexible approach to considering messy situations such as those found in social work management. Thus SSM offers a range of tools that are useful in developing organizational learning.

Complexity theory and management

Another relative newcomer to management theory is complexity. Mitleton-Kelly (2003: 24) identifies five main areas of research that have informed complexity theory:

> (a) complex adaptive systems at SFI and Europe; (b) dissipative structures by Ilya Prigogine and his co-authors; (c) autopoiesis based on the work of Maturana in biology and its application to social systems by Luhman; (d) chaos theory; and (e) increasing returns and path dependence by Brian Arthur and other economists

The universe is full of systems that are complex and constantly adapting to their environment, such as weather systems, immune systems and social systems. Complexity theory aims to provide insights into these types of systems, which it calls complex adaptive systems (CASs). A widely cited definition of a CAS is attributed to John Holland. (This is said to have been taken from Waldrop, 1993: 145).

> A Complex Adaptive System (CAS) is a dynamic network of many agents (which may represent cells, species, individuals, firms, nations) acting in

parallel, constantly reacting to what the other agents are doing. The control of a CAS tends to be highly distributed and decentralized. If there is to be any coherent behavior of the system, it has to arise from competition and cooperation among the agents themselves. The overall behavior of the system is the result of a huge number of decisions taken simultaneously by many individual agents.

Different authors see a number of related issues or properties of CASs. Mitleton-Kelly (2003) suggests that the following 10 principles apply to all CASs. Of these 10, four are principles (2–5) of all systems, not just CASs:

1 *Self-organization*: the system maintains its own organization. This differentiates a CAS from other types of systems. For example the human body (a CAS consisting of cells), while it remains alive, maintains its structure of arms, legs etc. and the relationships between them itself despite all its cells being replaced on a regular basis. This process is self-organization.
2 *Emergence*: the behaviour of a system is a property of it as a whole and cannot be predicted from analysis of the constituent parts; that is, the whole is more than the sum of its parts.
3 *Connectivity*: the elements of a system are connected to one another.
4 *Interdependence*: the behaviour of one element of a system has effects on other elements.
5 *Feedback*: the process by which the value of some property of a system is introduced as an input to the system's production of that property. Feedback can be positive and increase the amount of the property (the escalating screech of a microphone placed in front of its own loudspeaker) or negative (the regulation of temperature in a heating system by a thermostat). CASs typically have a complex mesh of positive and negative feedback loops.
6 *Far from equilibrium*: this means that the system is open and receives energy from outside its boundaries.
7 *Space of possibilities*: this suggests that a CAS is constantly undertaking a process of adaption to changing circumstances through changing itself or its behaviour.
8 *Co-evolution*: in adapting to its environment a CAS also changes its environment and the two, system and environment, change together or co-evolve.
9 *Historicity and time*: the current state of a system is dependent on its history of interactions because its structure will have been changed because of its history. In CASs this process of change through time is irreversible.
10 *Path-dependence*: this suggests that, as CASs are subject to positive as well as negative feedback, at any point in time there are many possible paths that a system can take and that the path taken will depend on an interplay between the state of the system and the stimuli in the environment. Thus a small stimulus may lead to a major change and vice versa.

If we consider an organization as a CAS this would suggest that we cannot predict the way that it would respond to a particular stimulus such as a management intervention. Its response would depend on a range of issues including its history, its current state, how it sees the intervention and so on.

A number of theorists use ideas drawn from chaos theory and apply these to CASs. These will be briefly discussed as they have been applied in some writing around social work (e.g. Black, Hinrichs and Fabian, 2007; Foote and Stanners, 2002; Stacey, 1997). One of these ideas drawn from chaos theory (Stacey, 1997) is that complex adaptive systems have effectively three behaviour types: chaotic; stable and unchanging; but innovative 'on the edge of chaos'. Thus there is a suggestion from these writers that we need to move organizations towards the edge of chaos – though what organizational behaviour, in the mathematical context, constitutes the edge of chaos is a moot point.

A further idea is that the agents in a CAS act on the basis of schema (simple rules that govern their actions); a concept that links to the idea in chaos theory that order can emerge from chaotic behaviour such as the emergent patterns of flocking birds through the individuals acting on simple rules. Some adherents of complexity theory still adhere to this idea thus:

> The science of complexity is concerned with the behaviour of non-linear network systems consisting of large numbers of agents in which each agent employs some sets of rules, which we will call schemas, to interact with other agents in the system to produce joint action. For example, a colony of ants is a complex adaptive system and so is a flock of birds . . . or a troop of baboons. And this is exactly what a human brain is (the agents being neurons), as well as the human mind (the agents being imaginal symbols), as well as a group, an organisation and a society (the agents being us).
>
> (Stacey, 1997: 185)

The issue with this approach is the implication that human group behaviour is rule bound in a similar way to that of a flock of birds.

The mathematical discipline of chaos theory (see Gleick, 1997) was taken up avidly by management consultants and academics in the 1980s and still occurs in some writing on the subject. This approach makes the assumption that these mathematical concepts are either a good metaphor for or directly applicable to organizational behaviour. However, there is a widely held view that it was disappointing in its results, and it has now been effectively subsumed as a subset of complexity theory. Thus Meek *et al.* (2007: 25) state:

> Complexity is now often distinguished from chaos by theorists interested in human behavior (Anderson, 1999; Lissack, 2002; McDaniel & Driebe, 2005; Mitleton-Kelly, 2003; Newell, 2001, 2003; Newell & Meek, 2000; Smedes, 2004), who now reject as inappropriate to human beings the mindless iteration of simple invariant rules underlying chaos theory. The

dominant model has become complex adaptive systems (CAS), which focus on the holistic patterns formed through human interactions.

Those applying complexity theory to organizations insist that their approach demands a complete mind shift from managers. They have to accept that the long-term future operation of their organization is inherently unknowable. This is because organizations and their environments are sensitive to small differences in initial conditions, which means that their behaviour is unpredictable. From such a standpoint long-term planning is untenable. In fact the strictures of long-term planning associated with the pursuit of a particular vision and objectives are seen as being likely to make the organization inflexible and unable to adapt to environmental changes. Because continuous transformation and emergent order is a natural state of CASs, managers can trust in emergence and make space and flexibility for their organizations to adapt. Management should have fewer hierarchies and promote working across boundaries.

Thus Minas (2005), talking about change management in mental health services, suggests the need for whole systems working (see next chapter for a discussion of whole systems approaches) including joint budgets and a system-wide perspective. In this approach people should be encouraged to work across boundaries and disciplines wherever feasible. He also suggests the need to replace detailed specifications of work and procedures with minimum specification – a few simple and flexible rules that specify principles of the approach (see also Plsek and Wilson, 2001, for a discussion of minimum specifications in a range of health care settings). Managers should also encourage diversity in order to allow the organization to explore its space of possibilities (e.g. Minas, 2005). Thus it challenges the view that consensus in organizations is a good thing and suggests that shared vision is likely to lead to groupthink. These classical management ideas are likely to reduce the creativity and learning necessary for organizational survival. Similarly it suggests that organizational politics need to be fostered to promote diversity and allow co-evolution to take place.

Strengths and weaknesses of complexity theory

Complexity theory is itself still in its early days and little work has been done on moving beyond its focus on natural systems (Mitleton-Kelly, 2003). The strong claim that organizations are complex adaptive systems governed by the mathematical laws of chaos has little or no empirical evidence to support it apart from some suggestive computer models (Jackson, 2003; Rosenhead, 1998). The suggestion that the application of the mathematics of chaos theory to organizations has been disappointing (Local Government Management Board, 1996) and the movement away from the mathematical basis suggested by Meek *et al.* (2007) above may be thought to leave it with little to distinguish it from other systemic theories. Jackson locates it among functionalist theories, which do not challenge the underpinning values of capitalism. Thus Jackson (2003: 123) states:

> Its advocates sometimes claim that it represents an advance on systems thinking. This is nonsense. With its emphasis on holism, emergence, interdependence and relationships, complexity theory is definitely a systems approach. Indeed, previous work in the systems field, on informal groups, group working, autonomous work groups, double-loop learning, organizations as information processing systems, open systems and 'turbulent field' environments, seems to cover much of the territory that complexity theory wants to claim as its own. In fact many of the ideas behind complex adaptive systems are directly informed by Humberto Maturana's work on self-referential systems which is widely used in systemic approaches to organisations and will be discussed later. Besides these criticisms of its theoretical basis there is still little in the way of methods to aid managers.

However complexity has captured the imagination of a wide range of writers in organizational theory in health care and here it has been among the strongest of the challengers to the command and control approaches seen in new managerialism, even gaining some credibility in government circles. The values within it certainly promote a trusting and a more egalitarian and less controlling approach than classical management. Similarly, the belief that organizational solutions to problems will emerge, if there is flexibility and sufficient diversity, has much in common with humanist principles. Its use of ideas from physical and biological systems undergoing turbulence offers a range of interesting metaphors for organizations that challenge linear rational understandings of change. Likewise it offers challenges to traditional management concepts such as shared vision, the need for a strong organizational culture and the need for top-down control. Complexity theorists acknowledge the turbulence of the organizational environment, seeing it as leading to a need for greater levels of cooperation between different enterprises. Thus, unlike many organizational theories, their focus is not on competition with other organizations but on cooperation, trying to bring about greater participation, partnership and decision making in 'multiagency settings'.

Postmodernism and management

Debates still rage over whether the postmodern is to be understood as a historical period following modernity or as an epistemological position with varying descriptions from being an emancipatory countermovement to a nihilist anti-humanist revolt. Postmodernism, as it appears as an influence on studies of organizations, is not simply any theoretical position that is not modernist, but draws specifically on the works of postmodern theorists such as Derrida, Foucault, Baudrillard and Lyotard. There are as many postmodern theories as there are postmodernists so this section can only give a brief introduction to some ideas from this area. One of the distinguishing characteristics of postmodernism in philosophy and the humanities generally is that it reduces the emphasis on fixed meanings and precise structures of measurement, and instead emphasizes discourses, which dynamically shape and are shaped by the perceptions, concepts and participation of those using them. Jackson (2003: 255) suggests that this:

> was developed because the dominating and 'totalizing' discourses of modernism . . . are seen as suppressing difference and creativity. The postmodern systems approach by contrast emphasizes the exceptional, seeks to make a space for suppressed voices to be heard and hopes to unleash creativity and a sense of fun by engaging people's emotions.

There is no general agreed definition or framework for a postmodern approach to management. However, Hassard suggests '5 key epistemological notions' which are relevant to the conceptual framework for postmodernism in organisations. These five key epistemological notions are 'representation', 'reflexivity', 'writing', 'différance' and 'de-centring the subject' (Hassard, 1993: 11). The following discussion of these notions gives a brief overview of the concepts.

Representation

This key notion is that postmodernism rejects the idea that knowledge is representational of an externally existing, transcendental reality and that language provides value-free, objective descriptions of it. Thus Gergen says (1992: 215) 'We should view these bodies of language we call knowledge in some lighter vein – as ways of putting things, some pretty others petty – but in no way calling for ultimate commitments, condemnations, or profound consequences.' This viewpoint thus challenges the use of empirical approaches in management since it is seen to represent not an accurate representation of reality but rather a process of professional self-justification.

Reflexivity

The postmodernist notion of reflexivity suggests that 'we must also possess the ability to be critical of our own intellectual assumptions' (Hassard, 1993: 12). This notion also implies a rejection of grand narratives such as that of historical progress or scientific progress.

Writing

According to Hassard, the idea of writing concerns the way we create order in our environment. In this sense writing relates to the structure of representations rather than the meaning of communications. Writing is seen as a process that is undecidable. The meaning of a text always defers to other texts and to the reader for its meaning. Cooper (1989: 491) thus states: 'we have seen that we are actually "inhabited" by writing and its contradictions. Among other things, this . . . destroys the idea that the subject is a more or less rational, self-contained unit.'

Différance

This is Derrida's term for a concept which has two areas of meaning: that concepts continually defer to other concepts in order to have meaning (the meaning is referential – it is not contained in the text itself); and that concepts are defined in terms of being an extracted half with the concept differing from its opposite. Cooper (1989) describes one aspect of différance as being comparable to the concept of 'information' in information theory. Bateson's idea that information is news of difference that makes a difference (and hence not a representation of the external world) can be seen to have similarities with Derrida's ideas.

De-centring the subject

This concept stems from Derrida's rejection of an independently existing, isolated, subjective self. This is a challenge to the traditional western view in which actions are carried out on the basis of a personalized subjective core of awareness coordinated by a knowing self. Derrida suggests that consciousness is never a direct and unmediated experience. The subject is always undecided and undecideable and exists in a system of relations between different strata. Thus the rationality of the subject is denied and along with it many of the presuppositions of science.

Because of the many versions of postmodernism there are many different interpretations of what postmodern organizations might be like. Some common ideas are that it challenges and reverses power hierarchies and the oppression of minorities. Thus Boje and Dennehy say:

> The promise of postmodern management is to get rid of management. To empower a diversity of people from women, to minorities, to handy-capable, to gays who have been marginalized by center-planned, center-organized, center-led, and center-controlled enterprises. In postmodern management, small is beautiful; temporary coalitions of small groups is power; social problems can be dealt with better by the oppressed than by the bureaucratic oppressors.
>
> (Boje and Dennehy, 1999: 41)

Thus a strength for social work management of postmodern writing is that it values the voices of those who are marginalized and suggests a different approach to power.

We will now look at the work of Gareth Morgan as an example of the use of postmodern ideas in management. Morgan has used ideas from postmodern thinkers along with a range of other theorists and philosophers to build an approach to working with organizations that stresses the importance of the assumptions and images we have of organizations for the way we operate within them. He suggested (Morgan, 1986, 2006) that a range of metaphors underpinned organizational theories, looking at them as machines, brains, cultures, political systems, psychic prisons and so on. The implication of considering this range of metaphors to reflect on organizational issues was that each brought forth its own complementary and competing insights, each with its own strengths and weaknesses. He suggested that most management theories limit themselves to one perspective and seldom reflect on the implications of the metaphors. He went on to propose that the assumptions and metaphors that underpin our thoughts and actions shape the worlds we live and thus there is a possibility, which he called 'imaginization', that we can become more effective in understanding the part that we take in shaping organizational life. He states:

> In coining the word Imaginization my intention is to break free of this mechanical meaning by symbolizing the close links between images and actions. Organization is always shaped by underlying images and ideas; we organize as we imaginize; and it is always possible to imaginize in many different ways.
>
> (Morgan, 1986: 343)

In his book *Imaginization* (1993) Morgan takes further his idea that it is possible to change organizations by helping people to create new metaphors for them. He builds an approach to work in organizations that promotes 'Imaginization'. In this he identifies three key principles (Morgan, 1993: 284–94).

1: 'The interconnection between "reading" and "writing"'

This principle is based on the metaphor of social reality as a text. Drawing on the work of Derrida (1978), he suggests that organizational realities can be considered as living texts that are continually being 'written' and 'read' (Morgan, 1993: 283). His basic idea is that metaphors can help people in organizations to write and read their organizations in new and different ways. His book invites 'you to become your own theorist, using images and metaphors to engage in a continuous construction and deconstruction of meaning in your encounters with everyday reality' (1993: 283).

He thus suggests that new ways of reading the organization can lead to its transformation and new ways of writing it. Each organization can be read in a variety of ways that depend on the range of assumptions and perspectives that the reader brings. Imaginization is intended to help people to become and remain open to the possibility of many different interpretations and hence meanings in any situation, and suggests that such a position leads to new writing of the organizations in ways that are more flexible and adaptable to change.

2: How images can be used as 'mirrors' and 'windows'

According to Morgan, this principle draws significantly on the work of Watzlawick and the Mental Research Institute (Watzlawick *et al.*, 1974; further ideas from this group will be discussed later in the chapter when we discuss the work of Gregory Bateson, who was a key member of this group). In particular it uses Watzlawick *et al.*'s concept of reframing, in which there is an attempt to change the conceptual or emotional framework within which a situation is experienced in order to change its meaning. However, it would appear that this is a 'loose' use of Watzlawick's concept of reframing. Morgan uses metaphors in his consultancy mainly through encouraging those involved to think metaphorically about various aspects of their situation and only occasionally by introducing his own metaphors. The idea of using metaphors is that they are open – the interpretation of them is very much up to the 'reader' – and they also encourage different or new ways of thinking about situations.

One of the basic ideas underlying Morgan's principle of mirroring – using metaphors to give new perspectives on an organization – is based on the idea drawn from the biologists Maturana and Varela (1980), also discussed later when we consider organizations as networks of conversations, that systems create their own boundaries through a process of self-reference or in their terms self-organization. He suggests this is based on the idea that the identity of a system is its most important product, which contrasts with ideas about systems that focus on goals and objectives. This led to Morgan's view that focusing on an organization's goals and objectives was likely to be unproductive. Focusing on the idea that self-referential systems interact with their environments in ways which maintain self-identity, he goes on to argue:

> if you wish to change a system, it may be more important to work on its sense of identity rather than on the goals it is trying to achieve. If one can affect a system's basic sense of identity, one creates a potential for the system to reorganize its understanding of its environment. If you only try to change goals and objectives, the system's understanding of the environment may remain unchanged.
>
> (Morgan, 1993: 327)

3: Imaginization as personal empowerment

This principle is a call for individuals to act in new and different ways through changing their individual worldviews through Imaginization. Morgan suggests that the alternative is a view that no-one can have influence and all are powerless in the face of cultural, economic and social forces:

> I believe that our innate imaginizing capacities can serve us well in tackling some of the major social and organizational problems of the current time ... We need new metaphors that can help us remake ourselves, our society, and our relations with planet Earth.
>
> (Morgan, 1993: 293–4)

An action-learning approach

Morgan describes his approach to the use of imaginization as one of 'Action-Learning', but here he starts to draw on theories other than postmodernism. He suggests the need for a strong facilitating role whilst trying to allow participants to shape its content through being aware of the facilitator's own influence on the interactions. He guides his activities 'using a loose quasi-ethnographic style of research' (1993: 300). His basic protocol for this consists of the following five injunctions (Morgan 1993: 301):

1 'Get inside'

   This is the ethnographic rule that the researcher needs to understand the situation in its own terms, trying not to influence the situation whilst getting data.

2 'Adopt the role of a learner'

   This is a reinforcement of the above suggesting the need to suspend judgement and not bring hypotheses to the situation as they pre-orient the research.

3 'Map the terrain'

   This covers the attempt to create a 'rich description' (Morgan 1993: 301) of the situation keeping track of experience, what is said, and what is happening. This description continues to be redrawn throughout the research.

4 'Identify key themes and interpretations'

   This relates to point 3 and is part of the process of 'developing an evolving "reading"' (Morgan 1993: 301) of the situation.

5 'Confirm, refute, and reformulate throughout'

   This injunction reinforces the idea that the process of action-learning is not seen as linear and requires an approach in which meaning is continuously evolving.

Morgan supplies interesting and illuminating examples of his use of imaginization in organizations and how this has empowered people to increase their control over their lives at work. Whilst his approach attempts to be empowering, it is unclear what other values its use should promote; and, although Morgan discusses the current trends such as downsizing and the use of cheap labour in third world countries, he does not link this directly to the use of the approach in a particular setting. There are thus no guidelines for when and where the approach should be applied.

Other approaches to postmodern management include Taket and White's (2000) approach. This is based around what appears an essentially linear four-point framework:

1 Deliberation One, which includes selecting participants, defining the purpose/objectives, and exploring the situation;
2 Debate, including identifying options, researching options (including consulting widely on options), and comparing options;
3 Decision, involving deciding on action and recording decisions;
4 Deliberation Two, which consists of monitoring and evaluating.

However they suggest that the implementation is more an art than a science. For it to be carried out in the spirit of postmodernism it has to ensure the widest possible range of views, acknowledge and allow differences of opinion, and challenge 'truths'. The approach uses a range of methodologies from different theoretical paradigms, mixing and matching as required by the context. Thus they provide a framework and some favourite recipes but stress the need for innovation and flexibility in their application.

Strengths and weaknesses of postmodern approaches

Critics of postmodernism suggest that it can have no value base, as one value system is as good or as bad as another and no view is better than another view. Similarly they would ask how you can trust a viewpoint that rejects all truths, which must necessarily include its own. It can even be disputed whether postmodernism provides an alternative approach. Whereas some use its ideas as part of consulting practice, others as a framework within which to use methodologies such as soft systems thinking, it is questionable whether such a diverse and challenging set of ideas can produce new managerial approaches. There is also doubt about its ability to be used within organizations that have great disparities of power and are still part of modernism with its focus on goals and consensus rather than postmodernism's celebration of conflict (Jackson, 2003: 272).

Certainly, postmodernism does not offer concrete methods or approaches but it does stress the importance of participative planning and the inclusion of excluded and minority voices. It offers a way of critically analysing organizations and their operations that challenges managerialist and centralist tendencies. Through writers such as Bauman (1993) the idea that postmodernism has no ethical basis is strongly refuted. He thus argues:

What follows is that contrary to both the popular opinion and hot-headed 'everything goes' triumphalism of certain postmodernist writers, the postmodern perspective on moral phenomena *does not reveal the relativism of morality*. Neither must it call for, or obliquely recommend, a 'nothing we can do about it' disarmament in the face of an apparently irreducible variety of ethical codes. The contrary is the case.

(Bauman, 1993: 14)

We will discuss further the ethics of management from a pluralist perspective in Chapter 8, but we agree with Bauman that reflective-pluralist approaches in fact offer very effective tools for understanding and acting on ethical issues. This is particularly so in postmodern thinking, which is focused on the idea that there is a greater diversity of stakeholders needing to be involved in decision making and have a more democratic framework for management whereby leaders are servants of the organization.

Critical systems theory

A further area of systems ideas to be discussed is that of 'Critical Systems Theory' (CST) and its application through 'Total Systems Intervention' (TSI) (Flood and Jackson, 1991a,b). This draws particularly on the Critical Theory of Jürgen Habermas (1984). A key element of CST has been a critique of the hard (positivist) systems approaches as well as the soft (interpretivist) systems approaches:

Critical systems thinking began with critiques of earlier systems approaches, examining their theoretical foundations, their history, the assumptions embedded in them, and who they serve.

(Schecter, 1991: 214)

The major criticism of the soft or interpretive systems approaches echoes the one made above, that interpretive systems approaches are unable to deal with issues of power, social control and social change (Jackson, 1982). Critical systems theory has sought to establish a position based on a philosophy of emancipation and enlightenment, and also of 'pluralism' with regard to systemic frameworks (Schecter, 1991).

Jackson (1991) puts forward the 'five commitments' of CST. These are critical awareness, social awareness, methodological pluralism, theoretical pluralism, and human emancipation. By 2000 this had been transformed into three (Jackson, 2000), with 'critical awareness' swallowing 'social awareness', and 'methodological pluralism' and 'theoretical pluralism' usually treated together. Critical awareness relates to the need to focus on the strengths and weaknesses of systems theories as well as to understand the assumptions and values that enter into systems designs. This also involves knowledge of the societal and organizational climate that determines the choice of particular approaches. The aim is to be conscious of the social consequences of different systems methodologies. Methodological and theoretical pluralism stems from an argument for pluralism – instead of seeing the different methodologies as competing for the same area of usage, this commitment suggests that different methodologies have different areas of strengths and applicability, and they thus might be used in a complementary rather than competing fashion. There is also a rejection of the idea that different paradigms are incommensurable (Burrell and Morgan, 1979). Rather it is seen that different elements of the systems movement, in fact, represent different rationalities which should all be respected and no one paradigm should be allowed to subsume all the others. The final commitment to human emancipation seeks: 'to achieve for all individuals the maximum development of their potential. This is to be achieved by raising the quality of work and life in the organizations and societies in which they participate' (Jackson, 1991c: 67).

Critical systems theory thus sets itself no small task. Not only is its intention to change the organisations in which it is used, but it is also intending to change society. It can be seen that CST adopts a clear Habermasian critical modernist position. Following the attack of the postmodernists on grand narratives this final aim has been somewhat reassessed and Jackson (2003: 306) says that critical systems thinkers are now very circumspect about using the phrase 'human emancipation'. He suggests they have accepted that Habermas's universalist position, based on the notion of the 'ideal speech situation', has been undermined. Instead, it has become more normal for CST practitioners and writers to talk in terms of achieving 'local improvement'.

The basis of TSI is to implement the commitments of CST in practice. The approach has three stages: 'Creativity', 'Choice' and 'Implementation'; these phases, however, are seen as part of an iterative process with movement back and forth between them. The creativity phase consists of using organizational metaphors based on Morgan's writing (1986): 'to help managers think creatively about their enterprise' (Flood and Jackson, 1991b: 46). The metaphors are based on different theoretical views of organizations and are discussed in detail in Morgan (1986). Examples include the organization as 'machine', 'organism', 'brain', 'culture', 'team', 'coalition' and 'prison' (Flood and Jackson, 1991c: 326). These images or metaphors are intended to highlight different political and human aspects or organizational structures of the organization's functioning. Managers are helped to think creatively about the organization by getting them to think about which of Morgan's metaphors reflects current thinking about organizational strategies and structures; what alternative metaphors might be more desirable and help make sense of the organisation's difficulties and concerns (Flood and Jackson, 1991c: 326)? Jackson (2003: 288) suggests that the following questions are useful when considering metaphors:

- What metaphors illuminate this problem situation?
- What main concerns, issues and problems are revealed by each metaphor?

- In the light of the metaphorical analysis, what concerns, issues and problems are currently crucial for improving the problem situation?

From the use of metaphors a dominant metaphor for the organization emerges which highlights the main areas of concern and interest. In addition other metaphors may highlight less central concerns but are also of use in the later phases. The choice phase uses the 'system of systems methodologies' (Flood and Jackson, 1991c: 45) to choose an appropriate methodology or set of methodologies using the knowledge of the metaphors underlying the operation of the organization. The third phase, implementation, uses the methodologies chosen in the choice phase to achieve specific proposals for change.

The application of CST through TSI is described by Jackson (2003: 273–99). It has also been substantially and robustly criticized by Tsoukas (1993), who suggests, drawing on Bateson, that the model's use of the system of systems methodologies involves a confusion of logical types. It is also suggested that as a model of complementarism it 'is not merely eclectic; it is the triumph of atheoretical common sense' (Tsoukas, 1993: 67). Tsoukas is particularly critical of the way in which TSI appears to ignore the very criticisms that it has made of other methodologies in its application of them. From their postmodern perspective, Taket and White (2000) see TSI as an approach that seeks to tame pluralism and diversity rather than embracing and celebrating them. The emphasis is on rigour and formalized thinking, which produces a tension with the supposed purpose of employing a plurality of methodologies and methods. From the point of view of constructivism CST's complementarism ignores the fact that each of the different systems approaches that are considered implies a different rationality and its introduction into an organization will bring forth a domain of reality. Thus CST suggests that, for example, hard systems approaches can be used to achieve technical mastery over social processes within the framework of complementarism, but at the same time it is founded on a criticism of the ontological and epistemological assumptions that hard systems approaches contain (Tsoukas, 1993: 61 gives a fuller critique of this issue). Thus CST is founded on the belief that application of any of these frameworks can be carried out within the framework of TSI without the problems that CST itself identifies in their use elsewhere, simply because TSI then allows the user to follow this up with the use of another theoretical approach. Thus it can ignore its own criticisms of these methods whilst they are used within its own paradigm.

A second criticism of TSI is its utopian nature. If TSI takes its task of improving society through management consultancy seriously, then it risks continually setting itself the task of solving insoluble problems whilst ignoring real difficulties faced by members of the organization. Tsoukas suggests that the evidence from the real world application of TSI shows that the critical aspect of the approach and its concern for emancipation 'turn out to be merely rhetorical ornaments' (Tsoukas, 1993: 69).

Another criticism of CST is made by Mingers (1992), who points out that a critical approach based on Habermas must have the intention of 'emancipation from an unequal and repressive society' (Mingers, 1992: 6). Critical systems theory's aims both to emancipate people and to 'facilitate the management task' (Flood cited in Mingers, 1992: 5) are clearly at odds with critical theory, according to which the management task would be seen as part of the control of the workforce by oppressive elites. This criticism is at the heart of the problems of CST. Whereas CST is critical of systems methodologies it is uncritical of organizations, and its analysis leaves untouched the fundamental role of the organization in the perpetuation of the society whose subjects CST aims to emancipate.

In favour of CST and its application through TSI is that it raises the issue of ethics in the application of systems approaches in organizations and provides a framework for selecting systems approaches that tries to take into account and promote empowerment within the organisation. Although there are still doubts about whether empowerment is adequately dealt with and whether TSI is merely a rehash of other approaches that could be achieved by common sense, at least the issues of oppression and emancipation are given prominence.

The new epistemology and organizations as networks of conversations

This section will cover ideas that come from a revolution in systems thinking and particularly management methodologies stemming from the work of Gregory Bateson and Humberto Maturana. Systems ideas changed in the 1970s with the recognition of the need to take account of the observer's participation in the system being observed. This reflexive turn has been termed second-order cybernetics (von Foerster, 1974). This change in systems thinking meant that observations started to be seen as dependent on the properties of the observer – not only their sense apparatus but also the beliefs or worldviews that shape what they are able to see and how they will respond. By the 1980s a number of systems writers were using the term 'constructivism' (Watzlawick, 1984) or 'social constructionism' (Hoffman, 1992) to describe their underpinning philosophy. This change in underlying philosophy will be familiar to readers with knowledge of family therapy, in which Hoffman (1985: 385) called it the 'new epistemology'. Like postmodernism and many different sociological and philosophical conceptions, constructivism concludes that we experience not a single stable reality but what Maturana (1988) has termed the multiversa – the idea that there are many realities each experienced as real with real consequences for our actions. He thus says:

> Science, a political doctrine, a particular religion, and many, many other creations that appear as particular cultural systems, constitute such domains. . . . we can observe that in each cognitive domain we . . . operate as if in a

> domain of objective (absolute) reality whose relativity can only be asserted if we step out and [reflect on it].
>
> (Maturana, 1988: 46)

For example a social work team that, in its responses to child protection, adopts a 'forensic gaze'(Parton, Thorpe and Wattam, 1997) will bring forth a domain in which many behaviours in families are seen in terms of evidence of abuse and will respond with decisions about investigation. This may be completely different from a team that believes that many child protection referrals are statements of concern for a child which reflect the need for support or help (see Bilson, 2002, and Thorpe *et al.*, 2007, for examples of the difference these two views can make to child protection practice).

This move to a constructivist epistemology leads to some key issues in management as well as in leadership, as has been seen in Chapter 3. Constructivism stresses the need to act cooperatively with others and to co-construct understandings of any problems or their solutions. This chapter will now consider the application of these systems ideas to social work management. Bilson and Ross (1999) propose a set of principles underpinning a systemic understanding based mainly on the writing of Gregory Bateson. These provide a framework for reflecting on responses to difficulties faced by organisations such as those providing social work. The principles are as follows.

Epistemology

The term 'epistemology' is used by Bateson (1979) to refer to the set of beliefs and basic premises that underlie action and cognition. Thus Bateson suggests that epistemology attempts to specify 'how particular organisms know, think and decide' (Bateson, 1979: 250). This use of the term is broader than the traditional philosophical reference to the set of analytical and critical techniques that define boundaries for processing knowledge. The research into teams in social care (e.g. Pithouse, 1987; Hall, 1997; White, 1998) shows how epistemologies or cultures in local teams support the creation of the tacit practices of occupations, organizations and teams. These local epistemologies are based on assumptions that are, in most cases, unexamined and taken for granted. They create the 'reality' of the work environment and shape what it is possible to do or to see. Problems can arise because the epistemology maintained within a team or organization can lead to people becoming trapped in a net of self-validating actions based on unexamined premises. Through the lens of the team or organization's epistemology moral or ethical issues that are apparent from another viewpoint may go unseen. The epistemology may thus maintain oppressive or poor practice.

For example, a study of levels of contact between parents and looked-after children (Bilson and Barker, 1998) found that there were dramatically different levels of contact between teams in the same local authority. These differences could not be explained by the nature of the children's problems or family situations or a range of factors often associated with lower levels of contact. Teams with high levels of contact were different from their neighbours in their belief that social work with families was a matter of partnership rather than rescue from parents. These assumptions that underpinned the cultures of these teams supported major differences in practices with important implications for children's wellbeing.

This principle thus proposes the need for managers to aid their team and organization to find ways to reflect on epistemologies and to avoid certainty in actions.

Circularity

A fundamental issue for Bateson's epistemology is the idea that the world of nature does not operate on simple linear causation but on circular or more complex chains of causation. By this he means that simple formulations of the form 'A causes B' do not accurately describe what happens in the natural world. In circular models of causation A has an effect on B; B has an effect on C; and so on around the circuit eventually having an effect on A. In such a system there is no simple cause and effect. It is possible to *punctuate* this sequence to suggest that A has caused B, or, if a different starting point is chosen, it can be said that B caused the chain of events that caused A. Bateson (1973: 262) uses the term 'punctuation' to demonstrate that a particular description is one of a number of different and equally valid descriptions of the interactional sequence, which depends on the starting point and order in which the sequence is described. Because of this view of causality, systems that have this circularity are termed *mutual-causal*.

A key issue raised by the concept of circularity is the need for a reconceptualization of power and control (for a fuller discussion see Bilson, 2004). Even discussing power is not simple. For example, whereas the concept is widely used there is no agreed definition of it (Mingers, 1992: 8; Morgan, 1986: 158). This principle challenges a linear cause-and-effect relationship between events and behaviour in social systems. The principle of circularity suggests that an understanding of the interactions and behaviour of members of organizations needs to be based on the acknowledgement of their interconnectedness and that this cannot be explained in terms of linear notions such as cause and effect. It proposes that organizations cannot be directly controlled either from within or without. In social work management this means that organizational problems are maintained by current interactions with the organization and its environment and that the actions of the manager have to be considered as possibly maintaining these problems.

This principle challenges rational linear approaches to management, including target setting and performance indicators frequently used in social work and health organizations. Although organizations will adapt to control through rigidly set targets this is unlikely to improve the quality of services or promote adaptability of the organizations to the changing environments in which they operate. Bateson (1973: 462) suggests this type of approach to control is 'epistemological lunacy and leads inevitably to various sorts of disasters.' He particularly warns against fixing any one particular variable in a dynamic system 'because fixing the value of any variable will in the end disrupt the homeostatic process' (Bateson and Bateson, 1988: 119).

Respect for ecology

This principle suggests that there is a delicate balance between organizations and their environment developed through interactions over time. Bateson, in his work *Mind and Nature* (1979), concluded that animals co-evolve with their environment. Thus approaches based on this principle would challenge the view of organizations being in competition with their environment. An approach that respects ecology will aim to promote an organization's ability to flexibly adapt, but will also expect that this adaptation will affect and create change in the environment. Central to this is the need to enable organizations to increase their flexibility and range of responses.

Respect for the ecology also requires an ability to see problems from a range of different perspectives and in social work this includes those of service users as well as other organizations and government. However, given the interconnectedness of ecologies, change in one part of an ecological system will affect other parts. Thus ecological approaches to problems do not need to work with all elements of an ecology but will consider how even small changes within an organization can affect both it and the ecology in which it operates. Adaptive interventions aim to introduce small changes to the current pattern of behaviour of the system aimed at changing the way it operates. These small changes can disrupt the current patterns, leading to major changes in the organization and in its ecology.

Information and pattern

Bateson defines information as news of difference that makes a difference (Bateson, 1979: 98). This stresses the idea that information is relational and not absolute and also that what makes a difference is 'news'. Bateson equates news of difference to meaning (1979: 110). A key idea in identifying differences is pattern creation. The observer creates a distinction that brings forth a particular pattern, which may be one of many immanent in the observed phenomena. Pattern is qualitative, not quantitative, and is about relationships. The creation of pattern is linked to context or relevance. Bateson suggests that we do this through stories. He thus says:

> What is a story that it may connect the As and Bs, its parts? And is it true

that the general fact that parts are connected in this way is at the very root of what it is to be alive? I offer you the notion of *context*, of *pattern through time*.

(1979: 15, original emphasis)

This principle suggests that managers and organizational staff need to find ways of constructing patterns in the descriptions of the practices of organizations and particularly to identify those that have negative consequences for the ecology in which they operate. The principle also suggests the need to provide feedback that encourages new responses to these patterns, and that this requires a focus on quality, not quantity. Managers and organizational staff need to become adept at telling stories.

Organizations as networks of conversations

We will now look at a further aspect of the new epistemology through the theories and writing of Humberto Maturana. These have had a wide impact on a range of managerial approaches. Many of the ideas in complex adaptive systems owe a debt to Maturana's theorizing (see for example Mitleton-Kelly, 2003; Espejo, 2003; Capra, 1997; Ruiz, 1996) and in particular his writing about self-referential systems. However, he rejects the direct application of this aspect of his theories to organizations, saying that in treating organizations as systems we lose the fact that they are made up of humans. Instead he proposes that we should consider them as networks of conversations. This aspect of his work has been less taken up, although we feel that it offers a way of looking at areas such as emotions in organizations that a standard systemic approach does not offer. There are a small number of writers who have developed this area, including Maturana and Bunnel (1998), Winograd and Flores (1987a,b, Kensing and Winograd, 1991; Winograd, 2006); Taylor and Robichaud (2004); Ford (1999); Ford and Ford (2003) and Bilson (1997; Bilson and White, 2004; Bilson and Thorpe, 2007; Bilson and Dykes, 2009), who has applied these ideas specifically to social work organizations.

In considering organizations as 'networks of conversations' (Maturana, 1988; Bilson, 1997) this approach draws specifically on Maturana's biology of cognition. In using the term 'conversation', we are referring not simply to speech but to a much more encompassing and interlocking network of behaviours: an embodied 'dance' between participants that involves the use of language, interlocking patterns of behaviour, and is braided in emotion. The latter is an important point because in the western cultural tradition the role of emotions is played down in an attempt to maintain 'rationality'. This biological view is rather that emotions both determine and are determined by interactions in the conversation. In particular we move between conversations emotionally and attention to emotions is an essential part of working with organizations.

One implication of the above is that a change in a system is through a change in the network of conversations that the members of the system generate. From this viewpoint the culture of a particular human system, be it a team, an organization or a nation is a manner of living in conversations that brings forth a particular world. Cultures have developed through the history of the closed network of conversations that constitute them and are learned (actually lived) by new participants in these conversations. Culture shapes all of our experiences, as Maturana (2007: 113) states:

> Experiences are distinctions that we make of what happens in us or to us as languaging beings . . . and since a culture is a closed network of conversations, we necessarily live the consequences of these experiences in our living according to the culture in which we live them, which is where they are features of the world that we live.

Thus culture develops over the history of the organization or team and shapes not only what can be done but also how things are experienced. It is passed on and maintained in the ongoing conversations through a range of emotional, verbal and non-verbal interactions that shape the behaviour and worldview of participants. These cultures are based on assumptions that are mostly unexamined and taken for granted. They create the work environment and shape what it is possible to do or to see. In work they constitute the 'way we do things here' that is learned by new entrants to an organization or team. Because of this people are resistant to cultural change, as Stafford Beer (1975: 11) argues: 'individuals are highly resistant to changing the picture of the world that their culture projects to them.'

A key aspect of western capitalist culture has been identified with concerns with effectiveness, efficiency, production and so on, which restrict choice, attempt to control outcomes, often removing human judgement, and, thus, essentially limit the humanness of our participation in the world of work (Lipsky, 1980; Ritzer, 1992; Dykes 2005a,b, 2006). This is at the root of proceduralized approaches such as the scientific-bureaucratic one described in the last chapter, which are prevalent in social work in the United Kingdom. Ritzer asserts that this leaves us in what the sociologist Max Weber called an 'iron cage of rationality' (Lassman, 1994: xvi). Similarly Maturana and Bunnell (1998), from their biological perspective, note that such systems 'restrict the possibility for acting out of awareness' and that they demand that 'we behave like robots'. The alternative approach suggested here is to let go of the desire to control and instead aim to increase responsibility and vision through inspiration and promoting critical reflection.

An organization can be seen to have multiple networks of conversations and cultures that will shape local responses to attempts to change practices in social work. From such a standpoint there can be no single method for promoting change applicable to all organizations and all situations within an organization. Instead biologically informed systems theorists such as Humberto Maturana,

Stafford Beer and Gregory Bateson suggest that we need to open a space for reflection and release the restrictions on individual judgement. As Maturana and Bunnell (1998: para. 143) state:

> As we release these restrictions, as we let humans be humans, without this demand of robotizations, then creativity, cooperation . . . and co-inspiration appear. If we have the same inspiration we don't need control, we have freedom, and we have responsibility. In a way all these reflections lead us to discover that we can do all we wish to do together as a co-inspiration when we let human beings appear.

Methodology

Bilson and Ross (1999) propose a methodology for management based around these Batesonian principals. The emphasis in this methodology is almost complementary to that of Checkland's SSM. Whereas Checkland predominantly focuses on analysis and building conceptual models of the system, Bilson and Ross predominantly focus on how interventions in an organization can be structured with relatively less explanation of how to analyse organizational issues. Their approach is to provide illustrations and case studies frequently drawing on systemic practice with families and the work of other family systemic practitioners such as Evan Imber-Black (1986, 1988) and Maria Selvini Palazoli (Selvini Palazoli *et al.*, 1986) who also applied Bateson's ideas in families and organizations. However, they warn that these methodologies need to be carefully adapted to the organizational context. Later work by Bilson developed the idea of reflexive conversations (Bilson, 1997; Bilson and Thorpe, 2007), which have been used in a range of social work settings to stimulate change. This provides a more embodied perspective, which has a greater emphasis on emotional engagement. We will first cover Bilson and Ross's approach before looking at reflexive conversations.

A central focus for this approach is the epistemology that supports the actions of a team or organization, and the aim is to find ways to help people to critically reflect on it. This critical reflection aims to open up a space for new and more ethical action. A number of approaches to identifying issues that need to be worked with are suggested. Some of these are concerned with reflecting on interactions within a group of staff. This may be done by dealing with some agreed problems, or identifying issues through research and reflection. Examples show that this might be done through having conversations with members of the organization and others involved or undertaking research but also through reading adverts, policies and service descriptions as well as social work files. Bilson and Ross suggest a need to reflect on the patterns of interactions and the language used in these writings. In particular it is important to read for what Cohen called social control talk (Cohen, 1985). Thus they advise not to read material for its literal sense but that it is important to read it for clues about the assumptions that underpin it and reflect the epistemology:

> Analysis of written communications can play a major role in identify-
> ing issues of epistemology . . . The choice of language, the images and
> metaphors which the reader elicits from them, are an important source of
> information about the nature and types of beliefs the authors may have.
> It is important to read them in a way which tries to listen to the beliefs
> or images that underpin them and how they characterise those who are
> written about.
>
> (Bilson and Ross, 1999: 124)

They use two of Bateson's ideas to help with the identification of epistemologies. The first is the creation of pattern and the second is the idea that
information is 'news of difference'. An example of this can be seen in a study
of files carried out by Bilson (1997) in an agency where he was a manager. This
pointed to older people being taken into residential homes in what appeared to
be a pattern of admitting older people to residential care in the belief that they
were lonely, isolated and depressed in their own homes and that residential care
would rescue them from this. This pattern emerged from reading the files of
the most recent entrants to residential care. Had the reader shared these beliefs
about the need for rescue, the pattern would not have become information as it
would be 'obvious' that people should enter care for this reason. However, for
most people admission does not cure loneliness but rather increases it.

Bilson has developed these ideas suggesting the need for reflexive conversations (Bilson, 1997). A reflexive conversation thus seeks to focus attention on
the tacit assumptions that shape practice. The approach recognizes the central
role of emotion in human reasoning (Damasio, 1994; Maturana, 1988) and
works with emotions to help participants to debate some of the historically and
culturally situated beliefs that shape their understandings. The management
intervention in the case above used a reflexive conversation. This took the form
of a workshop and used techniques and concepts drawn from family systemic
practice to engage participants in critical reflection. It used the methods of
reframing, metaphor and constructivist approaches to research (also see Bilson,
1997, or Bilson and Thorpe, 2007, for a more recent example). Following
the seminar there was a reduction in admissions to homes and a range of new
services developed. This approach uses a range of methods and concepts often
drawn from family systemic practice that are adapted for work in organizations. These include:

- *reframing*: the idea that a situation can be placed in a new context by
  changing the conceptual and/or emotional setting in which the situation
  is viewed and thereby ascribing new or different meaning – for example a
  child's behaviour can be 'hyperactive' or 'energetic';
- *fit*: this is the idea that for communications or actions to be 'heard' they

need to have a resonance with those of actors in the system (i.e. they need to have similarities on a range of levels such as using a similar vocabulary and emotional tone);

- *metaphor*: using metaphors bypasses conscious mental 'sets' (Cade 1982: 136) and has a formative impact on 'the construction and embellishment of meaning, and on the development of theory and knowledge of all kinds' (Morgan, 1993: 277).

The approach here draws on family systemic practice, which has a tradition of working with problems by focusing on interactions between members during the sessions. This has led to a strong focus on the inter-personal skills of dealing with interactional processes in the 'here and now'. A key aspect of this approach is emotional engagement with participants. The subject of emotions in studies of organizations is 'usually either completely ignored or very narrowly conceived' (Flam, 1993: 58; see also Hosking and Fineman, 1990; Fineman, 1993; Putnam and Mumby, 1993). Putnam and Mumby (1993: 36) see emotion as 'the process through which members constitute their work environment through negotiating a shared reality.' This approach suggests that change in an organization involves aesthetic seduction: emotional engagement and invitation to reflection on an alternative appreciation of underpinning assumptions and their implications. The epistemologies maintained in a network of conversations are, by their very nature, self-fulfilling and rationally complete (Maturana, 1988). The development of reflexivity cannot therefore be based on rational argument and seeks to engage participants emotionally through a range of approaches including telling stories and metaphor and through awareness of one's own emotions and those of the participants.

Strengths and weaknesses

Although the ideas of Bateson and Maturana have been widely influential in organizational theory they can be very complicated and difficult. Bateson (1958) warns of the danger of 'misplaced concreteness' whereby someone might assume that descriptions such as those offered by economics or sociology are more than ways that scientists arrange data and can in some sense have an objective existence. Both he and Maturana suggest that problems would be created if ideas such as considering organizations as networks of conversations were believed to exist in some more concrete sense than as an explanatory model for our experience of organizational life. Whereas this approach does provide a framework within which one can reflect on one's actions, it does not prescribe particular actions in given circumstances, nor does it provide a method. The idea that this approach would do so is an example of 'misplaced concreteness'. The practice guidelines and examples given by Bilson are intended to illustrate how such a high-level theory can inform the actions needed to deal with problems without specifying a particular method or specific approach. Thus it provides more a way of reflecting on actions than specific guidance on what to do. Thus, if the question of the limitations of this approach for an understanding of problems in human service organizations is crudely put, then at one level of analysis it can be said that it is not useful at all. These ideas will not change government policy, provide funds for new projects or protect an elderly person from abuse by her relatives.

A strength of this approach is that it stands astride a major rift in current organizational theory and practice: that between modernist and postmodernist approaches. Although it is based firmly on biology and might be accused of being a 'grand theory' by postmodernists, it is firmly pluralist and challenges realist interpretation. Thus Habermas (1981: 385) claimed that, with the adoption of ideas based on Maturana's modern biology, the battle between the 'objectivists' and the 'subjectivists' loses its point. The approach also challenges the current emphasis on rationalism and places emotions at the centre of its practice. This leads to an ethical approach (Bilson 2006) with an emphasis on responsibility, which will be discussed further in Chapter 8. Although this does make issues such as inequalities of power central to the approach it offers no simple solutions. Adopting this framework does not lead to any single or unified model of practice; rather it challenges professional certainties.

Conclusion

The approaches covered in this chapter offer new and different perspectives on social work management. Although they all are underpinned by complex theoretical frameworks they also offer concrete approaches. However, this may prove difficult for managers as the approach of many social work organizations to their problems is often anti-theoretical: 'Social work often tries to reject theoretical constructs as too remote from the "real world". Its practitioners, theoreticians and managers assume that epistemological issues do not matter, that only what is done is important' (Ross, 1987: 208).

This pragmatic or common-sense approach to dealing with problems can clearly be seen to be at odds with the deep, philosophical underpinnings of the reflective-pluralist approaches. Forden's comments illustrate the way in which the complexity of systems theory was distorted through over-simplification in its application in social work:

> From the point of view of most social workers there is probably no need to spend much time inculcating the elaborate jargon of general systems theory. Part of the need for the jargon is checked by the attempt to cover such a wide range of systems. Social workers are only concerned with a limited range, and it is sufficient to make use of such terms from the social sciences that can easily be applied to most human systems. Simple models can be derived from systems theory and provide a framework for analysis, without

having to study General Systems Theory itself. Both Goldstein and Pincus and Minahan demonstrate this.

(Forden, cited in Ross, 1987: 211)

However, the 'simple models' derived in this way left out essential components of systems theory such as interconnectedness and feedback and did much to prevent the development of these ideas in the social work management literature. The search for 'simple models' is still evident in social work management and is typified by a 'cookery book' or 'ready remedies' approach to theory that we see in publications such as the SCIE's practice workbook on social care governance, elements of which we discussed in Chapter 2. If the application of reflective-pluralist approaches leads to similar 'simple models' then this will be at the expense of sacrificing key elements and principles in the same way as happened in the application of General Systems Theory in social work. Thus, whereas the complexity and theoretical nature of reflective-pluralist approaches allow them to do justice to the complexity of human systems, at the same time their complex nature is ironically the major barrier to wider application. This chapter has sought to give an introduction to these complex ideas. Each of these has its own substantial literature and we can do no more in this chapter than give overviews and general principles, which we hope are not over-simplifications. However, we would want those wishing to apply one of these approaches to their practice to read further and get a deeper understanding of their intricacies. As we shall discuss in detail in the next chapter, we are concerned that in some cases, such as the current discussion of Whole Systems Approaches, we are yet again seeing this over-simplification and a rush to apply ideas not properly grasped. In the next chapter we will also discuss some important issues in social work and consider the implications of adopting a reflective-pluralist approach to management and leadership. We hope this will help in thinking about the problems on which reflective-pluralist approaches can shed new light and justify to readers any effort involved in understanding them.

7 Challenges for social work management and leadership

So far in this book we have looked at theories and approaches to management and leadership, categorizing them as rational-objectivist or reflective-pluralist. In this chapter we will look further into the implications of these perspectives for the management and leadership of social work. As will be clear from the previous chapters, these approaches are based on very different assumptions about the nature of management and leadership and they thus provide very different perspectives on how to carry out the varied tasks of managing or leading an organization. In looking at their implications for social work we will focus on specific issues that we see as having particular implications for management and leadership.

Our position is that social work organizations have major differences from those for which managerial theories have been developed. Unlike many businesses, social work has no simple product that is bought or sold or even a simple service. Social work also has a wide range of varied stakeholder groups, as with other public service organizations. Some of the interests of these different stakeholder groups conflict at times with one another. Also social work deals with endemic tensions between, for example, caring for the individual and the family or the wider community, which again may conflict at times. The purpose of social work and its value in people's lives is constantly discussed within and beyond the profession. For all these reasons, there are particular challenges for the managers and leaders of social work organizations. The distinctiveness of social work organizations and their fundamental values are succinctly summarized in this quotation from a social services manager:

> The meat and drink of this organization is people's lives, you know and the way – the meaning of life – you could walk into any room in this building and you, you would not be surprised by people sitting round and talking about the meaning of life and they wouldn't be doing it because they'd seen a good film the night before or read a good book. It's because it's actually central to the task that we're trying to achieve and I think that is something that people coming from – sectors or industries that are not people centred,

that are product centred – is actually quite a difficult thing to learn.

Social Work manager

(Lawler, 1992: 216)

Also the services social work provides include those for some of the most excluded and vulnerable people. In some cases these services are provided on a compulsory basis and often there is stigma attached to being a recipient. In many cases the role of social work is to mediate or represent those who are excluded and to try to support those who may be oppressed. Thus, although there has been a push from the government to take a more business-like approach and to have a stronger customer focus, the adoption of these market-oriented ideas does not fit easily within the social work environment. Unlike many businesses, social work has the aim of decreasing user demand and user dependence. It is concerned with de-marketing rather than marketing, with promoting independence rather than dependence. It does not set out to attract and retain customers in the way of many commercial organizations. Its aim also is to advocate change in the wider social world, not simply to deliver 'products' to 'customers'.

In addition to this difference in the nature of the organization and of its users, there are particular problems in the nature of the work that social work is intended to perform. Human services organizations often have to deal with what have been called 'wicked problems' (Rittel and Webber, 1973), which have no simple solution, indeed they have many different potential solutions. The idea of wicked problems was suggested by Rittel and Webber in 1973 around the same time that Ackoff (1974) reported a similar phenomenon that he called a 'mess'. Rittel and Webber contrast a wicked problem with a tame one. Tame problems in management have a solution that can be identified using the classical management methods of linear problem solving involving the linear steps of data gathering, data analysis, solution formulation, and solution implementation. In contrast wicked problems are incomplete, contradictory and changing, with complex interdependencies that are often unique to the local setting of the problem. One such problem that has frequently led to criticisms of social work and restructuring of social work organizations is how best to protect children from harm, whether caused directly by or through the negligence of their parents. This has consistently led to criticisms of children's services and its management over many years and across the English-speaking world. Others among a range of wicked problems include dealing with the overlaps between health and social care and dealing with the care of 'dangerous' individuals in the community.

Thus the nature of a social work organization, its users and the complexity of its tasks mean that it is different from the organizations that are more generally the subject of organizational theory. In particular these differences demonstrate that social work operates in an environment that is fraught with uncertainty; it is particularly turbulent; and issues of inequality and power are at the core of most of its business. To that extent social work has a more directly political dimension to its work than most other organizations. Because of this we contend that management and leadership in a social work context is less suitable for those approaches that fall within the rational-objectivist category and yet, paradoxically, we think these approaches have been dominant, as a consequence of the managerial and marketization agendas, at least in terms of implementing national government policies in which a command and control approach using targets and tight objectives is increasingly dominant.

In what follows we will consider a number of issues of current importance for management and leadership in social work. In this consideration we will note the dominant assumptions being made according to our framework and highlight, where appropriate, the value of considering the issue from another perspective. The six issues we will consider are listed below:

- Women in social work management

  In this section we discuss the profile of the profession and the under-representation of women at senior management levels in social work and the issue of gender and styles of management.

- Managing organizational change

  This section considers how change is implemented in social work organizations.

- Culture

  Linked to the above, this section focuses on understandings of culture and cultural change.

- Joined-up working and whole system approaches

  The recognition of the need to work closely with a range of organizations and professionals is at the core of much social work. We will look in this section at how this is approached and particularly the whole systems approach, which has become a major element of social work policy and provision in the UK.

- Managing practice

  The focus of this section is the particular and continuing concern with managing social work practice in teams and also the supervision of professional work.

- Evidence-informed practice

  This section discusses the concern with developing professional practice and approaches to how evidence might inform practice.

There are clear overlaps and inter-relationships between these topics, as we will note, but structuring the discussion in this way enables us to examine each in some detail before drawing the issues together. In considering these issues we cannot be comprehensive. Our aim is to give indications of how reflective-pluralist theories and approaches might help to give a different perspective and create a space for different actions.

Women in social work management

The issue of gender within management and leadership is important and receiving increasing attention both generally and in social work. In the social work context, this attention ranges from discussions over feminine and masculine management styles (Chernesky, 2003; Dewane, 2008), and their relative effectiveness, to data and commentaries on the demographic profiles of social work managers (Berg *et al.*, 2008). In relation to management and leadership styles, Foster (1999) points out the 'catch-22' position that faces women managers in and beyond social work, in that stereotypical management behaviours are seen to represent broadly masculine qualities and conflict with behaviours consistent with women's gender identity.

> The woman who adopts a masculine style and behaviour is perceived as having been incorporated and criticised for assuming the status of an honorary man, while the woman who retains a caring or service orientation risks being criticised for failing to conform to the models expected of a manager. In the context of Social Services Departments, the association of management with the authority of position and social work with the authority of expertise fits (perhaps too) neatly with the essentially gendered nature of the presentation of the occupations themselves and the anticipated gender of the occupants of the respective roles.
>
> (Foster, 1999: 322)

Similarly Berg *et al.* (2008) note that the development of managerialism in social work and other public service organizations from the 1970s onwards placed a premium on stereotypical masculine managerial styles:

> This [managerialism] is also thought to have affected social work, an area of provision often seen as appropriate for the employment of women . . . even though there are those who have identified a potential mismatch between the macho image of the new management . . . and the supposedly transformative styles of women and their positioning in care functions.
>
> (Berg *et al.*, 2008: 114)

So it may be that valued styles associated with feminine approaches to management are being over-ridden by an imported, more masculine culture. However, Dewane (2008) notes that the stereotypical feminine approach to management and leadership has both advantages and drawbacks.

Women's relational style can both help and hinder their effectiveness as leaders (Allison & Allison, 1985). One study identified nine categories in which women excel as managers: concern for people, sensitivity to the needs of female workers, investment in workers, a cooperative orientation, a global perspective, openness in communication, recognition of inequities, concern for the quality of the environment, and use of intuition (Chernesky, 1996). These qualities make for a nurturing, receptive, empowering, and inclusive environment but can also result in one in where productivity suffers.

(Dewane, 2008: 1)

It is important to point out here the danger of being restricted by stereotypical views, which view men and women as separate yet homogeneous groups, each exhibiting its distinctive and different style. Writers such as Eagly and Johannesen-Schmidt (2001) point out contrasting approaches in studies of men and women in leadership roles: approaches that focus on difference and those that focus on similarities. They also point out the inconclusive nature of much research into gender and leadership effectiveness and the considerable influence of organizational context, making authoritative generalization difficult. We have noted that approaches to management and leadership tend to deal in generalities and much of the popular literature concerning gender and leadership follows that trend. Much of it also takes the rational-objectivist approach. In relation to style, it may be more helpful to think of masculine and feminine styles, which are available to and used by both men and women, rather than assuming each style belongs to each gender specifically. Taking a more relative-pluralist approach would enable us to incorporate the voices of both men and women in management and leadership positions and those who aspire to such positions to include their interpretations of gender and its influence and importance in social work organizations.

Whereas it is misleading to assume that men and women have exclusively different approaches to management and leadership, it is less problematic to consider the numerical detail of men and women in different management and leadership positions. Such data themselves can be said to be objective though their interpretation can be made from different perspectives. Social work is a profession that employs a preponderance of women (National Minimum DataSet for Social Care [NMDS-SC], 2008). Is the level of women employed in the profession represented in management and leadership positions in social work organizations? Writing in 1999, Foster presents the contemporary situation as being that approximately 20 per cent of UK Directors of Social Services were women, the proportion having risen to that level from 10 per cent between 1987 and 1992 and remaining constant until 1999. However, she argues that the extent of their influence, even for those who achieve such positions, is limited:

> Women in senior management positions have overcome the difficulties presented within the opportunity structure, at least in terms of having achieved such roles. Nonetheless, the power sources to which they have access may, I suggest, still be affected by their gender. Women occupying senior management roles present a challenge to the wider power structure within society, as well as to the image of management as an occupation.
>
> (Foster, 1999: 317)

Some years on, although there appears to be some progress in this area, it is still the case that there are disproportionately few women in senior management positions within social work. Recently with the separation of children's and adult services, the previous body that represented Directors of Social Services (the Association of Directors of Social Services, ADSS) was superseded by two bodies representing senior managers in both children's and adults' services: the Association of Directors of Children's Services Ltd (ADCS) and the Association of Directors of Adult Social Services (ADASS). The profiles of senior managers in these groups still indicate an under-representation of women in comparison with other grades in the profession. Recent information on women among the ranks of senior managers in children's social work reports that 'Women make up 83% of the workforce and are represented in this proportion at all grades including managerial. However at Senior Management level males make up 35% of the workforce' (NMDS-SC, 2008: 1); and in relation to the top level of management in social work in adult services: 'Perhaps unsurprisingly this pattern of female under-representation is repeated when looking at Directors of Adult Services. Of the 166 full members of the Association of Directors of Adult Services only 76 were women i.e. 46%' (NMDS-SC, 2008: 4).

Berg *et al.* (2008) note that women are disadvantaged in two respects in relation to career progress towards management. First, they often start their social work careers from a lower organizational baseline in comparison with male counterparts; that is, they tend to have entered social work at a very low level. Second, they are more likely to have taken greater responsibility for the care of their own children than their male partners and worked part-time and/or with career breaks in comparison with the male work pattern of full-time, continuous employment. In many respects social work as a profession and social work organizations place a more positive value on emancipatory employment practices than might be found in some other areas of work. Nevertheless, as Coulshed and Mullender (2006) point out, structural issues in our society might still affect career advancement for work in social work:

> since some of the obstacles that work against women in other employment sectors, such as lack of qualifications and permanent jobs, do not apply in social work, the key barriers to women's advancement clearly must boil down to these discriminatory attitudes and unequal family responsibilities. Women who do make it in management are more likely to be single or

divorced and without children than their male counterparts (Balloch *et al.* 1995). New female entrants to the profession are no less ambitious than male (Murray 1997), so the challenge is there for organizations to help them make it to the top.

(Coulshed and Mullender, 2006: 208)

Dewane (2008) comments on the difficulties experienced by some women managers in experiencing pressure through trying to be responsive to those both above and below them in the organizational hierarchy and suggest personal strategies for dealing with potentially conflicting interests from these groups. Through the adoption of such strategies, she argues, women can succeed and develop their careers. Berg *et al.* (2008) come to a more pessimistic conclusion regarding the future prospects of a greater proportion of women amongst the ranks of senior social work managers, due to wider societal norms, the gendering of careers and general employment practices:

> There seems little sign of a decisive challenge to the prevailing, gendered, structuring of careers, and managerialism within social work, and which has, within management and organizations more generally, been identified as setting women at a disadvantage, compared to men ... For these reasons, it seems that although women are in a majority at middle manager level, it is less likely that they will become senior managers. Despite the absence of equal chances of advancement social work does nevertheless provide opportunities for some women to pursue managerial careers.
>
> (Berg *et al.*, 2008: 114)

In summary there are robust data that indicate an under-representation of women in senior management posts in social work. There are also less robust data on masculine and feminine styles.

A more reflective-pluralist approach to this topic would involve recognizing that the issue of individual and group difference – difference of perception and experience – can be explored within social work organizations through more detailed and open dialogue. This has potential beyond improving access to management positions for all staff, beyond addressing the more obvious barriers to career progress. It has the potential to enrich the conduct of management and leadership by seeing these as less static roles or functions and to develop new perspectives through the dialogue itself. Other approaches such as those based on postmodernism discussed in Chapter 6 would suggest the need to find ways to empower the voices of women.

The feminist approach to leadership discussed in Chapter 3 not only identifies some different approaches to management activity that fit well with the nature of social work organizations but also suggests that there is a mechanism whereby such behaviour is 'disappeared' (written off in various, often gendered, ways). Managers, both male and female, can promote the valuing of such approaches by using the strategies of naming, norming, negotiating and networking suggested by Fletcher (2004) and discussed in Chapter 3.

Managing organizational change

We made comment in Chapter 2, in relation to managerialism, on the ways in which social work organizations have had to change, along with others in the health and local government sectors, as part of the modernizing agenda. Such changes have involved changes to organizational structures, internal procedures and geographical boundaries. There has also been change in relation to function, with social workers becoming 'care managers' (Harris, 2003) and, as we said, the allocation of purchaser or commissioner and provider functions. In England a major range of reorganizations has taken place, with the previous generic social services departments being replaced by new adult services and children's services departments. In addition there have been changes at institutional level with the establishment of organizations such as the General Social Care Council and SCIE. It is not the nature of the change that is our focus here but the approach to introducing such and other changes within social work. There has been an impetus to change in other less specified ways in addition to structural or operational methods as summarized by Seden (2008):

> the planned changes to organizations continue, and usually have the aim of making interprofessional collaboration easier, as it is argued that this gives better services to people who need them. The drivers for organizational change are therefore less about the shape of individual organizations and more about how organizations can learn to work together. Paradoxically however, this can have the opposite effect as the fast pace of change can derail professionals.
>
> (Seden, 2008: 180)

Organizational change can be approached in a number of ways (see for example Collins, 1998; Senior and Fleming, 2006). If we take Morgan's (2006) metaphors of organizations as machines and as organisms we can see immediately the different ways in which change would be introduced according to each different metaphor. Using the machine metaphor, this implies that change is introduced by changing part of the machinery: perhaps replacing one part with another, adding other bits onto the machine or replacing one mechanism with a newer, more effective version. It is something that can be planned in advance and implemented whilst leaving the rest of the process unchanged; only that bit of the machine which is changed or replaced is affected in any significant way. In the organic metaphor we would imagine a seedling being planted whose roots and shoots would develop in particular ways, in response to the growing conditions. So the metaphor we use will fundamentally influence the way change is viewed.

Dustin (2007) notes how the process of McDonaldization, which we discussed earlier, is a broader phenomenon in our society but affects social work organizations through the way change is introduced and as part of the nature of that change itself. In other words, our society is strongly influenced by processes of mass production and that approach to production is being introduced into social work, through fragmenting the tasks of social work and dividing them amongst different individuals (such as commissioner and provider). The way the changes are being introduced is similarly a reflection of the role of managers in mass production contexts. What is seen by managers as a more efficient means of organizing and delivering services takes precedence over the views of professional workers: 'economic efficiency is the priority and managers are responsible for promoting economic efficiency' (Dustin, 2007: 24). Thus policy makers and managers design and implemented standardized processes with little consideration of the complexities of either the service that is affected or the change process itself.

For example, a study of older people's services (Bilson and Thorpe, 2007) showed that, following organizational changes to implement care management in an English local authority, care managers had started to create packages of services for people living in the community using statutory and private providers without reference to the social or emotional needs of the people served. One effect of this for service users was that they were confused and concerned by having a constantly changing stream of carers as different providers were swapped in and out in line with purchasing rules.

Our view is that much change is proposed using, unconsciously, the machine metaphor, that is, from a rational-objectivist perspective. This sees change as being a fairly straightforward, manageable process, taking place through a number of orderly steps. Any opposition to this is seen largely as 'resistance', the expression of which is to be expected but is not legitimized as offering a valid alternative: it is something to be managed. It is for this reason that we believe such change can have the opposite effect to that intended, as Seden states above and as shown in the example of care management.

In Chapter 6 we discussed a range of approaches to organizational change that do not use the machine metaphor. These included soft systems theory, which considers organizations as systems and attempts to stimulate organizational learning through surfacing the nature of the problem and engaging key staff in a constructive debate about possibilities of change; complexity theory, in which organizations are viewed as adaptive networks and problems are dealt with by stimulating adaptation and the emergence of a solution through, for example, the use of minimum specification (Plsek and Wilson, 2001); postmodern approaches, which aim to stimulate change by promoting diversity; and critical systems theory, which deliberately uses a range of metaphors chosen for the particular organization and its problem. In the example of older people's service discussed above, an approach based on understanding organizations as networks of conversation was used to bring about changes (Bilson and Thorpe,

2007). This last approach used emotional engagement and a reflective conversation to change the local culture. This subject of cultural change is the subject of the next section.

Organizational culture

There is much exhortation throughout the public sector to address and improve organizational cultures in line with the attempt to 'modernise' services (Hafford-Letchfield, 2006b). Thus the Scottish Executive's website states boldly: 'Transformation of social work services to better meet people's needs requires major cultural change, as well as visionary leadership at national and local levels' (socialworkscotland.org, 2009). The term 'organizational culture' is used to refer to factors such as beliefs, behaviour, values and practices, which together establish the environment for professional practice and service delivery. The focus on culture often comes from a strategic leadership approach according to which some authors suggest that the job of leaders is to 'impose' a culture on an organization. Thus Hill and Jones (1995: 366) say:

> organizational culture is created by the strategic leadership provided by an organization's founder and top managers. The organization's founder is particularly important in determining the culture because the founder 'imprints' his or her values and management style on the organization.

However, the term 'culture' has many definitions (Brown, 1998) and can be interpreted or analysed from different perspectives (Martin, 1992; Cameron and Mah Wren, 1999; Alvesson, 2002). A fundamental difference among these interpretations is that some argue or imply that culture is an organizational attribute – something the organization has – whereas others infer that it is less superficial and represents what the organization is (Ormrod, 2003). Franks provides a summary of these approaches:

> Functionalists see culture as a variable (like structure) which affects the way an organization 'works'. In other words culture is something an organization *has*; if you can change the culture you can change inter alia productivity, levels of conflict and behaviour. By contrast, the interpretive school sees culture as a root metaphor (a fundamental image of the world under study); in other words organizations *are* cultures. Culture is a subjective experience and the concept of cultural change (as understood by the functionalist school) as a means to an organizational end, is a meaningless construct.
>
> (Franks, 2001: 18, our emphasis)

The difference of interpretations is important as it informs practice as noted in relation to different groups in health and social care services:

this research suggests that [these] groups are investing 'culture' with disparate meanings. The danger of mutual misunderstanding in these circumstances is obvious; for example the theories of change that might be implicit in these different meanings might vary significantly.

(Peck *et al.*, 2001: 325)

Difficulties arise in trying to institute change if culture is seen to be founded on beliefs and values: are these open to influence and, if so, what time-scales are involved? If culture is to be seen to represent what the organization *is*, then any change initiative must perforce be radical. At best, an organic process may be more appropriate here: planting the seeds of a new culture and helping that growth, rather than assuming a new culture can simply replace the old. Some writers see the diffuse interpretations of culture as being a less than helpful refuge in some respects, in that culture is used as a 'residual category': it describes an aspect of organizations or professions that is seen as the way to explain issues, behaviours or attitudes that cannot be accounted for otherwise. 'Fundamentally "culture" remains an unexplained catch-all, which appears to offer little of pragmatic value to [political change] programmes' (Ormrod, 2003: 229).

Brown (1998) notes that work on organizational climate was the foundation for writing on organizational culture, though now climate receives less attention. However, writers such as Glisson and Hemmelgarn (1998) believe climate might be a more powerful issue than is commonly appreciated in affecting social work service delivery. They use the distinction made by Denison (1996: 624), who argues that:

> Culture refers to the deep structure of organizations, which is rooted in the values, beliefs, and assumptions held by organizational members. Meaning is established through socialization to a variety of identity groups that converge in the workplace. Interaction reproduces a symbolic world that gives culture both a great stability and a certain precarious and fragile nature rooted in the dependence of the system on individual cognition and action. Climate, in contrast, portrays organizational environments as being rooted in the organization's value system, but tends to present these social environments in relatively static terms, describing them in terms of a fixed (and broadly applicable) set of dimensions. Thus, climate is often considered as relatively temporary, subject to direct control, and largely limited to those aspects of the social environment that are consciously perceived by organizational members.

The study by Glisson and Hemmelgarn (1998) indicates that organizational climate was a more significant factor than culture in delivery of high-quality children's services. With the increase in the need to work in inter-disciplinary ways and in partnership with other agencies, they argue that focus has often been inter-organizational rather than intra-organizational. Climate is defined as 'the individual employee's perception of the psychological impact of the work environment on his or her own well-being' (Glisson and James, 2002: 769). This in turn is seen to relate directly to the quality of service provided. This could be an important consideration if we accept that culture itself is difficult to influence directly and, even then, the relationship between the nature of the intervention and the intended outcome is tenuous at best.

The view of culture taken by SCIE, especially its amenability to change by leaders, is interesting to note: 'Leaders need to have a strategic vision and an understanding of social care governance. They will *determine* the culture, structures and resources required to take this agenda [governance] forward' (Simmons, 2007: 13, our emphasis). This clearly implies a view of culture as a possession or attribute of the organization, not as something more fundamental. However, there is recognition that this is a complex process and that the participation of others in this process of change is crucial:

> Developing the right culture is one of the biggest challenges and will take 'dynamic leadership, time and commitment from all levels of the organization' (Governance in the HPSS, 2003). This will only develop if there is a commitment to organizational learning, support for an open and fair approach, partnerships and collaboration with other professionals, service users and carers.
>
> (Simmons, 2007: 13)

Once again the way that the issue of culture is understood leads to disparate approaches and aims. For example, according to Jackson (2003: 122), approaches to change based on complexity theory suggest that the 'existence of a strong, shared culture that stifles innovation must be avoided at all costs.' Thus this approach sees culture as potentially a force for conformity that can limit the organization's ability to adapt and change. Similarly, postmodern approaches would seek to promote diversity rather than shared organizational culture. Other reflective-pluralist perspectives are informed by the recognition that change can be brought about initially, though at relative small scales, through dialogue between individuals around new ways of operating. The view of organizations as networks of conversations particularly focuses on culture, seeing it as reflecting a manner of living that brings forth a particular world. This is open to change through reflection, though achieving this is not a simple procedure and requires emotional engagement and opportunities to make visible the usually unexamined assumptions (for example about what is good practice) that underpin it. From this point of view, although cultures can be very difficult to change, the actual nature of change is sudden rather than gradual. Thus, in the case of the older people's organization discussed in the example above, a reflexive conversation was held, one of its aims being to promote reflection on the culture of not considering the social and emotional needs of service users (for details see Bilson and Thorpe, 2007). Following this there was rapid change across the organization.

The issue of organizational, team and professional cultures is particularly important when considering change beyond the boundaries of one organization and into the area of working across boundaries of professions and organizations, which we will discuss in the next section.

Joined-up working and whole system approaches

Clarke and Stewart (1997) suggest that a new generation of wicked problems was recognized in the United Kingdom during the 1990s, which required new forms of policy response. This was seen as influential on the New Labour government's focus on 'joined up government'. This idea that a range of problems that are difficult to resolve require joined-up action has been identified in a range of countries. Ling (2002), for example, suggests this is the case in Australia, Canada, The Netherlands, New Zealand, Sweden and the United States.

Thus inter-agency work forms a central theme in criticisms that arise in child protection inquiries. Thus Lord Laming's report, stimulated by the death of Baby P in England, states:

> Despite considerable progress in interagency working, often driven by Local Safeguarding Children Boards and multi-agency teams who strive to help children and young people, there remain significant problems in the day-to-day reality of working across organizational boundaries and cultures, sharing information to protect children and a lack of feedback when professionals raise concerns about a child. Joint working between children's social workers, youth workers, schools, early years, police and health too often depends on the commitment of individual staff and sometimes this happens despite, rather than because of, the organizational arrangements. This must be addressed by senior management in every service.
>
> (Laming, 2009:10)

It is in this context of a need for joined-up work that the idea of the whole system approach gained ground. Developments in social policy are often intended to have a 'whole systems approach' and problems are often seen to arise because of poor communication and coordination between different professions and public services. Thus the Audit Commission's (2002: 8) *Integrated Services for Older People: Building a whole system approach in England* states:

> The need to work across organisational boundaries in order to deliver joined up services is a key theme of public policy. However, it is not always clear what this means in practice. A whole system approach benefits everyone, from older people to partner agencies and the staff who work within them.

The report goes on to cite a number of UK policies that call for better interagency working and require a whole system approach (2002: 9–10). Similarly Jones and Bowles (2005: 642) state that 'mental health policy emphasizes whole systems working.' In the United States as in the UK, whole system approaches are widely used, for example in promoting healthy communities.

In the field of children's services the statement of the joint position paper (produced by the organizations representing chief officers of social services, the National Health Service, police, education and local authorities as well as a range of voluntary sector children's services organizations) for a dynamic 'whole system approach' shows the widespread acceptance of the whole system concept. Likewise in the United Kingdom the governmental organizations responsible for developing the social work and social care workforce (Skills for Care and the Children's Workforce Development Council) have developed their strategy for continuing professional developments and they state 'Skills for Care and CWDC are committed to a "whole systems" approach to implement the CPD strategy' (McDonnell and Zutshi, 2006: 9).

Finally, the SCIE has carried out a knowledge review entitled 'Improving social and health care services' (Fauth and Mahdon, 2007), providing a review of literature on key practices and processes needed to promote effective organizational change and improvement. This again advocates a whole system approach, seeing it as an 'overarching aspect to organizational change' and concluding that 'Improvement in social care requires a whole systems, emergent framework' (Fauth and Mahdon, 2007: 4, 6).

We are interested to consider the whole system approach because we feel it shows that, despite this recognition of the systemic nature of these problems, attempted solutions are based on mechanistic understandings of organizations and are mostly not even systemic (Chapman, 2004). Some authors refer to writers on the systemic theories we discussed in Chapter 6, for example the Audit Commission (2002: 11) briefly mentions Senge's work on systems thinking, Complexity Theory and complex adaptive systems. Jones and Bowles (2005: 642) suggest that the concept can be traced back to Checkland's Soft Systems Methodology. However, these theories play very little role in the practice that is derived from the concept. Thus the Department of Health's document *Discharge from Hospital: Pathway, process and practice* (DH, 2003b: 15) is fairly typical in defining the commonly understood characteristics of whole system working as:

- Services are responsive to the needs of the individual patient/client/tenant/carer.
- All stakeholders accept their inter-dependency and the fact that the action of any one of them may have an impact on the whole system.
- There is agreement between the stakeholders as to the vision of the service(s), the priorities, the roles and responsibilities, the resources, the risks and the review mechanisms.

- Those using the system do not experience gaps or duplication in provision.
- Relationships and partnerships are enhanced.

It can be seen that the only characteristic in the list above that has anything to do with systemic ideas such as those presented in Chapter 6 is the criterion that a system is composed of interdependent parts. However, interdependency is a fundamental property of a system and requires no acknowledgment or agreement as suggested in the list. The other statements are aspirational rather than system characteristics and it will be seen that concepts such as a shared vision and agreed roles come from classical and strategic management theories as were discussed in Chapter 5. The practice approaches put forward in whole systems literature offer many practical suggestions on how to run large group meetings, sound principles to involve services users in planning, and an approach that in some cases genuinely involves staff at a range of levels and from a range of disciplines in discussion. However, they do not represent systemic practices of the sort discussed in Chapter 6. Thus the Audit Commission's (2002: 12) whole systems approach suggests that at a strategic level, for senior managers, it means:

- engaging with older people as citizens and users of public services to enable them to help shape local services;
- having a strategic vision that is shared with others; and
- having a broader view of all the services and interventions that older people need to access, where these are available and how they fit together.

As will be clear these 'strategic' actions do not represent systemic approaches. It is thus unsurprising that these whole system problems have proved very difficult to resolve. Whether they surround child protection or services for older people they have stubbornly resisted various attempts to solve them. This section started by suggesting that the idea of a whole system approach came as a response to wicked problems. This accords with our view that the perceived poor performance of social work and health care in certain areas occurs because of complex problems that involve multiple stakeholders, cannot be resolved with traditional rational objective analytical approaches to problem solving, and have no simple or straightforward solutions. As mentioned earlier the Australian Public Service Commission has produced a report assessing the need for new approaches to planning and policy making to deal with 'wicked problems'. These problems not only run across the boundaries of organizations, but have a number of other facets. They have the following complications (Australian Public Service Commission, 2007: 4–5):

- They are difficult to clearly define.
- Have many interdependencies and are often multi-causal.

- Attempted solutions often have unintended negative consequences.
- They rapidly evolve and change.
- They have no clear solution.
- They are socially complex.
- They hardly ever sit conveniently within the responsibility of any one organisation.
- Involve changing the behaviour of individuals or groups.
- Can be characterised by chronic policy failure.

The stakeholders of a wicked problem often have radically different world-views leading to different and often contradictory understandings of the problem and approaches to its solution. We suggest that the whole system approach, although recognizing the cross-organizational nature of wicked problems, in the main does not recognize the range of these other complications, which are at the root of why these problems are so resistant to attempts to solve them. Because of this serious limitation the whole systems approach tends to treat wicked problems as if they are simply tame ones on a larger scale, and is thus unable to deal with them. In England and Wales the lack of success of one initiative after another attempting to solve problems such as 'how to deal with the care needs of an increasingly aging population' or 'how best to protect children from harm from their parents' has led to an escalation of attempted policy solutions until the focus is on major reorganizations, attempts to control from the top down by setting targets and performance indicators, increasing external control structures and other attempts to 'drive through' change – an escalation of managerialist attempted solutions that all draw on rational objective approaches. This escalation takes the form of what has been called a 'more of the same loop' (Watzlawick *et al.*, 1974) in which attempted solutions escalate and make the original difficulties worse; sometimes the solutions even become the problem.

So what can be suggested as possible ways forward? The Australian Public Service Commission (2007: 11) says something that will by now be familiar to the readers of this book:

> Wicked policy problems are difficult to tackle effectively using the techniques traditionally used by the public sector. Traditional policy thinking suggests that the best way to work through a policy problem is to follow an orderly and linear process, working from problem to solution . . . The consensus in the literature, however, is that such a linear, traditional approach to policy formulation is an inadequate way to work with wicked policy problems . . . Linear thinking is inadequate to encompass such interactivity and uncertainty.

Many of the systems approaches discussed in Chapter 6 arose from the need to find more flexible approaches to deal with wicked problems. Thus, for example, critical systems thinking uses its pluralist methodology to ensure that a range of perspectives are brought to bear on wicked problems, or messes (Ackoff, 1974), as they are sometimes called in the systems literature. It also adopts a process that aims to deal with multiple stakeholders with different perspectives on a problem. Similarly the starting point for complexity theory is that the behaviour of organizations (if they are considered to be complex adaptive systems) is inherently unpredictable and this leads away from linear planning approaches. Its theoretical basis offers a direct challenge to silo mentality and it specifically aims to promote working across boundaries. The approaches based on considering organizations as networks of conversations are also well placed for the analysis of problems in which the different worldviews of stakeholders are all too apparent. A key element of this approach is creating reflection on the assumptions that bring forth particular views of the world. None of these approaches, however, is simple to use. They do not offer 'ready remedies' and all require detailed knowledge and understanding of often complex theories. The danger is that they will be used in the simplistic fashion we have seen in whole systems approaches so far. If that is the case they will not provide the powerful tools needed to deal with these complicated issues so often faced in managing social work.

Managing practice

The SCIE's guide to managing practice (SCIE, 2003) suggests that those managing practice have the following core responsibilities: managing the primary tasks and activities of the organization; determining whether standards of practice are consistently maintained; supporting staff engaged in complex, personally demanding practice; and ensuring that staff continue to develop their practice. Managers carry out this work through supervision and team management.

Supervision

Traditionally supervision is carried out on a one to one basis between a manager and practitioner, though it can be carried out on a group basis. Social work supervision is thought to be one of the most important factors in determining job satisfaction levels of practitioners and the quality of service to clients (Tsui, 2005, gives a review). There is wide acceptance in the literature of the idea that supervision has three main functions: administrative, educational and support. These have developed from both the managerial context of social work and its history of therapeutic practice. The administrative function aims to monitor implementation of agency policy and service delivery; the educational function aims to develop the values, knowledge and skills of frontline social workers; and the support function attempts to raise the morale and job satisfaction of staff (Kadushin and Harkness, 2002). Tsui (2005: 486) suggests that this combination of functions makes 'social work supervision unique and humanistic'. However, according to the SCIE guide to managing practice (SCIE, 2003), supervision has fallen into disrepute for two main, but contradictory, reasons: first it is criticized for being a semi-private activity that focuses on the individual supervisee's needs and not on the benefits for the service user; and second it 'has become procedurally driven, checking compliance rather than positively challenging accepted custom and practice'. This latter position stresses the administrative function and leads to supervision in which the relationship between practitioner and supervisor is likely to be a hierarchical and prescriptive one and in which managers focus predominantly on compliance with procedural and fiscal requirements. Current guidance therefore appears to be following a rational-objectivist approach with a particular emphasis on the achievement of performance standards, such as completion of a specific number of assessments within a particular timeframe. Dustin (2007) highlights that the focus on managers is now on performance and output rather than on reflection, in a quote from one of her research respondents:

> I personally would love a supervision where one can also have reflection and also to be able to be honest about the issues you are facing, the way you're considering or resolving them, but it's very much down to targets and actions.
>
> (Dustin, 2007: 64)

It could be argued that this development represents a move away from a reflective-pluralist approach that characterized aspects of social work and supervision previously. Both in social worker interactions with service users and in interactions between supervisors and the social worker, the aspect of the relationship between the parties was previously regarded as important. The supervisor role now appears to be much more akin to a production line supervisor, overseeing effort and standards of output, than a supportive supervisor of professional practice and development. As another of Dustin's respondents comments: 'We are on the production lines very clearly' (2007: 67). In Chapter 4 we saw how leadership within that perspective has a less hierarchical and less certain approach and thus a supervisor would see her- or himself not as an inspector but as a participant in meaningful dialogue who is able to proffer support and advice on the basis of professional experience. Such a role may be more suited if we accept the uncertainties and complexities of social work intervention and its outcomes. Similarly, if supervision is to fulfil its educational and support functions, acknowledgement must be made of the importance of discussion and reflection. Social workers thus need time and encouragement to reflect if they are to learn from their experiences and impart that learning to others. The reduction of time allocated to this will result in greater priority being given to the achievement of objective performance, important in its own right but only a part of professional practice and development.

Teams

Over the past two decades and more there has been considerable attention given to teams involving different professional groups – multi-disciplinary teams – which remains an important element of service currently in the era of partnership and joined-up working. The concept of groups and team-working has an established history within social work:

- as a form of organization: departments structured into social work teams both generic and specialist;
- as a means of supervision and learning: supervisory and development discussions and analyses based on groups and teams;
- as a form of intervention/service provision: a team of workers delivering services in collaboration with each other.

Furthermore the notion of teams plays an important part in the culture of the organization and the part both might play in developing evidence-based practice (Lawler and Bilson, 2004). Payne (2006) notes that there are many different interpretations of teams and team working. Finlay and Ballinger provide a definition of teams for the context of social care and health care. A team is:

> A group of individuals, with varying backgrounds, perspectives, skills and training, who work together towards the common goals of delivering a health or social service. Ideally team members collaborate and value one another's different contributions.
>
> (2008: 149)

There are different ways in which teams can be constituted, ranging from one in which all members have an equal part in discussion and decision making to one in which decisions are made by one 'team leader' or senior professional after discussion and consultation with the team. There is also the issue of to what extent the team is there to decide on a course of action and the allocation of resources, from which point each professional separately delivers his or her particular input into the service and reconvenes to review progress. This is a different approach from one where responsibility for the service is shared collectively.

Finlay and Ballinger report on the classification of different models of teams within this context but rightly note that many teams operate as a combination of these different categories and that their work 'is too complex to be easily classified' (ibid.: 153).

One of the factors that might influence how a team is constituted and how it operates is the degree of certainty or predictability there is about the possible course of action open to the team. In a context of relative certainty, clarity about the nature of task and its causal factors, together with clarity about what intervention is needed and what the outcome will be, it will be easier to operate through one nominal decision maker: a rational-objectivist approach is appropriate. The team process will be relatively clearly described and roles allocated appropriately. To that extent this process requires little complex interaction. In the less certain context a more dynamic set of interactions is more appropriate; there are different potential causal factors, interventions and possible outcomes. In the former, decision making is limited to a small number of people within the team, even to one person. In the latter, it involves the group as a whole. In some circumstances, for example a multi-disciplinary team working with a medical issue, the team may decide on a course of action, based on the diagnosis of one or more members of the team. The prognosis is agreed and actions set in motion. The team may not reconvene or only so do at the end of the process. In such respects the actions and the need for them are fairly clear, as are the outcomes. In less predictable situations, such as mental health services, the situation may be subject to rapid and at times dramatic change. The way in which the team operates, communicates, makes decisions etc. may need to be very different. The role of the user of services in such a team differs too and is an important variable. In such a situation it is more important to elicit subjective views of teams with multiple interests and perspectives: a more reflective-pluralist view.

There is often the assumption made that team working and team-based services have distinct advantages over independent professional work but the evidence demonstrates this to be a partial view. Finlay and Ballinger (2008) summarize such evidence and as a result pose three general questions in relation to teams in social care: do teams provide a more comprehensive service; are they more cost efficient; and are they more positive for professionals to work in? In all three cases the answer is very qualified. Teams do have advantages but also disadvantages – for their professional members, for service users and in terms of cost effectiveness. Thus team-based solutions are not a panacea for solving practice and organizational problems.

Returning to the reflective-pluralist and rational-objectivist distinction, team working can again often be founded on objectivist approaches without taking sufficient regard of the inter-personal dynamics and intra-personal perspectives. We have argued elsewhere the potential of the team as a focus for development, particularly in relation to evidence-based practice and the need for teams to question their own modus operandi:

> We therefore argue that, if we are to develop the capacity of social workers to evaluate whether they want to make changes to tacit foundations of their practice and base decisions on available evidence, we need techniques to help them reflect on their tacit assumptions.
>
> (Lawler and Bilson, 2004: 201)

The guidance issued for managers of multi-professional teams (DES, 2006: 3) aims to isolate:

what is important and distinctive about the abilities required by managers of multi-agency or integrated children's services. It is intended as a definitive document on which managers themselves, human resources professionals, providers of leadership and management development and others will draw.

The complexity of inter-professional working, particularly as policy continues to evolve, is recognized. Thus there are lists of priority concerns for managers of such teams, including headings such as 'Achieving Outcomes' and 'Providing Direction'. There are elements within the guidance that indicate an openness to other perspectives, often conspicuously absent in other guidance for managers. The document recognizes, first, that teams are complex arrangements of professionals that do not readily lend themselves to linear approaches of standard management techniques and, second, that other perspectives exist and need to be voiced. So team managers need to:

> Work with the team to seek out different perspectives on the needs of children, young people and their carers and the professionals with whom they interact, to identify opportunities for service improvement.
>
> (DES, 2006: 7)

In addition teams, including their managers and their component members need to be encouraged to reflect on their own assumptions and foundation so that they can:

> Understand one's own and others' backgrounds and values, and using this to develop approaches and processes that enhance delivery and support the concept of mutual accountability.
>
> (ibid.)

Such guidance perhaps demonstrates the possibilities of exploring the different perspectives available rather than remaining blinkered by one perspective. Overall we can see the value, in relative predictable circumstances with identifiable goals, of a rational-objectivist approach to teams, with clearly delineated roles and responsibilities. In this circumstance the team leader may be focused on supporting each team member and ensuring the team works to agreed procedures. In less clear situations, though, adopting a reflective-pluralist approach to team working would be more appropriate, for example in assessing complicated circumstances and/or in more dynamic, changing situations. Here it may be more appropriate for the team leader to focus on involving all members and in eliciting their views and opinions before appropriate actions are decided.

Evidence-based practice

The roles of teams and culture noted above are also relevant in relation to evidence-based practice in social work, a concept that is currently the subject of considerable debate, ranging from the actual nature of evidence through to the problems associated with the transfer of research findings to the 'messy' world of social work practice (Bilson, 2005). This debate is increasingly important as government initiatives in a number of countries attempt to promote a more 'scientific' approach to social work policy and practice. In a knowledge review published by the SCIE titled *Improving the use of research in social care practice* the authors (Walter *et al.*, 2004) identified three models that 'embody different ways of thinking about and developing the use of research in social care' (p. xvii). These models are:

- *The research-based practitioner model*: In this model it is the role and responsibility of the individual practitioner to keep abreast of research and use it to inform everyday practice. This model stresses professional autonomy to change practice based on research and thus values professional education and training as an important foundation for research use. The assumption here is that research use is an individual domain.
- *The embedded research model*: In this model standards, policies, procedures and tools are used to embed research in the systems and processes of social care. In this way policy makers and service delivery managers are responsible for ensuring research is used. Research-based guidance and tools are promoted through funding decisions, performance management and regulatory regimes. This approach is virtually that identified by Harrison (1999) as the 'scientific-bureaucratic' model.
- *The organizational excellence model*: In this model the social care organization promotes research use and the key responsibility thus lies with leaders and managers to promote an organizational culture that is 'research-minded'. Research findings are locally adapted, often in partnership with researchers, and research use is developed through learning within organizations.

The knowledge review included a systematic review of the literature considering over 3,000 academic papers as well as consultations with a wide range of practitioners and educators. Despite this it could identify little evidence that any of the three models is effective. The authors go on to propose a 'whole systems' approach 'for enhancing research use in social care' (Walter *et al.*, 2004: xviii). This did not draw on the extensive literature of systems theory and cybernetics (Bilson and Thorpe, 2007; and see Chapter 6), instead relying on common-sense ideas that do not address what, in this literature, has long been recognized as the counterintuitive nature of change in human systems (Forrester, 1971).

One particular attempt to promote evidence-based practice in social work is that of Sheldon *et al.* (2005), who report on a survey of over 1,000 social work staff in England. Although they find social work staff have enthusiasm for the idea of evidence-based practice they suggest that there is also a worrying lack of knowledge of evaluative research. This is not dissimilar to the findings of a smaller survey in the United States (Mullen and Bacon, 1999). Sheldon *et al.* (2005) also report on the results of their attempts to promote greater understanding and use of research through their work with a number of social care departments in England. This was assessed by means of two questionnaire surveys of staff in the partner social care departments (the one mentioned earlier in 1998 prior to the intervention and the other in 2002) covering over 1,000 staff in each survey. The second survey took place after widespread attendance at research discussion groups and seminars promoting evidence-based practice, increases in the availability of research summaries, publications and databases, and the commitment of the agencies to be part of this programme. The outcomes of these surveys are surprising. Rather than demonstrating increased discussion of research in the key meetings assessed by the research, the surveys showed that discussion of research *fell* in departmental meetings (52 per cent reported discussion 'often' or 'sometimes' in 1998, reduced to 36 per cent in 2002) and supervision (40 per cent reported discussion 'often' or 'sometimes' in 1998, reduced to 20 per cent in 2002). Even the number who said they had knowledge of a piece of evaluative research fell from 43 per cent in 1998 to 36 per cent of respondents in 2002 (Sheldon *et al.*, 2005: 27–35). Despite the brave face put on these results, focusing on some minor improvements – 'promising trends indicating steady change . . . have to be a cause for a modest celebration' (Sheldon *et al.*, 2005: 42) – these key measures indicate that in these authorities the approach of promoting research awareness and increasing availability and access to research was associated with reported *decreases* in discussion or knowledge of research.

There is a complicated picture here, as the issue of 'evidence' is still the topic of debate within social work. At one level, one can see the importance of rational-objectivist research findings and their application to practice. However this model of evidence is very difficult to apply in the area of social work, where, for example, the application of large-scale, randomized controlled trials is largely impracticable and thus the availability of objective evidence will be limited. The purpose of evidence-based practice is clear: 'in common with many management practices, it is an attempt to limit uncertainty in decision-making in individual cases' (Lawler and Bilson, 2004: 427) but, given the difficulties, amongst other factors, of identifying and agreeing causality in social work, the application of evidence to practice will also be restricted. Thus it would be inappropriate to rely exclusively on rational-objectivist research in this context. To do so would be to ignore the wealth of experience and tacit knowledge that informs social work practice. In this respect reflective approaches need to be included, in addition to more objective evidence in evidence-informed practice. The means to do this are through a combination of the elements referred to in the previous sections above, namely supervision, to allow expression and examination of tacit knowledge, and team working, in which a collective understanding and culture of learning can develop.

Summary

In this chapter we have examined a number of topical issues within social work management. It is clear from the topics we have highlighted here that this continues to be a changing and uncertain context for practitioners, managers and leaders as well as for service users. Each of the above issues will continue to develop and change over time. We can estimate what some of those changes and developments will be, but there will be others that we cannot yet be aware of. It is within this context of uncertainty that we feel it is important for managers and leaders to be open to different perspectives in order to deal with and to make sense of current complexities and to retain sufficient flexibility to be able to respond to unknown future developments. We know that, with further research and developments in technology and knowledge in other areas, we will bring more certainty to some areas of public service in the longer term. The search for and application of that knowledge will, in some cases, be appropriately driven by rational-objectivist approaches. In this chapter we have given indications of how the reflective-pluralist approaches can start to shed new light on some of the most difficult and pervasive problems in social work management. Reflective-pluralist theories and approaches are, we believe, critical for social work managers and leaders both now and in the future to maintain a range of services that are appropriate to the needs and demands of service users and that meet the expectation of other stakeholder groups in the broader society.

Some of the issues for social work management and leadership discussed here will remain of significance over time; others will wane in importance or be joined by additional factors as change in the organizations and the broader environment come to bear on social work managers and leaders. We noted, at the beginning of this chapter, the distinctive nature of social work services and the implications that this has for management and leadership in social work. We also noted the significant and enduring element of values that underpin social work intervention and social work organizations. In the final chapter we take these issues one step further and discuss the implications of reflective pluralist approaches and methods for developing an ethical approach to management and leadership in social work, which can build on the approaches we have examined in the chapters to this point.

8 Towards ethical management and leadership in social work

In the last chapter we discussed a number of key areas in the application of management and leadership theory to social work and suggested ways in which the approaches that fall into our reflective-pluralist classification can offer perspectives on key tasks and issues from which to consider management and leadership anew. In this final chapter we want to consider the way ahead for managers and leaders who wish to apply these approaches and what they say about an ethics for social work management and leadership.

As discussed earlier, there are particular challenges for social work managers and leaders that are different from the challenges facing managers in other contexts. Much of the general concern of management throughout the past century has been the search for control and regulation. The managerialist developments in the public services over the past two decades have been a continuation and expansion of this. However social work practice is not a straightforward area to try to regulate or manage. First, social work aspires to being a profession with the attendant levels of autonomous decision making – professional autonomy is in tension with management in any context. Second, as in other organizational contexts, social work practice is enmeshed in a web of power dynamics but, unlike most other contexts, much social work intervention is directly focused on reducing inequalities including those due to power. Social work's aim of emancipation, challenging inequalities, inequity and oppression, does not sit easily with managerial regulation and control. Although some current policy aspirations of user empowerment, choice and personalized care may aim to respond to some of these major issues, as seen in previous chapters they are frequently framed from within a particular market ideological position and they do not address either structural inequalities or the part that social work plays in systems that oppress people. In addition there is the perennial tension associated with addressing significant human need (though increasingly this is expressed as user demand, which is arguably related but different) with finite resources.

The dual responsibilities of social workers and their managers, both to service users and to their own organizations, itself creates potential for conflicting interests. There are arguments that the development of managerialism has been to the detriment of social work practice values (Hughes and Wearing, 2007) but, as these authors also acknowledge, there is a need to manage these tensions, as both practice and organizational interests are legitimate.

In addition social work deals with situations in which people's lives are sometimes at risk. When a tragedy occurs, be it a child murdered by parents, a carer murdered by their mentally ill relative, or an old person dying because of lack of care, there is great public concern and flurry of activity. Scott Snook in his analysis of a friendly fire incident over Iraq in April 1994 saw similar issues in a range of incidents:

> The practical frustration springs from our duty as responsible practitioners to identify a logical source of the tragedy so that it can be isolated and fixed. Such tragic outcomes simply cannot happen without *something* breaking, without *someone to blame*. In the face of such frustration, our hunger for action is almost palpable. With incidents involving the loss of life, when no compelling account immediately presents itself, we become overwhelmed by the urgent requirement to fix something, anything . . . When a single tragic incident such as this one is followed by flurries of wide-ranging organizational action fired in shotgun-sprayed blasts such as these, this suggests that either the conditions contributing to the accident were extremely complex or not fully understood, or both.
>
> (Snook, 2001: 9, original emphasis)

The shotgun-sprayed blasts of activity and desire to find something or someone to blame will be familiar to those working in social work. For example in England following the death of Victoria Climbié there was a clamour for 'heads to roll' and there were wide-ranging changes including new laws, a wholesale national reorganization of social work, changes to the information systems implemented to track children at risk, to say nothing of a report with 108 detailed and wide-ranging recommendations. As we now know, such activities do not prevent further deaths but sadly neither do we consider that they may be counterproductive. We thus rarely consider, in our anger and sadness at what has occurred, that our desire to blame and to 'prevent such a tragedy from ever occurring again' might itself be part of the problem or even make things worse.

This chapter will consider these issues and start to outline an approach for considering the ethical consequences of management and leadership. Social work practice has its own ethical dilemmas (Bilson, 2006; McBeath and Webb, 2002; Houston, 2003; Hugman, 2003) and a number of professional ethical frameworks. It is our intention here not to detail those but to consider ethical management and leadership practice and how that might be guided and informed and work in practice. As the major themes within this book indicate, we have a preference and argue for a critical and reflective approach to management and leadership generally and hence for the same approach regarding management and leadership ethics. Such an approach cannot therefore be constrained by using one static framework or rule system. In keeping with the value placed on subjective experience detailed in earlier chapters, we feel that ethical management is a dynamic process, wherein the values of individuals and groups play an important and often unacknowledged role. Thus we agree with Briskman and Noble when they say:

> It is our contention that the notion of an all-encompassing code of ethics which emphasises universality, inclusiveness and conventional conceptualisations of community in fact mutes the diverse interests and plurality of voices characteristics of modern pluralist societies.
>
> (Briskman and Noble, 1999: 58)

This is not to ignore the value of external frameworks or codes of ethics in that they can be helpful in illustrating generic values, demonstrating transparency, and gaining and maintaining stakeholder support overall. However, the values of individual social workers and their managers are themselves crucial, particularly how they see the role and nature of social work itself. Their individual and group views on issues of inclusiveness, liberation, emancipation, meeting users' needs and demands, and a range of other issues are all influential in the organisation and delivery of social work services.

Current ethical frameworks and codes of practice

We will focus on managers and their values and the influence of local context in due course but first we will consider the ethical frameworks and codes of practice operating across social work. The definition of social work given by the British Association of Social Workers is similar to the international definition and those found in a number in codes from social work professional bodies in other countries. It explicitly declares its value base:

> The social work profession promotes social change, problem solving in human relationships and the empowerment and liberation of people to enhance well-being. Utilising theories of human behaviour and social systems, social work intervenes at the points where people interact with their environments. Principles of human rights and social justice are fundamental to social work.
>
> (BASW, 2002: 1)

Thus change and social justice form important foundations for social work practice and organization. This is further detailed in the list of values provided in the code of practice, the first two of the list being served by the remaining three: human dignity and worth; social justice; service to humanity; integrity; and competence (BASW, 2002: 2). This follows closely the same values declared in the context of bio-medical ethics by Beauchamp and Childress (2001). The code provides details of each of these values and principles and is a thoughtful and helpful document in many respects, detailing the various stakeholders in social work services and the potential conflicts of interests between different parties at times, in practice. Included in the code is a section that relates to the ethical responsibilities of social workers with different organizational roles including those of management. Such a framework is helpful to a certain extent in detailing the intentions or aspirations of social work managers but its generality cannot cover all the complexities of management practice. A potential difficulty here is that not all managers of social work are social workers or members of the British Association of Social Workers.

In the UK as in many other countries, social work has become subject to regulation with adherence to a code of practice or code of conduct being the basis for social workers being allowed to practice. Thus in the UK the General Social Care Council (GSCC) has published a code of practice that is applicable to all social workers and employers providing social work services in the United Kingdom. It starts by laying down six duties, saying that social care workers must:

1 Protect the rights and promote the interests of service users and carers;
2 Strive to establish and maintain the trust and confidence of service users and carers;
3 Promote the independence of service users while protecting them as far as possible from danger or harm;
4 Respect the rights of service users whilst seeking to ensure that their behaviour does not harm themselves or other people;
5 Uphold public trust and confidence in social care services; and
6 Be accountable for the quality of their work and take responsibility for maintaining and improving their knowledge and skills.

(GSCC, 2002: 11)

This has some aspects of the principles of the professional code of ethics but it can be seen that it takes a far less emancipatory and more prescriptive approach. The code goes on to lay down more detailed prescriptions for what a social worker must do by breaking each of these key duties into four or five elements. Orme and Rennie (2006: 341) point to the underpinning rational-objectivist nature of such an approach:

> Ethical codes at worst suggest that individuals cannot be trusted to make moral choices. At best they blunt rather than reinforce individual moral responsibility (Bauman, 1993: 34). As such, they may well contribute to the technicist, managerialist approach to practice.

However, when it comes to employers the rational-objectivist framework becomes stronger still. First the purpose of the code is described as follows: 'The code requires that employers adhere to the standards set out in their code, support social care workers in meeting their code and take appropriate action when workers do not meet expected standards of conduct' (GSCC, 2002: 2). Thus in moving from the code of practice for social workers to that applying to employers we see a move away from principles (albeit more limited than those of the professional code) to an approach of top-down regulation. The code of practice lays down the following five responsibilities for employers:

1 Make sure people are suitable to enter the workforce and understand their roles and responsibilities;
2 Have written policies and procedures in place to enable social care workers to meet the General Social Care Council (GSCC) Code of Practice for Social Care Workers;
3 Provide training and development opportunities to enable social care workers to strengthen and develop their skills and knowledge;
4 Put in place and implement written policies and procedures to deal with dangerous, discriminatory or exploitative behaviour and practice; and
5 Promote the GSCC's codes of practice to social care workers, service users and carers and co-operate with the GSCC's proceedings.

(GSCC, 2002: 6)

From within this perspective such a code may be seen to reflect a shared vision (Bisman, 2004). However, the code of practice goes on to lay down even more detailed prescriptions for employers to follow and it will be seen from the above that this is strongly framed within the rational-objectivist framework, in which workers are controlled through prescriptive procedures, clear lines of accountability and communication of values and vision from the top down. In the next section we will consider why we feel that a different approach is needed and how this can help to develop compassionate concern and enable us to deal more sensitively with ethical concerns in our daily practice.

Why do we need a reflective-pluralist approach to ethics?

As will be seen from the above, the codes of practice start from an understanding of the nature of social work and go on to identify values and principles, and with the approach of central registration they have come to lay out rules of conduct. These rules and principles, as suggested by Bauman, come to reflect, not ensure, good practice (1993: 221). Thus, as Bauman suggests (1993: 11), codes of practice take a similar form to law. Like law they strive to define the 'proper and 'improper' actions in those situations on which they have a view. In doing this they seek to provide unambiguous definitions and clear-cut rules for the choice between proper and improper practice and leave no 'grey area' of ambivalence or the possibility of multiple interpretations. Bauman (1993: 11) sees the implication of this legalistic approach being that: 'it acts on the assumption that in each life-situation one choice can and should be decreed to be good in opposition to numerous bad ones, and so acting in all situations can be rational while the actors are, as they should be, rational as well.'

Like Bauman we think there is a need for an approach that takes into account the spontaneous nature of everyday work in which social worker managers and leaders undertake their ethical actions. We believe that situations are contingent and ambiguous and that our actions therefore cannot be prescribed. Hughes and Wearing develop this point in relation to social workers, which we see as being equally applicable in relation to management and leadership practice:

> [I]t is possible to recognise that in some situations there may be no clearly identifiable right course of action. The actions we claim to be virtuous and right may not be the ones we are able to choose and follow through with [sic]. Organisation contexts increase this moral complexity because the competing interests within and without the organisation – such as those of clients, staff, volunteers, funding bodies, managers – are often difficult to accommodate.
>
> (Hughes and Wearing, 2007: 177)

In this respect then ethical management practice is dynamic and cannot offer certainties in a social context that is itself changing rapidly and continuously. We thus agree with Bauman (1993: 11) when he says 'The moral self moves, feels and acts in the context of ambivalence and is shot through with uncertainty.'

Examples of this uncertainty can be found in many aspects of work in social work organizations. Consider, for example, the issues in providing care for elderly, infirm people. There are tensions between care of the elderly person and his or her caregiver's needs, such as need for respite; those tensions are situated in a context of finite financial and professional resources. In such a situation, the ethical concerns cannot be resolved by reference to prescribed rules of practice. What is more, an appropriate decision one month may be less appropriate the following month because of the dynamics involved in the situations of all concerned.

We thus see negative aspects of general codes of behaviour, of general values and of competency frameworks in that they tend to reduce complicated and inter-related knowledge, behaviours, experience, contexts etc. to technical standards. There is great value in clarity in social work but there is a danger that, on occasion, the search for clarity leads to over-simplification.

Principles for ethics in social work management

Having discussed the need for a different approach we will now move on to start to share some thoughts about how such an approach might be developed. In rejecting the rationalist approach of codes of practice we are suggesting not that the alternative is irrational, rather that it is essentially human and operates in a changing local context. In our view it is in this area that the reflective-pluralist approaches provide insights in relation to ethics. It will be apparent that such an approach will value the different viewpoints provided by pluralism and also attempt to promote reflection. We believe that ethics consists of acting with compassionate concern (Varela 1992, Bilson 2006). Varela poses a crucial question:

> How can an attitude of . . . compassionate concern be fostered and embodied in our culture? It obviously cannot be created merely through norms and rationalistic injunctions. It must be developed and embodied through disciplines that facilitate the letting-go of . . . habits and enable compassion to become spontaneous and self-sustaining.
>
> (Varela, 1992: 73)

In order to consider this we will now propose two contrasting principles for ethics. These are respect and responsibility:

- *Respect*: we recognize that the cultural viewpoints of others are equally valid and equally ungrounded as our own. Isaacs (1999: 4) says: 'An atmosphere of respect encourages people to look for the sense in what others are saying and thinking. To respect is to listen for the coherence in their views, even when we find what they are saying unacceptable.'
- *Responsibility*: we are in a condition where we reflect and act on our preferences. Thus 'being responsible . . . means to be in a certain state of attention and mindfulness: one's activities match one's desires in a reflected way' (Maturana in Poerksen, 2004: 74–5).

These two principles are intended to help us to promote reflection on our actions and to increase our capacity for compassionate concern. Maturana says respect is a gaze that accepts difference. However, to accept difference does not imply that you have to accept what people do. In fact the recognition of ill-treatment or cruelty requires responsible action unless our concern for the other is obscured by some other emotion: 'If we recognise abuse we cannot escape the ethical concern that such a recognition entails, otherwise we would not have recognised it' (Maturana, 1988: 78–9). Maturana thus points to responsibility arising in our recognition of ill-treatment or cruelty. He suggests that if we then do not take responsible action it is because of some competing desire which we value more highly than our concern for others. Thus, if we do recognize some form of ill-treatment or cruelty and we do not take responsible action, perhaps because we feel powerless, we cannot escape our concern and we risk losing self-respect and dignity. When we don't take responsibility we tend to be in emotional turmoil. Thus the principle of respect requires recognition of the humanness of others even when, from our own ungrounded perspective, we find their actions to be wrong or even repellent. Respecting others opens up a space for dialogue, whereas lack of respect prevents dialogue.

Respect is built on self-respect. Self-respect is an emotional sense of well-being in which one's own legitimacy arises without need for justification. It is possible to act with respect towards others only if one has the wellbeing that self-respect brings. We agree with Didion's often quoted statement that: 'The willingness to accept responsibility for one's own life is the source from which self-respect springs' (cited in Schwatz and Daylle, 2009: 7).

Responsibility implies that one is able to answer for one's conduct and obligations and able to choose for oneself between right and wrong. It takes place in reflection. It involves being aware of the possible consequences of what one does in relation to others, and acting according to whether one wants or does not want those consequences. Thus a starting point is awareness of the possible effects we may have on others. This does not imply an ability to predict things – we may be wrong in our assessment of consequences. It also involves acting on this awareness.

The implications of these two principles for ethics in social work management will be discussed under the following headings: action and emotion; culture and values; power and control; and mistakes and blame.

Action and emotion

The starting point for considering the implications of reflective pluralism for ethics is that ethical conduct is pervasive. From this point of view all our behaviour in interaction with others has an ethical dimension because it changes the lives of those with whom we interact. Thus we are immersed in ethics. It is therefore in the area of what managers actually do in their day to day activities that the reflective-pluralist perspective provides important insights.

This does not mean that we are constantly aware of the ethical nature of our actions. We agree with Maturana, who suggests that we have ethical *concerns* only when we perceive a breakdown in human respect. Thus the basis for ethical concerns is an emotional response to the consequences of the actions of ourselves or others:

> Ethics, therefore, have to do with our emotions, not with our rationality. No doubt we use reason to justify our ethical concerns, and we speak as if there were transcendental values that validate our arguments against what we consider unethical behaviour [however]. What determines whether we see a given behaviour as unethical, and that we act accordingly, is an emotion: love, mutual acceptance, empathy – and not reason.
>
> (Maturana, 1988: 73)

It has long been recognized that human emotions are a fundamental part of social work practice and hence of its management. How we recognize and respond to our own emotions and those of our colleagues, staff and service users is an integral part of professional practice and organizational life. We are now suggesting that the recognition of ethical concerns in a situation is emotional rather than rational. If we are to improve our ability to act ethically we thus need to be aware of our emotional responses to situations as we act within them.

In Maturana's writing, love is the emotion (bodily disposition for action) in which the other is seen without judgement. He is thus referring not to erotic love but to a much broader concept: the emotion that creates social interaction. Thus he says that 'Love means to live in a community that is supported by self-respect and mutual respect' (Maturana in Poerksen, 2004: 71). The implications of this view of love for social work management concern our own ability to see the legitimacy of others as well as the need to make this visible to others. Thus, for example, when producing a court report a key issue is that people write about the subject in a way that makes their humanity visible to the magistrates or judges who will read it.

A further issue is the relationship between emotions and rationality. Maturana suggests that our experience of emotions is immediate and we tend towards empathy. However, we may rationalize away our emotions of empathy (or other emotions). For example, on seeing a service user who is asking for money I may feel empathy but say to myself: 'if I give money to her she'll only spend it on drink'. In this way we rationalize away the conflict between our actions and our emotion of empathy, though this frequently leaves us with a feeling of unease.

Reflection on emotions

Thus as managers we need to pay attention to and develop means for reflection on our emotions. This will help us to become more attuned to the recognition of ethical concerns as well as to recognize when we rationalize away our empathy. This puts awareness of our emotions at the centre of ethical practice (this has a similarity with feminist ethics: Clifford, 2002; Parton, 2003). To identify ethical concerns we therefore need to develop our ability to reflect on emotions such as those of unease, anger or tension that might indicate that we are experiencing an ethical dilemma. Different emotions can be associated with different sorts of ethical issues. Emotions of certainty in the face of opposition to someone else's position can provide clues to our lack of respect for the other. Feelings of certainty often occur when we lose respect for the other and fail to see them, or when we want to make them do something that they do not want to do.

Love, as the emotional underpinning of social coexistence, is the basis of respect. It is possible to identify signs that we are acting towards people through some other emotion by reflection and by listening to our rationalizations and descriptions. When we are not seeing someone we use stereotypes, talk about them in the third person or simply do not take them into account. Although to see someone and to act with respect may lead to a different understanding of their actions, it is not to condone them, particularly when they harm others. But respect opens up the possibility of communication and change. We can become aware of our failures of respect by listening to how we refer to others in conversations and our inner dialogues and can use this awareness to reflect on what we are doing.

Since emotion is central to ethics, we need to find ways to reflect upon our emotions in our day to day practice as managers. Our suggested approach to reflection on emotions is not the introspective one of many therapies. Instead it focuses on how we might become aware of emotions through attention to our physical states, actions and awareness of the other as they occur. Work in drama training gives a clue to how we might learn to do this (D. Wright, 2005; Pippen and Eden, 1997). Pippen and Eden argue: 'while emotions may begin in bodily chemical reactions, it is in the domain of behaviour that we detect them. We identify love, aggression, fear, and playfulness in ourselves and others through the things we do' (1997: 69). They go on to argue that 'the most useful attitude [is] . . . one of reflective self awareness of the motor-sensory process . . . and, simultaneously, heightened awareness of the "other"' (1997: 57). Because of this they advocate the extensive use of body-based learning techniques such as Feldenkrais and Alexander Technique. A similar approach was proposed in the early days of groupwork and gestalt therapy by authors such as Schutz (1973) and Perls (1974).

Culture and values

Individual managers have their own histories, experiences, personalities and values, which are bound to influence their everyday actions directly and indirectly, consciously and unconsciously. These values are developed through interplay between our subjective experience and the fact that we are immersed in the culture of the society and the groups with whom we share our lives. Just as individuals have different values, which shape the way they see ethical issues, the cultures in which we live also reveal some issues whilst they hide others.

Our ability to act in oppressive and inhumane ways is often associated with a culture or individual values that dehumanize or make invisible the subject of our actions. Soldiers are trained not to see their combatants as fellow human beings, and oppressive regimes strive to make those they oppress appear non-human. The way in which the culture of the community or group in which we are operating shapes how we see things and our view of the possible responses to them is mainly invisible – like wearing a lens that brings distant objects into focus, whilst we see through it we do not see it. This is illustrated in the way much of social work practice is based on tacit understandings developed socially in teams and professions (e.g. Taylor and White, 2000). Tacit understandings are the 'right things to do' that are so obvious they are never questioned or the 'how we do things here' that we learn when we enter a new social situation. To create reflection on our tacit understandings is not easy because they are what we see as obvious, common sense, taken for granted, and thus go mainly unquestioned. We seldom question these understandings, even when our actions based on them fail to have the expected outcomes. For example in a child care team that assumed that children needed to be rescued from their parents there was a pattern of placements that placed children further away and in more restrictive conditions as the 'absconding' of the children increased (Bilson and Ross, 1999). The absconding was seen not as a challenge to the team's assumption about the need for contact with parents, but instead as an indication that they had not distanced the child enough.

Reflection

Many approaches to anti-oppressive practice in social work stress the need for critical consciousness, which is seen as the process of continually reflecting upon and examining how personal biases, assumptions and cultural worldviews affect the ways difference and power dynamics are perceived (e.g. Sakamoto and Pitner, 2005). As will have become apparent from the discussion above, reflection on culture and worldviews is also central to the approach to ethics being developed here. The picture drawn from the reflective-pluralist position is that changes between cultural value systems are more fluid than the anti-oppressive approaches would suggest. They are influenced by cultures within teams, organizations and other groups as well as by the underlying societal or professional culture, and thus they change as we move from one social situation to another. The way these cultures affect what we do becomes visible through everyday practices. Thus approaches to developing ethical social work need to encourage reflection on their actions by managers and this includes finding ways to reflect on the effects of their participation in the cultures of the teams and organizations in which they work. At the same time managers have a key role in helping those they work with to similarly develop greater powers of reflection.

Thus an important element of ethical practice for managers is to find ways to reflect on organizational and team cultures and how they shape what we do and see. As mentioned above, this is not simple, particularly as we do not see what we do not see. Schön (1987) suggests that professional activity has three different aspects: knowing-in-action, reflecting-in-action and reflecting-on-action. Knowing-in-action is the skilled performance of practice and requires no explicit reflection whilst it is being done. This routinized approach to practice is described as follows: 'spontaneous, skilful performance [which] we are characteristically unable to make explicit' (Schön, 1987: 25). It is only when we become aware of some breakdown in knowing-in-action that we resort to reflection-in-action. This leads us to question our knowing and to experiment, trying new approaches to the situation. The third element is reflection-on-action. This occurs later when we reflect on what has happened and try to make sense of it and extend our knowledge for future activity. In this way Schön sees professional practice as akin to artistry.

In our writing above about awareness of emotions and listening to internal dialogues we have been outlining some of the ways in which we think managers can encourage mindfulness in their practice in a way that will increase their ability to engage in reflection-in-action, thus increasing their awareness of when the routine practice has ethical implications and maybe hides some lack of respect or of responsible action. We also feel that there is a need for reflection-on-action and for managers to find time and space to consider the effectiveness of what they have done and its implications. However, there is also a need to find ways to step outside the limitations of culturally bound practices. Taylor and White (2000) term this wider type of reflection reflexivity. It includes Schön's three aspects of professional activity but has a deeper understanding of the culturally bound knowledge that informs our actions. Thus they define reflexivity as follows:

> We use it not only to encompass reflection but also to incorporate other features. For us the 'bending back' of reflexivity is not simply the individualized action in the manner suggested by reflective practice, rather it is the collective action of an academic discipline or occupational group . . . it implies that they subject their own knowledge claims and practices to analysis. In other words, knowledge is not simply a resource to deploy in practice, it is also a topic worthy of scrutiny.
>
> (Taylor and White, 2000: 205–6)

One approach to this wider approach of reflexivity is to research local practices and the explanations that shape them as a basis for reflection within teams and organizations (Bilson and Thorpe, 2007; Bilson, 1997; Bilson and White, 2004). Such research could be carried out by practitioner–researchers or in partnership with researchers or service users as part of promoting reflexivity and reflection-on-practice. The key issue is that the research promotes reflection that is not solely rational but needs to address our emotional commitment to what we do and how we see things. For example, a recent study of services for older people in a local authority (Bilson and Thorpe, 2007) led the researchers to see that local teams were not addressing social issues in their work but were focusing on medical or practical problems. The missing social dimension led, for example, to patterns of work with families with an older relative suffering from dementia that focused on physical support rather than emotional or social support. The research showed that this frequently resulted in breakdowns, with the person with dementia admitted to long-term care following rejection by his or her family. A reflexive conversation was undertaken in the manner, and using the approaches, described in Chapter 6 (see Bilson and Thorpe, 2007, for a description).

In addition to seeking to reflect on their own tacit assumption, social workers, managers and leaders can use research and everyday contacts to make service users visible to, or to challenge the views of, members of wider oppressive systems, which might include their own agencies or outside bodies such as courts.

Mistakes and blame

We will now consider mistakes and blame, though this can only be a limited exploration of this complex area. We noted above that when there is a tragedy and lives are lost there is a natural desire to find someone or something to blame. Our feeling is that social workers' mistakes or errors are often treated in a more punitive fashion than other professions such as the police or health visitors who are sometimes jointly implicated. It is possible to think of many reasons why this may be so. It may be because of the vulnerability of the people with whom we deal; because of the emotions that these deaths raise; because people find it hard to believe that the person murdering or raping a child would not immediately appear to be some sort of monster; or that our profession is seen to be weak, under-trained and inadequate. None of this is an excuse for poor or dangerous practice. However it is worth thinking about implications of reflective-pluralist approaches for managers and leaders dealing with errors or mistakes.

As we discussed in Chapter 3, the notions that appear in the different versions of systems theory and complexity theory that in social systems there is circular or mutual causation (Bilson and Ross, 1999) and that the behaviours of social systems (and individuals) are unpredictable have a significant impact on how errors might be considered. If we are dealing with self-reinforcing loops of causation then what appears from one analysis to be a cause will, from another, be an effect. And how this will be seen depends on the assumptions and viewpoint of the observer. We also know that such loops suddenly and unpredictably go into 'runaway', as anyone who has put a microphone in front of a speaker will testify. It is thus unsurprising that the application of the linear logic of blame to this sort of complex causal system is fraught with difficulties.

A further issue is that mistakes only happen in retrospect. If I do something that is a genuine mistake then, at the time I do it, I do not know that I am making a mistake. It is only on reflection, and with reference to something I did not know at the time – perhaps the outcome of what I did – that I can recognize my original actions as a mistake. In this respect why punish someone if they made a mistake? This is not to say that it is not possible that a tragedy may occur because a social worker acted out of malice or was knowingly neglectful of his or her duties.

Scott Snook's (2001) analysis of the friendly fire incident over Iraq in April 1994 once again provides a basis for reflection. As an investigative journalist he wanted to find a cause, someone to blame. However, after lengthy investigation he was unable to turn up any simple cause or person to be blamed. The situation was complex. He reports in his book how he used the theories of Weick (1995) on sense-making, which we discussed in Chapter 4, to analyse the nature of the errors. A key element of this was that he felt that a standard rational objective approach, and what we know about how people interpret and make sense, would lead to a question that would focus on the decision maker rather than the complex context within which the tragedy occurred:

> I could have asked, 'Why did they *decide* to shoot?' However, such a framing puts us squarely on a path that leads straight back to the individual decision maker, away from potentially powerful contextual features and right back into the jaws of the fundamental attribution error. 'Why did they decide to shoot?' quickly becomes 'Why did they make the *wrong* decision?' Hence, the attribution falls squarely onto the shoulders of the decision maker and away from potent situation factors that influence action. Framing the individual-level puzzle as a question of meaning rather than deciding shifts the emphasis away from individual decision makers toward a point somewhere 'out there' where context and individual action overlap . . . Such a reframing – from decision making to sensemaking – opened *my* eyes to the possibility that, given the circumstances, even *I* could have made the same 'dumb mistake.' This disturbing revelation, one that I was in no way looking for, underscores the importance of initially framing such senseless tragedies as 'good people struggling to make sense,' rather than as 'bad ones making poor decisions.'
>
> (Snook, 2001: 206–7, original emphasis)

Thus, for managers and leaders dealing with a mistake, the framing of the question behind the investigation is a powerful force to lead us to certain types of conclusions rather than others. And particularly to the recognition by this hard-nosed journalist that, given the context, he might well have made the same dumb mistake; something that we have heard said many times from social workers following another tragedy.

Reflection

For managers the reflective-pluralist approaches and the principle of respect would suggest a need to frame the question around tragedies as simply 'people struggling to make sense' rather than focusing on decision making with its implication of a rational and detached weighing of possibilities. The situations with which social work has to deal are emotionally charged and complex. We are often charged with trying to prevent something from happening that is, in prospect, essentially unpredictable. The response of inquiries into tragedies is frequently the top-down application of yet more procedures that try to constrain and control. Our discussion of reflective-pluralist approaches throughout this book will have made it clear that we feel that such command and control approaches are precisely the wrong ones for dealing with complex situations. We need to promote responsibility rather than constrain it and we need to have respect for all those (social workers and managers alike) who undertake these onerous tasks.

At the same time the implications for the more mundane arena, in which mistakes also happen, are similar. To reduce mistakes we need to increase the ability of ourselves and our workers to be sensitive and mindful in our practice. We need to encourage reflection and learning and this requires us to respect our staff and to provide the maximum capacity for them to develop responsibility. We also need, as we have already discussed, to ensure that the cultures within which they work do not limit their ability to see the humanity of those with whom we work or the harm they may be causing.

Power and control

Within the rational-objectivist theories, issues of power are generally the legitimate right of those holding senior management and leadership positions (see Chapter 3 for a discussion of power from this perspective). The issue of power has been a major area of debate in the application of reflective-pluralist theories and approaches to work with organizations. Within this field much of the work on how to deal with inequalities of power has drawn on Jürgen Habermas's later writings on the nature of rationality (see Midgley, 2000). Despite the increasing view of the centrality of power in the field of organization studies there is no agreed definition of it (Mingers, 1992: 8; Morgan, 1986: 158). Morgan points to the way that analysis in terms of power can lead to feelings of futility and disempower those wanting to attempt change:

> Like those writers who emphasize how the social construction of reality is embedded in deeper power relations, I too believe that we act on a stage shaped by deeply ingrained assumptions and discourses, where certain groups and individuals have much greater power than others to shape the infrastructure of what we do. Knowledge of these deeper power relations can be instructive. But the image that we live in a world shaped by forces over which we have little control is generally overwhelming. It tends to create complacency and feelings of futility.
>
> (Morgan, 1993: 275)

However, managers in social work, as elsewhere, have to face working in a situation where they may experience misuses of power and control. It will be evident that there can be no simple answer to this. In Chapter 3 we have seen the idea of power on the one hand as legitimized and on the other hand as being a problem that needs to be designed out of the organization. In reflective-pluralist theories there are many different ways of understanding power. We will focus here on two aspects that we feel are important and can shape an ethical approach without trying to comprehensively cover the different understandings of this complex but important issue. Foucault provides a useful description of these two aspects of power when he says:

> I exercise power over you: I influence your behavior, or I try to do so. And I try to guide your behavior, to lead your behavior. The simplest means of doing this, obviously, is to take you by the hand and force you to go here or there. That's the limit case, the zero-degree of power. And it's actually in that moment that power ceases to be power and becomes mere physical force. On the other hand, if I use my age, my social position, the knowledge I may have about this or that, to make you behave in some particular way – that is to say, I'm not forcing you at all and I'm leaving you completely free – that's when I begin to exercise power. It's clear that power should not be defined as a constraining act of violence that represses individuals, forcing them to do something or preventing them from doing some other thing. But it takes place when there is a relation between two free subjects, and this relation is unbalanced, so that one can act upon the other, and the other is acted upon, or allows himself to be acted upon.
>
> (Foucault, 1988: 2)

We will first consider power as it appears in relationships within an organization, much in the way that the quote above defines it. We will then consider coercive acts of power and the demand for obedience that are referred to as mere physical force, though we see a range of demands for obedience that fall short of physical force.

This idea that power is embedded in the relationships between those in an organization is common to several approaches. Thus, in his work on developing a view of power from a postmodern perspective, Gergen (1992: 221) says 'traditional conceptions of power as inhering either in individuals or in organizational flow charts must be abandoned' and he goes on to argue that 'power is inherently a matter of social interdependence.' For Gergen this means that achieving power is tied up in language. However the achievement of power creates isolated worlds within the different divisions, departments and teams:

> In doing so each develops local definitions of the real and the good and coordinates its actions around these definitions. However, as power of functioning is achieved within each group, signification is solidified – as it must be for reliable coordination of actions among persons. And, as local criteria of the real and the good are solidified, so do members of these divisions become insulated against the realities of the adjoining divisions.
>
> (Gergen, 1992: 221)

It will be seen from the above that this view fits with the idea of culture discussed above and not only relates to the development of local practices but also suggests that power is the source of 'solidified' conceptions of 'the real and the good'. Within this perspective power itself is not seen as being repressive but it leads to conflict or oppressions because of the failure to see the reality of others outside. At the same time societies and organizations can and do embed inequalities of power through institutions that maintain an imbalance in power in favour of certain groups or individuals.

Maturana suggests that power arises when there is obedience. He sees power as an act of submission to which individuals subject themselves. Thus he says (in Poerksen 2004: 65): 'we always do what we want to do, even though we may claim to be acting against our will or to have been compelled to do something.' Although we may say that we were forced to do something, this is an excuse we use to explain our obedience when we chose to do whatever it was in order to meet another desire. For example, if someone points a gun at me and asks me to raise my arms and stand against the wall I may choose to do that in my desire to stay alive. It may seem that saying that we choose submission is 'blaming the victims' but rather it is ultimately empowering. The recognition of choice does allow reflection on the possibility of doing something else. This is not to say that in the face of the gunman I should refuse to do as told, though it does make that a possibility. In fact Maturana's view is shaped by his experience of living under the Chilean dictator Pinochet in a regime that murdered many people. He says of his general demeanour during that experience, which included him being arrested and put into prison at great risk to his life:

> I decided to practise hypocrisy in order to stay alive and to protect my family and children. At the same time, I tried to move and behave in such a way as to avoid endangering my dignity and my self-respect. I kept away from certain situations, respected the curfew, did not discuss certain topics in the university. When the soldiers came and ordered me to raise my hands and to move up to the wall, I raised my hands and moved up to the wall. However, it was quite clear to me in those moments that the time would come when I would no longer be prepared to grant power to the dictator's regime.
>
> (Maturana in Poerksen, 2004: 66)

Interestingly, when he was arrested and talked his way out of prison by giving his gaolers a lecture and later when he challenged Pinochet directly by responding critically to his toast at a dinner party, he felt it was his maintenance of self-respect and dignity that protected him.

Reflection

The issue of power relates directly to our principles of respect and responsibility. The last quotation by Maturana shows how a key issue in dealing with coercion is the maintenance of self-respect and dignity, if necessary by hypocrisy (pretending to submit). Such a view keeps open the possibility of choice even in situations of extreme oppression; however, hypocrisy requires a state of awareness of the choice and the simulation of submission. It involves keeping alive the possibility of acting differently and the recognition of the oppression.

Another linked issue is that we suggest that, when acting in the face of coercion, it is important to assert one's responsibility and, through treating others with respect (this does not mean with deference, which is not respect), to invite them to act in full awareness of your fellow humanity. For example, in one social work department the senior management team ordered headquarters staff to drop all their work and come to a meeting. At the meeting they were told there was to be a reorganization that would substantially reduce the number of first line managers. They were threatened with disciplinary procedures and told that that the senior management team did not want to hear anything about why the reorganization wouldn't work; they simply had to implement it. This uncharacteristic intervention by the senior management team was felt to be a response to a continuing campaign from a senior politician who had recently been reported in the press as saying he thought the departments was top-heavy, needed to save money and would benefit from the loss of some 'men in suits'.

Within days of this announcement by the senior management team there was widespread dissent from the front-line teams with meetings held in which they passed votes of no confidence in the director, and a series of strikes was planned. One headquarters manager decided to act with respect and responsibility. Despite being warned by colleagues to keep her head down she carefully crafted a report, which started by saying that she appreciated how the director and his colleagues had always shown deep concern to ensure social work practice was properly supervised and their concern for proper procedures – all things that were true descriptions of their previous actions and showed her respect for the senior management team. This was accompanied by detailed information on the numbers of cases and their situations along with a careful and considered estimate of the implications for workloads for front-line managers. The report ended by saying that she was not sure if other data were available to the senior management team or if there were other ways they considered allocating the workloads but that she had felt it her duty to share her understanding of the situation with them as she knew they were careful in having an evidence base for their management. This also showed her understanding and respect for the senior management team, who had previously adopted a style of careful planning using similar data.

It is impossible to know what effect this single intervention had in the sudden about-face that followed shortly after the report was delivered. However, the report was soon in the hands of the trade unions, who praised the writer and said it gave them real ammunition for the negotiations. At the same time, the writer was praised by members of the senior management team, one of whom said he didn't know why the other managers hadn't been so helpful. Also the figures she had produced were used to plan a restructured service and the budget cuts were fully reinstated. The writer of the report had clearly acted with respect and responsibility and done this carefully. Luckily, this had a positive impact on her career. In other circumstances she might have faced disciplinary action or had her career aspirations side-lined, but she was aware of this when she wrote the report.

A second area for reflection comes from the view that power solidifies conceptions of the real and the good. This is a similar effect to that discussed in the section above on culture and values. It does once more raise the need to find ways to reflect on those things we hold to be true and good. As Foucault (1988: 12) said:

> In a sense, I am a moralist, insofar as I believe that one of the tasks, one of the meanings of human existence – the source of human freedom – is never to accept anything as definitive, untouchable, obvious, or immobile. No aspect of reality should be allowed to become a definitive and inhuman law for us.

Reflections on social work leadership and management

Management and leadership roles in social work are not easy, as our discussion in this final chapter clearly illustrates. The approach to management and leadership we are proposing is similarly not simple. It offers no cookbooks or simple recipes for what to do. We propose the need for a framework that is relativist and complex because this is the nature of the world in which social work managers and leaders must act. We acknowledge the need to have a framework of broad principles for social work practice and social work organization; amongst other reasons, to maintain the legitimacy of both in the public eye. And this is also required to make clear the principles on which social work services are delivered to those we try to help. We have two key concerns with the increasingly rigid framework being thrust on social work and its management:

First, there is an illusion, reinforced by successive reports into tragedies, that if we have sufficient guidelines, protocols and procedures we will avoid major incidents of harm or ill-treatment. We know that guidelines and procedures will not prevent tragedies; such is the nature of social work and the tensions with which it deals on a daily basis. New guidelines should promote flexibility and encourage responsible action by practitioners and their managers.

Second, and related to this last comment, a reliance on ever more detailed procedures and frameworks will in fact erode the ability of social workers and their managers to make judgements and act with ingenuity when they encounter situations for which there are no encompassing guidelines. It is at such times that managers and social workers need not only the skills of reflection-in-action but also the ability to reflect-on-action in order to enhance their capacity to deal with the complex and unexpected situations they will face in the future. We do not believe this is possible through reliance on rational-objectivist frameworks alone. Thus we require the perspective of reflective-pluralism if we are to develop a healthy and helpful profession. We are particularly concerned that social workers and their managers be given sufficient autonomy and resources to take appropriate actions. For their part social workers and their managers need the confidence to take responsibility, individually and collectively, for these actions.

Final comments

We need to make several short points in conclusion. This book has drawn on a wide range of approaches to management and leadership and it has omitted others. We have sought to show how the approaches discussed apply to the context of social work organizations. Our own interest in these topics has developed over time. As managers, social workers and academics we have examined many different points of view and engaged in debate about the theory and practice of management and leadership in social work. Our standpoint, as will be clear from the concluding two chapters, is that social work management and leadership are not straightforward roles. We believe that reflective approaches lead to a greater understanding of management and leadership in social work, which enables us to respond effectively to the diverse perspectives, interests and experiences not only of service users and their communities but also social workers and the wider public.

We have drawn on a wide range of theories and approaches to inform and help develop our own perspectives. We hope that this book has conveyed our passion and in turn has inspired the reader to delve further into management and leadership theories. We are concerned that some texts over-simplify management and leadership and attempt to provide step by step instructions. Similarly attempts to prepare those in the profession to take up leadership have a singular focus on competency and little or no emphasis on reflection, education and learning more broadly. Some element of skill development is useful and necessary but that is not the whole story. Competencies can aid us to undertake straightforward tasks, but where tasks are more complex people need flexibility of action and ingenuity, and these require learning of a different order.

Thus we have not taken a competency-based or 'how to' approach to management and leadership, nor have we tried to simplify them. Instead we have sought to stimulate the interest of the reader in learning more about the complexity of management and leadership. We do not believe that there is one correct way to undertake management and leadership and so we have offered a range of perspectives. Above all we believe in our human potential to understand complex situations and to respond with creativity and passion.

References

Ackoff, R.L. (1974) *Redesigning the Future*, New York: Wiley.

Alimo-Metcalfe, B. (2004) 'Leadership: A Masculine Past, but a Feminine Future?', *Gender and Excellence in the Making*, Brussels: European Commission.

Alimo-Metcalfe, B. and Alban-Metcalfe, R.J. (2001) 'The Development of a New Transformational Leadership Questionnaire', *Journal of Occupational and Organizational Psychology*, 74: 1–27.

Alimo-Metcalfe, B., Ford, J., Harding, N. and Lawler, J. (2000) 'Leadership Development in British Organisations (at the Beginning of the 21st Century)', *Careers Research Forum Report*, London: Careers Research Forum.

Alvesson, M. (2002) *Understanding Organizational Culture*, London: Sage.

Alvesson, M. and Sveningsson, S. (2003) 'The Great Disappearing Act: Difficulties in Doing "Leadership"', *Leadership Quarterly*, 14: 359–81.

Alvesson, M. and Willmott, H. (eds) (2003) *Studying Management Critically*, Thousand Oaks, CA: Sage Publications.

Ancona, D., Malone, T.W., Orlikowski, W.J. and Senge, P.M. (2007) 'The Incomplete Leader', *Harvard Business Review*, Feb.: 94–100.

Andersen, S.C. (2005) 'How to Improve the Outcome of State Welfare Services: Governance in a Systems-Theoretical Perspective', *Public Administration*, 83(4): 891–907.

Anderson, P. (1999) 'Complexity Theory and Organization Science', *Organization Science*, 10(3): 216–32.

Antonakis, J., Cianciolo, A.T. and Sterberg, R.J. (2004) *The Nature of Leadership*, Thousand Oaks, CA: Sage.

Argyris, C. and Schön, D.A. (1974) *Theory in Practice: Increasing Professional Effectiveness*, San Francisco: Jossey-Bass.

Argyris, C. and Schön, D.A. (1978) *Organizational Learning: A Theory of Action Perspective*, Reading, MA: Addison-Wesley.

Ashman, I. (2007) 'Existentialism and Leadership: A Response to John Lawler with Some Further Thoughts', *Leadership*, 3(Feb.): 91–106.

Ashman, I. and Lawler, J. (2009) 'Leadership and Authenticity: A Sartrean Critique', paper presented to the Leadership Track of the 2009 British Academy of Management Conference: The End of the Pier, Brighton, 15–17 September.

Audit Commission (2002) *Integrated Services for Older People: Building a Whole System Approach in England*, London: Audit Commission.

Audit Commission (2007) *Seeing the Light: Innovation in Local Public Services*, London: Audit Commision.

Australian Public Service Commission (2007) *Tackling Wicked Problems: A Public Policy Perspective*. Barton, ACT: Commonwealth of Australia, http://www.apsc.gov.au/publications07/wickedproblems.pdf, accessed 29 July 2009.

Avolio, B.J. (1995), *The Multifactor Leadership Questionnaire (Form R Revised)*, Palo Alto, CA: Mindgarden.

Barker, R.A. (1997) 'How Can We Train Leaders if We Do Not Know What Leadership Is?', *Human Relations*, 50(4): 343–62.

Bass, B.M. (1985) *Leadership and Performance beyond Expectation*, New York: Free Press.

Bass, B.M. (1997) 'Does the Transactional-Transformational Leadership Paradigm Transcend National and Organizational Boundaries?', *American Psychologist*, 52: 130–9.

Bass, B.M. and Steidlmeier, P. (1999) 'Ethics, Character and Authentic Transformational Leadership Behavior', *Leadership Quarterly*, 10(2): 181–217.

BASW (2002) *The Code of Ethics for Social Work*, Birmingham: British Association of Social Workers.

Bateson, G. (1958) *Naven* (2nd edition), Stanford, CA: Stanford University Press.

Bateson, G. (1973) *Steps to an Ecology of Mind*, New York: Paladin (first published 1972 Chandler Publishers).

Bateson, G. (1979) *Mind and Nature: A Necessary Unity*, New York: E.P. Dutton.

Bateson, G. and Bateson, M.C. (1988) *Angels Fear*, London: Rider.

Bauman, Z. (1993) *Postmodern Ethics*, Oxford: Blackwell.

Beauchamp, T.L. and Childress, J.F. (2001) *Principles of Biomedical Ethics* (5th edition), New York: Oxford University Press.

Beer, S. (1975) *Designing Freedom*, Toronto: Canadian Broadcasting Corporation.

Belbin, R.M. (1981 and 2004) *Management Teams: Why They Succeed or Fail*, London: Heinemann.

Bennett, N., Wise, C., Woods, P. and Harvey, J.A. (2003) *Distributed Leadership*, Nottingham: NCSL.

Bennis, W. and Nanus, B. (1985) *Leaders: The Strategies for Taking Charge*, New York: Harper and Row.

Berg, E.B., Barry, J.J. and Chandler, J.P. (2008) 'New Public Management and Social Work in Sweden and England: Challenges and Opportunities for Staff in Predominantly Female Organizations', *International Journal of Sociology and Social Policy*, 28(3/4): 114–28.

Berger, P.L. and Luckmann, T. (1966) *The Social Construction of Reality: A Treatise in the Sociology of Knowledge*, Garden City, NY: Anchor Books.

Bhaskar, R.A. (1998) *The Possibility of Naturalism* (3rd edition), London: Routledge (first published 1979).

Billing, Y. and Alvesson, M. (2000) 'Questioning the Notion of Feminine Leadership: A Critical Perspective on the Gender Labelling of Leadership', *Gender, Work and Organization*, 7(3): 144–57.

Bilson, A. (1997) 'Guidelines for a Constructivist Approach: Steps towards the Adaptation of Ideas from Family Therapy for Use in Organizations', *Systems Practice*, 10(2): 153–78.

Bilson, A. (2002) 'Family Support: Messages from Research', *Representing Children*, 15(1): 10–20.

Bilson, A. (2004) 'Escaping from Intrinsically Unstable and Untrustful Relations: Implications of a Constitutive Ontology for Responding to Issues of Power', *Journal of Cybernetics and Human Knowing*, 11(2): 21–35.

Bilson, A. (ed.) (2005) *Evidence-Based Practice in Social Work*, London: Whiting and Birch.

Bilson, A. (2006) 'Promoting Compassionate Concern in Social Work: Reflections on Ethics, Biology and Love', *British Journal of Social Work*, 37(8): 1371–86.

Bilson, A. and Barker, R. (1998) 'Looked after Children and Contact: Reassessing the Social Work Task', *Research, Policy and Planning*, 16(1): 20–7.

Bilson, A. and Dykes, F. (2009) 'A bio-cultural basis for protecting, promoting and supporting breastfeeding', in F. Dykes and V. Moran (eds), *Infant and Young Child Feeding: Cultural Challenges*, Chichester: John Wiley, pp. 32–42.

Bilson, A. and Ross, S. (1999) *Social Work Management and Practice: Systems Principles* (2nd edition), London: Jessica Kingsley Publishers.

Bilson, A. and Thorpe, D.H. (2007) 'Towards Aesthetic Seduction Using Emotional Engagement and Stories', *Kybernetes*, 36(7/8): 936–45.

Bilson, A. and White, S. (2004) 'The Limits of Governance: Interrogating the Tacit Dimension', in A. Gray and S. Harrison (eds) *Governing Medicine*, Maidenhead: Open University Press, pp. 93–106.

Binns, J. (2008) 'The Ethics of Relational Leading: Gender Matters', *Gender, Work and Organization*, 15(6): 600–20.

Bisman, C. (2004) 'Social Work Values: The Moral Code of the Profession', *British Journal of Social Work*, 34: 109–23.

Black, J.A., Hinrichs, K.T. and Fabian, F.H. (2007) 'Fractals of Strategic Coherence in a Successful Nonprofit Organization', *Nonprofit Management & Leadership*, 17(4): 421–41.

Blake, R.R. and Mouton, J.S. (1978) *The New Managerial Grid*, Houston TX: Gulf.

Block, P. (1996) *Stewardship: Choosing Service over Self-Interest*, San Francisco: Berrett-Koehler.

Blockley, D.I. and Godfrey, P (2000) *Doing it Differently: Systems for Rethinking Construction*, London: Thomas Telford.

Boje, D. and Dennehy, R. (1999) *Managing in the Postmodern World* (3rd edition), http://business.nmsu.edu/%7Edboje/mpwchap1.htm, accessed 15 January 2009.

Bolden, R. (2004) *What is Leadership?*, Leadership South West Research Report, Centre for Leadership Studies, University of Exeter, http://www.leadership-studies.com/lsw/lswreports.htm, accessed 2 March 2009.

Bolden, R., Gosling, J., Marturano, A. and Dennison, P. (2003) *A Review of Leadership Theory and Competency Frameworks*, University of Exeter: Centre for Leadership Studies.

Bolger, S., Corrigan, P., Docking, K. and Frost, N. (1981) *Towards Socialist Welfare Work: Working in the State*, London: Macmillan.

Briskman, L. and Noble, C. (1999) 'Social Work Ethics: Embracing Diversity?', in B. Pease and J. Fook, *Transforming Social Work Practice: Postmodern Critical Perspectives*, Abingdon: Routledge.

Brookes, S. (2008) *The Public Leadership Challenge: Full Research Report. ESRC Seminar Series End of Award Report*, RES-451–25–4273, Swindon: ESRC

Brown, A.D. (1998) *Organisational Culture*, London: Financial Times/Pitman.

Buber, M. (2002) *Between Man and Man*, London and New York: Routledge.

Buchanan, D. and Huczynski, A. (2007) *Organizational Behaviour: An Introductory Text* (7th edition), Harlow: Financial Times/Prentice Hall.

Burns, J.M. (1978) *Leadership*, New York: Harper.

Burns, T. and Stalker, G.M. (1961) *The Management of Innovation*, London: Tavistock.

Burrell, G. (1997) *Pandemonium*, London: Sage.

Burrell, G. and Morgan, G. (1979) *Sociological Paradigms and Organisational Analysis: Elements of the Sociology of Corporate Life*, London: Heinemann.

Cade, B.W. (1982) 'Some Uses of Metaphor', *Australian Journal of Family Therapy*, 3(3): 135–40.

Cameron, G. and Mah Wren, A. (1999) 'Reconstructing Organizational Culture: A Process Using Multiple Perspectives', *Public Health Nursing*, 16(2): 96–101.

Capra, F. (1997) *The Web of Life: A New Understanding of Living Systems*, New York: Doubleday.

Chapman, J. (2004) *Systems Failure: Why Governments Must Learn to Think Differently*, London: Demos.

Checkland, P. (1999) *Systems Thinking, Systems Practice: Revised Edition*, Chichester: John Wiley.

Checkland, P. and Scholes, J. (1990) *Soft Systems Methodology in Action*, Chichester: John Wiley.

Chernesky, R.H. (2003) 'Examining the Glass Ceiling: Gender Influences on Promotion Decisions', *Administration in Social Work*, 27(2): 13–18.

Clarke, M. and Stewart, J. (1997) 'Handling the Wicked Issues – A Challenge for Government', University of Birmingham, School of Public Policy Discussion Paper, Birmingham.

Clifford, D. (2002) 'Resolving Uncertainties: The Contribution of Some Recent Feminist Ethical Theory to the Social Professions', *European Journal of Social Work*, 5(1): 31–42.

Cohen, S. (1985) *Visions of Social Control: Crime, Punishment and Classification*. Cambridge: Polity Press.

Cole, G.A. (2004) *Management Theory and Practice*, London: Thompson Learning.

Collins, D. (1998) *Organizational Change: Sociological Perspectives*, London: Routledge.

Collins Essential English Dictionary (2006) London: HarperCollins.

Connor, R. and MacKenzie-Smith, P. (2003) 'The Leadership Jigsaw – Finding the Missing Piece', *Business Strategy Review*, 14(1): 59–66.

Cooper, D. (1999) *Existentialism: A Reconstruction* (2nd edition), Oxford: Blackwell.

Cooper, J.E. (2002) 'Constructivist Leadership: Its Evolving Narrative', in L. Lambert, D. Walker, D.P. Zimmermann, J.E. Cooper, M. Dale Lambert, M.E. Gardner and M. Szabo (eds) *The Constructivist Leader* (2nd edition), Oxford, OH: Teachers College Press, pp. 112–26.

Cooper, R. (1989) 'Modernism, Post Modernism and Organizational: The Contribution of Jacques Derrida', *Organization Studies*, 10(4): 479–502.

Coulshed, V. and Mullender, A. (2006) with D.N. Jones and N. Thompson, *Management in Social Work* (3rd edition), Basingstoke: Palgrave Macmillan.

Cunliffe, A. (2002) 'Social Poetics as Management Inquiry', *Journal of Management Inquiry*, 11(2): 128–46.

Daft, R.L. and Marcic, D. (1995) *Understanding Management*, Orlando, FL: Dryden Press.

Damasio, A.R. (1994) *Descartes' Error: Emotion, Reason and the Human Brain*, New York: Avon Books.

Denison, D.R. (1996) 'What *Is* the Difference between Organizational Culture and Organizational Climate? A Native's Point of View on a Decade of Paradigm Wars', *Academy of Management Review*, 21: 619–54.

Department for Education and Skills (DES) (2006) *Championing Children – A Shared Set of Skills, Knowledge and Behaviours for Those Leading and Managing Integrated Children's Services*, Nottingham: DfES Publications.

Department of Health (DH) (2003a) *The Victoria Climbié Inquiry: Summary Report of an Inquiry*, London: Department of Health.

Department of Health (DH) (2003b) *Discharge from Hospital Pathway, Process and Practice*, London: Department of Health.

Department of Health/Department of Education and Skills (DH/DfES) (2006) *Options for Excellence: Building the Social Care Workforce for the Future*, London: DH/DfES.

Department of Health Workforce Directorate/NHS Partners/Manchester University (2006) *HR High Impact Changes: An Evidence Based Resource*, London: Department of Health.

Derrida, J. (1978) *Writing and Difference*, London: Routledge.

Dewane, C.J. (2008) '10 Leadership Strategies for Women in Social Service Management', *Social Work Today*, 8(2): 38.

DHSSPS (2001) *Best Practice – Best Care – A Framework for Setting Standards, Delivering Services and Improving Monitoring and Regulation in the HPSS*, Belfast: DHSSPS.

Dodgson, M. (1993) 'Organizational Learning: A Review of Some Literatures', *Organization Studies*, 14(3): 375–94.

Drucker, P.F. (1954) *The Practice of Management*, New York: Harper and Row.

Drucker, P.F. (1974) *Management: Tasks, Responsibilities, Practices*, New York: Harper and Row.

Dulewicz, V. and Higgs, M. (2000) 'Emotional Intelligence: A Review and Evaluation Study', *Journal of Management Psychology*, 15(4): 341–72.

Dustin, D. (2007) *The McDonaldization of Social Work*, Aldershot: Ashgate.

Dykes, F. (2005a) 'A Critical Ethnographic Study of Encounters between Midwives and Breastfeeding Women on Postnatal Wards', *Midwifery*, 21: 241–52.

Dykes, F. (2005b) '"Supply" and "Demand": Breastfeeding as Labour', *Social Science & Medicine*, 60: 2283–93.

Dykes, F. (2006) *Breastfeeding in Hospital: Midwives, Mothers and the Production Line*, London: Routledge.

Eagly, A.H. and Johannesen-Schmidt, M.C. (2001) 'The Leadership Styles of Women and Men', *Journal of Social Issues*, 57(4): 781–97.

Elmore, R. (2000) *Building a New Structure for School Leadership*, Washington, DC: Albert Shanker Institute.

Emery, F. and Trist, E. (1965) 'The Causal Texture of Organizational Environments', *Human Relations*, 18: 21–32.

Espejo, R. (2003) 'Social Systems and the Embodiment of Organizational Learning', in E. Mitleton-Kelly (ed.), *Complex Systems and Evolutionary Perspectives on Organizations: The Application of Complexity Theory to Organizations*, Oxford: Pergamon, pp. 53–70.

Fauth, R. and Mahdon, M. (2007) 'Improving Social and Health Care Services', *SCIE Knowledge Review 16*, London: Social Care Institute for Excellence.

Fayol, H. (1916) 'Administration Industrielle and Generale – Prevoyance, Organisation, Commodidement, Coordination, Controle', *Bulletin de la Société de l'Industrie Minérale*, 10(3): 5–162.

Fineman, S. (ed.) (1993) *Emotions in Organizations*, London: Sage.

Finlay, L. and Ballinger, C. (2008) 'The Challenge of Working in Teams', in S. Fraser and S. Matthews (eds) *The Critical Practitioner in Social Work and Health Care*, London: Sage, pp. 149–68.

Fiol, C.M., and Lyles, M.A. (1985) 'Organizational Learning', *Academy of Management Review*, 10(4): 803–13.

Flam, H. (1993) 'Fear, Loyalty and Greedy Organizations', in S. Fineman (ed.) *Emotions in Organizations*, London: Sage.

Fleming, D. (2001) 'Narrative leadership: using the power of stories', *Strategy and Leadership*, Aug. 29(4): 26–34.

Fletcher, J. (2001) *Disappearing Acts: Gender, Power and Relational Practice at Work*, Cambridge, MA: MIT Press.

Fletcher, J. (2004) 'Invisible Work: The Disappearing of Relational Practice at Work', in *Ohio State University President's Council on Women's Issues 2004: Annual Report*, Ohio: Ohio State University, pp. 28–33.

Flood, R.L. (1990) *Liberating Systems Theory*, New York: Plenum Press.

Flood, R.L. and Jackson, M.C. (eds) (1991a) *Critical Systems Thinking: Directed Readings*, Chichester: John Wiley.

Flood, R.L. and Jackson, M.C. (1991b) *Creative Problem Solving: Total Systems Intervention*, Chichester: John Wiley.

Flood, R.L. and Jackson, M.C. (1991c) 'Total Systems Intervention: A Practical Face to Critical Systems Thinking', in R.L. Flood and M.C. Jackson (eds) *Critical Systems Thinking: Directed Readings*, Chichester: John Wiley.

Flynn, N. (1990) *Public Sector Management*, London: Harvester Wheatsheaf.

Foerster, H. von (1974) *Cybernetics of Cybernetics*, Urbana: University of Illinois.

Follett, M.P. (1934) *Creative Experience*, London: Longmans Green.

Foote, C. and Stanners, C. (2002) *An Integrated System of Care for Older People: New Care for Old*, London: Jessica Kingsley Publishers.

Ford, J. and Harding, N. (2007) 'Move Over Management: We Are All Leaders Now', *Management Learning*, 38: 475–93.

Ford, J. and Lawler, J. (2007) 'Blending Existentialist and Constructionist Approaches in Leadership Studies: An Exploratory Account', *Leadership & Organization Development Journal*, 28(5): 409–25.

Ford, J.D. (1999) 'Organizational Change as Shifting Conversations', *Journal of Organizational Change Management,* 12(6): 480–500.

Ford, J.D. and Ford, L.W. (2003) 'Conversations and the Authoring of Change', in D. Holman (ed.) *Management and Language: The Manager as a Practical Author,* London: Sage, pp. 141–56.

Forrester, J.W. (1971) 'Counterintuitive Behaviour of Social Systems', *Technology Review,* 73(3): 52–68.

Foster, A. (2004) 'Foreword', in Department for Innovation, Universities and Skills, *Bureaucracy Review Group Annual Report 2004,* London: Department for Innovation, Universities and Skills, http://www.dius.gov.uk/~/media/publications/2004BRGFirstAnnReport2–40–68, accessed 10 October 2008.

Foster, J. (1999) 'Women Senior Managers and Conditional Power: The Case in Social Services Departments', *Women in Management Review,* 14(8): 316–24.

Foucault, M. (1988) 'An Interview with Michel Foucault Conducted by Michael Bess', *History of the Present,* 4: 1–2, 11–13, http://www.vanderbilt.edu/historydept/michaelbess/Foucault%20Interview, accessed 31 March 2009.

Franks, A. (2001) 'Organisational Culture – Make of It What You Will', *Clinician in Management,* 10: 14–22.

French, J.P. and Raven, B.H. (1986) 'The Bases of Social Power', in D. Cartwright and A.F. Zander (eds) *Group Dynamics: Research and Theory* (3rd edition), New York: Harper and Row.

General Social Care Council (GSCC) (2002) *Employers of Social Care Workers: Codes of Practice,* London: GSCC.

General Social Care Council (GSCC) (2005) *Specialist Standards and Requirements for Post-qualifying Social Work Education and Training: Leadership and Management,* London: GSCC.

Gergen, K.J. (1992) 'Organizational Theory in the Post-Modern Era', in M. Reed and M. Hughes (eds) *Rethinking Organizations: New Directions in Organization Theory and Analysis,* London: Sage, pp. 207–26.

Giddens, A. (1999) *Runaway World: How Globalization is Reshaping Our Lives,* London: Profile.

Gill, R. (2006) *Theory and Practice of Leadership,* London: Sage.

Gleick, J. (1997) *Chaos,* London: Vintage.

Glisson, C. and Hemmelgarn, A. (1998) 'The Effects of Organizational Climate and Interorganizational Coordination on the Quality and Outcomes of Children's Service Systems', *Child Abuse and Neglect,* 22(5): 401–21.

Glisson, C., and James, L.R. (2002) 'The Cross-level Effects of Culture and Climate in Human Service Teams', *Journal of Organizational Behavior,* 23: 767–94.

Gold, J., Rodgers, H., Frearson, M. and Holden, R. (2003) 'Leadership Development: A New Typology', working paper, Leeds Business School and Learning and Skills Research Centre.

Goleman, D. (1996) *Emotional Intelligence,* London: Bloomsbury Publishing.

Goleman, D. (2001) *Working with Emotional Intelligence,* London: Pharmacia.

Grant, R.M. (2002) *Contemporary Strategy Analysis,* Oxford: Blackwell.

Greenleaf, R.K. (1970) *The Servant as Leader,* Indianapolis, IN: Robert Greenleaf Center.

Gregory, W. (2003) 'Discordant Pluralism', in G. Midgley (ed.) *Systems Thinking,* vol. 4, London: Sage: pp. 123–42.

Grint, K. (ed.) (1997) *Leadership: Classical, Contemporary and Critical Approaches,* Oxford: Oxford University Press.

Grint, K. (2005) *Leadership: Limits and Possibilities,* Basingstoke: Palgrave Macmillan.

Gronn, P. (2000) 'Distributed Properties: A New Architecture for Leadership', *Educational Management & Administration,* 28(3): 317–38.

Habermas, J. (1972) *Knowledge and Human Interests,* trans. J.J. Shapiro, London: Heinemann.

Habermas, J. (1981) 'Modernity versus Postmodernism', *New German Critique,* 22: 3–14.

Habermas, J. (1984) *The Theory of Communicative Action,* vols. I and II, Oxford: Polity Press.

Hafford-Letchfield, T. (2006a) *Management and Organisations in Social Work*, Exeter: Learning Matters.

Hafford-Letchfield, T. (2006b) 'Organizational Culture Is Crucial to Improving Social Care Management', *Community Care*, 3 August: 36–7.

Hall, C. (1997) *Social Work as Narrative: Storytelling and Persuasion in Professional Texts*, Aldershot: Ashgate.

Harris, J. (1998) 'Scientific Management, Bureau-Professionalism, New Managerialism: The Labour Process of State Social Work', *British Journal of Social Work*, 28: 839–62.

Harris, J. (2003) *The Social Work Business*, London: Routledge.

Harrison, S. (1999) 'New Labour, Modernisation and Health Care Governance', paper presented at the Political Studies Association/Social Policy Association Conference 'New Labour, New Health', London, September.

Harrison, S. (2002) 'New Labour, Modernisation and the Medical Labour Process', *Journal of Social Policy*, 31(3): 465–85.

Harrison, S., Moran, M., Wood, B. (2002) 'Policy Emergence and Policy Convergence: The Case of 'Scientific-Bureaucratic' Medicine', *British Journal of Politics and International Relations*, 4(1): 1–24.

Hassard, J. (1993) 'Postmodernism and Organizational Analysis', in J. Hassard and M. Parker (eds) *Postmodernism and Organizations*, London: Sage.

Helgeson, S. (1990) *The Female Advantage: Women's Ways of Leadership*, New York: Doubleday.

Hesselbein, F. (1996) 'Managing in a World that is Round', *Leader to Leader*, 2 (Fall): 6–8.

Hill, C. and Jones, G. (1995) *Strategic Management: An Integrated Approach* (3rd edition), Boston: Houghton Mifflin.

Hoffman, L. (1985) 'Beyond Power and Control: Toward a "Second Order" Family Systems Therapy', *Family Systems Medicine*, 3(4): 381–96.

Hoffman, L. (1992) 'A Reflexive Stance for Family Therapy', in S. McNamee and K.J. Gergen (eds) *Therapy as Social Construction*, London: Sage, pp. 7–24.

Hosking, D. and Fineman, S. (1990) 'Organizing Processes', *Journal of Management Studies*, 27(6): 583–604.

Houston, S. (2003) 'Establishing Virtue in Social Work: A Response to McBeath and Webb', *British Journal of Social Work*, 33: 819–24.

Howe, D. (1987) *Introduction to Social Work Theory: Making Sense in Practice*, Aldershot: Wildwood House.

Hughes, M. and Wearing, M. (2007) *Organizations and Management in Social Work*, London: Sage.

Hugman, R. (1991) *Power in the Caring Professions*, Basingstoke: Macmillan.

Hugman, R. (2003) 'Professional Values in Social Work: Reconsidering Postmodernism', *British Journal of Social Work*, 33: 1025–41.

Iles, V. and Sutherland, K. (2001) *Managing Change in the NHS*, London: NHS Service Delivery and Organisation Research and Development.

Imber-Black, E. (1986) 'The Systemic Consultant and Human-Service-Provider Systems', in L.C. Wynne, S.H. McDaniel and T.T. Weber (eds) *Systems Consultation – A New Perspective for Family Therapy*, London: Guildford Press.

Imber-Black, E. (1988) *Families and Larger Systems*, New York: Guildford Press.

Isaacs, W. (1999) 'Dialogic Leadership', *Systems Thinker*, 10(1): 1–5.

Jackson, M.C. (1982) 'The Nature of Soft Systems Thinking: The Work of Churchman, Ackoff and Checkland', *Journal of Applied Systems Analysis*, 9: 17–28.

Jackson, M.C. (1991) 'Five Commitments of Critical Systems Theory', in R.B. Blackham, R.L. Flood and M.C. Jackson (eds) *Systems Thinking in Europe*, London: Plenum Press.

Jackson, M.C. (2000) *Systems Approaches to Management*, New York: Kluwer/Plenum.

Jackson, M.C. (2003) *Systems Thinking: Creative Holism for Managers*, Chichester: John Wiley.

Jackson, N. and Carter, P. (1991) 'In Defence of Paradigm Incommensurability', *Organization Studies*, 12(1): 109–27.

Jeston, J. and Nelis, J. (2008) *Management by Process*, Oxford: Butterworth-Heinemann.

Johnson, D.W. and Johnson, F.P. (2003) *Joining Together: Group Theory and Group Skills* (8th edition), Englewood Cliffs, NJ: Prentice-Hall.

Jones, A. and Bowles, N. (2005) 'Best Practice from Admission to Discharge in Acute Inpatient Care: Considerations and Standards from a Whole System Perspective', *Journal of Psychiatric & Mental Health Nursing*, 12(6): 642–7.

Jones, C. (1983) *State Social Work and the Working Class*, London: Macmillan.

Joyce, P., Corrigan, P., and Hayes, M (1988) *Striking Out: Trade Unionism in Social Work*, Basingstoke: Macmillan.

Kadushin, A. and Harkness, D. (2002) *Supervision in Social Work* (4th edition), New York: Columbia University Press.

Kakabadse, A. and Kakabadse, N. (1999) *Essence of Leadership*, London: International Thomson.

Kanungo, R.N. and Conger, J.A. (1992) 'Charisma: Exploring New Dimensions of Leadership Behavior', *Psychology and Developing Societies*, 4: 21–38.

Kaplan, R. and Norton, D. (1992) 'The Balanced Scorecard – Measures that Drive Performance', *Harvard Business Review*, Jan./Feb.: 71–9.

Katz, A.M. and Shotter, J. (1996) 'Hearing the Patient's "Voice": Towards a Social Poetics in Diagnostic Interviews', *Social Science and Medicine*, 43(6): 919–31.

Kellerman, B. (2008) *Followership*, Boston: Harvard Business Press.

Kensing, F. and Winograd, T. (1991) 'The Language/Action Approach to Design of Computer-support for Cooperative Work: A Preliminary Study in Work Mapping', in R. Stamper, P. Kerola, R. Lee and K. Lyytinen (eds) *Collaborative Work, Social Communications and Information Systems*, Amsterdam: Elsevier.

Kirkpatrick, I. (2006) 'Taking Stock of the New Managerialism', *Social Work & Society*, 4(1): 14–24.

Klugman, D. (1997) 'Existentialism and Constructivism: A Bi-polar Model of Subjectivity', *Clinical Social Work*, 25(3): 297–313.

Kotter, J.P. (1990) *A Force for Change: How Leadership Differs from Management*, New York: Free Press.

Kotter, J.P. and Heskett, J.L. (1992) *Corporate Culture and Performance*, New York: Free Press.

Kouzes, J.M. and Posner, B.Z. (2002) *The Leadership Challenge: How to Get Extraordinary Things Done in Organizations* (3rd edition), San Francisco: Jossey-Bass.

Lambert, L. (2002) 'Leading the Conversations', in L. Lambert, D. Walker, D. P. Zimmerman, J. E. Cooper, M. D. Lambert, M. E. Gardner and M. Szabo (eds) *The Constructivist Leader*, New York: Teachers' College Press, pp. 63–88.

Lambert, L., Walker, D., Zimmerman, D. P., Cooper, J. E., Lambert, M. D., Gardner, M. E. and Szabo, M. (eds) (2002) *The Constructivist Leader*, New York: Teachers' College Press.

Laming, Lord (2009) *The Protection of Children in England: A Progress Report*, London: The Stationery Office.

Land, F.F. (2000) 'Evaluation in a Socio-Technical Context', in R. Basskerville, J. Stage and J.I. DeGross (eds) *Organizational and Social Perspectives on Information Technology*, Boston: Kluwer Academic Publishers, pp. 115–26.

Langan, M. (2000) 'Social Services: Managing the Third Way', in J. Clarke, S. Gerwitz and E. McLaughlin (eds) *New Managerialism New Welfare?*, London: Sage.

Lassman, P. (ed.) (1994) *Weber, Max. Weber: Political Writings* (Cambridge Texts in the History of Political Thought). Ed. and trans. R. Speirs, Cambridge: Cambridge University Press.

Lawler, J. (1992) *The Social Services Manager*. PhD thesis, University of Bradford.

Lawler, J. (2000) 'The Rise of Managerialism in Social Work', in E. Harlow and J. Lawler (eds) *Social Work, Management and Change*, London: Ashgate, pp. 33–56.

Lawler, J. (2007) 'Leadership in Social Work: A Case of Caveat Emptor?', *British Journal of Social Work*, 37(1): 123–41.

Lawler, J. and Bilson, A. (2004) 'Towards a More Reflexive Research Aware Practice: The Influence and Potential of Professional and Team Culture', in A. Bilson (ed.) *Evidence-based Practice and Social Work: International Research and Policy Perspectives*, London: Whiting and Birch, pp. 190–211.

Lawler, J. and Ford, J. (forthcoming) 'Conversations and Learning: Narrative and Development in Practice', in J. Gold, R. Thorpe and A. Mumford (eds) *Gower Handbook of Leadership and Management Development* (5th edition), Farnham: Gower.

Le Grand, J. and Bartlett, W. (eds) (1993) *Quasi-markets and Social Policy*, Basingstoke: Palgrave Macmillan.

Legge, K. (1989) 'Human Resource Management – a Critical Analysis', in J. Storey (ed.) *New Perspectives on Human Resource Management*, London: Routledge.

Legge, K. (2005) *Human Resource Management: Rhetorics and Realities*, Basingstoke: Macmillan.

Ling, T. (2002) 'Delivering Joined Up Government in the United Kingdom: Dimensions, Issues and Problems', *Public Administration*, 80(4): 615–42.

Lipsky, M. (1980) *Street-Level Bureaucracy: Dilemmas of the Individual in Public Services*, New York: Russell Sage Foundation.

Lissack, M. (ed.) (2002) *The Interaction of Complexity and Management*, Westport, CT: Greenwood Publishing Group.

Local Government Management Board (1996) *The Complexicon: A Lexicon of Complexity*, London: Local Government Management Board.

Lukes, S. (2005) *Power: A Radical View*, Basingstoke: Palgrave Macmillan.

McBeath, G. and Webb, S. (2002) 'Virtue Ethics and Social Work: Being Lucky, Realistic and not Doing One's Duty', *British Journal of Social Work*, 32: 1015–36.

McDaniel, R. and Driebe, D. (eds) (2005) *Uncertainty and Surprise in Complex Systems: Questions of Working with the Unexpected*, New York: Springer.

McDonnell, F. and Zutshi, H. (2006) *Continuing Professional Development Strategy for the Social Care Workforce*, Leeds: Skills for Care.

McGregor, D. (1960) *The Human Side of Enterprise*, New York: McGraw-Hill.

McLaughlin, K., Osborne, S. and Ferlie, E. (eds) (2002) *New Public Management: Current Trends and Future Prospects*, London: Routledge.

Manthorpe, J. and Iliffe, S. (2005) 'Timely Responses to Dementia: Exploring the Social Work Role', *Journal of Social Work*, 5(2): 191–203.

Marshall, J. (2000) 'Revisiting Simone de Beauvoir: Recognizing Feminist Contributions to Pluralism in Organizational Studies', *Journal of Management Inquiry*, 9: 166–72.

Martin G.P., Phelps K. and Katbamna, S. (2004) 'Human Motivation and Professional Practice: Of Knights, Knaves and Social Workers', *Social Policy and Administration*, 38(5): 470–87.

Martin, J. (1992) *Cultures in Organizations: Three Perspectives*, Oxford: Oxford University Press.

Martin, V. and Henderson, E. (2001) *Managing in Health and Social Care*, London: Routledge.

Martinez, M.N (1997) 'The Smarts that Count', *HR Magazine*, 42(11): 72–8.

Maturana, H.R. (1988) 'Reality: The Search for Objectivity or the Quest for a Compelling Argument', *Irish Journal of Psychology*, 9: 25–82.

Maturana, H. (2007) 'The Biological Foundations of Virtual Realities and their Implications for Human Existence', *Constructivist Foundations*, 3 (2): 109–14.

Maturana, H.R. and Bunnell, P. (1998) 'Biosphere, Homosphere, and Robosphere: What Has That to Do with Business?', http://www.solonline.org/res/wp/maturana/index.html, accessed 8 May 2008.

Maturana, H. and Varela, F. (1980) *Autopoesis and Cognition: The Realization of the Living*, Dordrecht, The Netherlands: D. Reidl.

Mazutis, D. and Slawinski, N. (2008) 'Leading Organizational Learning through Authentic Dialogue', *Management Learning*, 39: 437–56.

Meek, J.W., De Ladurantey, J. and Newell, W.H. (2007) 'Complex Systems, Governance and Policy Administration Consequences', *Emergence: Complexity and Organization*, 9(1–2): 24–36.

Midgley, G. (2000) *Systemic Intervention: Philosophy, Methodology, and Practice*, New York: Kluwer.

Minas, I. H. (2005) 'Leadership for change in complex systems', *Australasian Psychiatry*, 13: 33–9.

Mingers, J. (1992) 'Recent Developments in Critical Management Science', *Journal of the Operational Research Society*, 43(1): 1–10.

Mintzberg, H. (1975) 'The Manager's Job: Folklore and Fact', *Harvard Business Review*, 55(4): 49–61.

Mintzberg, H. (1978) 'Patterns in Strategy Formation', *Management Science*, 24(9): 934–48.

Mintzberg, H. (1987) 'Crafting Strategy', *Harvard Business Review*, 87(4): 66–75.

Mintzberg, H. and Quinn, J. (1996) *Evaluating Business Strategy* (3rd edition), Upper Saddle River, NJ: Prentice-Hall.

Mitleton-Kelly, E. (2003) *Complex Systems and Evolutionary Perspectives on Organizations: The Application of Complexity Theory to Organizations*, Oxford: Pergamon.

Mohan, B. (2002) 'The Future of Social Work Education: Curricular Conundrums in an Age of Uncertainty', *Electronic Journal of Social Work*, 1: 1–10.

Morgan, G. (1986) *Images of Organization*. Thousand Oaks, CA; London: Sage.

Morgan, G. (1993) *Imaginization*, Beverly Hills, CA: Sage.

Morgan, G. (2006) *Images of Organization* (2nd edition), Thousand Oaks, CA; London: Sage.

Muldoon, S. (2004) 'Is Symbolic Interactionism the Fifth Paradigm of Leadership?', School of Business Working Paper Series, Victoria University of Technology, http://www.business. vu.edu.au/mgt/pdf/working_papers/2004/wp11_2004_muldoon.pdf, accessed 23 July 2009.

Mullen, E.J. and Bacon, W.F. (1999) 'A Survey of Practitioner Adoption and Implementation of Practice Guidelines and Evidence-Based Treatments', paper presented at the 2nd International Inter-Centre Network for Evaluation of Social Work Practice Conference, Stockholm, Sweden, 10–15 June.

Mullins, L.J. (2007) *Management and Organisational Behaviour* (8th edition), Harlow: Financial Times/Prentice Hall.

National Minimum DataSet for Social Care (2008) *NMDS-SC Briefing Issue 5 (February 2008) – Age and Gender*, Leeds: Skills for Care.

Newell, W. (2001) 'Theory of Interdisciplinary Studies', *Issues in Integrative Studies*, 19: 1–25.

Newell, W. (2003) 'Complexity and Interdisciplinarity,' in L.D. Kiel (ed.) *Knowledge Management, Organizational Intelligence and Learning, and Complexity*, Oxford: EOLSS Publishers.

Northouse, P.G. (2007) *Leadership: Theory and Practice* (4th edition), London: Sage.

O'Brien, M. and Penna, S. (1998) *Theorising Welfare: Enlightenment and Modern Society*, London: Sage.

Ochberg, R.L. (1994) 'Life Stories and Storied Lives', in A. Lieblich and R. Josselson (eds) *Exploring Identity and Gender: The Narrative Study of Lives*, Thousand Oaks, CA: Sage, pp. 113–44.

Open University (2008) *T306_2 Managing Complexity: A Systems Approach – Introduction*, http://openlearn.open.ac.uk/course/view.php?name=T306_2, accessed 30 July 2009.

Orme, J. and Rennie, G. (2006) 'The Role of Registration in Ensuring Ethical Practice', *International Social Work*, 49(3): 333–44.

Ormrod, S. (2003) 'Organisational Culture in Health Service Policy and Research: "Third Way" Political Fad or Policy Development?', *Politics and Policy*, 312: 227–37.

Osborne, D. and Gaebler, T. (1993) *Reinventing Government: How the Entrepreneurial Spirit is Transforming the Public Sector*, New York: Plume Books.

Parker, M. (2004) 'Structure, Culture and Anarchy: Ordering the NHS', in M. Learmonth and N. Harding (eds) *Unmasking Health Management: A Critical Text*, New York: Nova Science, pp. 171–85.

Parton, N. (2003) 'Rethinking Professional Practice: The Contributions of Constructivism and the Feminist Ethic of Care', *British Journal of Social Work*, 33: 1–16.

Parton, N. (2004) 'From Maria Colwell to Victoria Climbié: Reflections on Public Inquiries into Child Abuse a Generation Apart', *Child Abuse Review*, 13: 80–94.

Parton, N., Thorpe, D. and Wattam, C. (1997) *Child Protection: Risk and the Moral Order*, Basingstoke: Macmillan.

Pascale, R.T. (1984) 'Perspectives on Strategy: The Real Story behind Honda's Success', *California Management Review*, 26: 47–72.

Payne, M. (2005) *Modern Social Work Theory*, Basingstoke: Palgrave Macmillan.

Payne, M. (2006) *Teamwork in Multiprofessional Care*, Basingstoke: Macmillan.

Peck, E., Towell, D., and Gulliver, P. (2001) 'The Meanings of "Culture" in Health and Social Care: A Case Study of the Combined Trust in Somerset', *Journal of Interprofessional Care*, 15(4): 319–27.

Perls, F.S. (1974) *Gestalt Therapy Verbatim*, New York: Bantam Books.

Pettigrew, A.M., Woodman, R.W. and Cameron, K.S. (2001) 'Studying Organizational Change and Development: Challenges for Future Research', *Academy of Management Journal*, 44(4): 697–713.

Pippen, J. and Eden, D. (1997) *Resonating Bodies*, Brisbane: QUT.

Pithouse, A.(1987) *Social Work: The Social Organisation of an Invisible Trade*, Aldershot: Avebury Gower.

Plsek, P.E. and Wilson, T. (2001) 'Complexity Science: Complexity, Leadership, and Management in Healthcare Organisations', *British Medical Journal*, 323: 746–9.

Poerksen, B. (2004) *The Certainty of Uncertainty: Dialogues Introducing Constructivism*, Exeter: Imprint Academic.

Popper, K. (1972) *Objective Knowledge: An Evolutionary Approach*, Oxford: Clarendon Press.

Poulter, J. (2005) 'Integrating Theory and Practice: A New Heuristic Paradigm for Social Work Practice', *Australian Social Work*, 58(2): 199–211.

Pugh, D.S. and Hickson, D.J. (2007) *Writers on Organizations*, Harmondsworth: Penguin.

Putnam, L.L. and Mumby, D.K. (1993) 'Organizations, Emotions and the Myth of Rationality' in S. Fineman (ed.) *Emotions in Organizations*, London: Sage, pp. 36–57.

Pye, A. (2005) 'Leadership and Organizing: Sense-Making in Action', *Leadership*, 1(1): 31–49.

Raelin, J.A. (2003) *Creating Leaderful Organizations: How to Bring Out Leadership in Everyone*, San Francisco: Berrett-Koehler.

Reder, P. and Duncan, S. (2003) 'Understanding Communication in Child Protection Networks', *Child Abuse Review*, 12: 82–100.

Rickards, T. and Clark, M. (2006) *Dilemmas of Leadership*, Oxford: Routledge.

Rittel, H. and Webber M. (1973) 'Dilemmas in a General Theory of Planning', *Journal Policy Sciences*, 4: 155–69.

Ritzer, G. (1992) *The McDonaldization of Society*, Thousand Oaks, CA: Pine Forge Press.

Roethlisberger, F.J. and Dickson, W.J. (1964) *Management and the Worker*, New York: John Wiley.

Rosenhead, J. (1998) 'Complexity Theory and Management Practice', LSE Working Paper 98.25, London School of Economics.

Ross, S. (1987) *Systems Interventions in Child Care*. PhD Thesis, University of Keele.

Ruiz, A.B. (1996) 'The Contribution of Humberto Maturana to the Sciences of Complexity and Psychology', *Journal of Constructivist Psychology*, 9(4): 283–302.

Sakamoto, I. and Pitner, R.O. (2005) 'Use of Critical Consciousness in Anti-Oppressive Social Work Practice: Disentangling Power Dynamics at Personal and Structural Levels', *BJSW Advance Access*, 21 March 2005, doi:10.1093/bjsw/bch190.

Salovey, P. and Mayer, J.D. (1990) 'Emotional Intelligence', *Imagination, Cognition, and Personality*, 9: 185–211.

Sbarcea, K. (2003) *Living Leadership: The Dance between Chaos and Stasis: A Guide for*

Complexity Leaders, http://www.thinkingshift.com/page.php?key=26, accessed 11 August 2008.

Schecter, D. (1991) 'Critical Systems Thinking in the 1980s: A Connective Summary', in R.L. Flood and M.C. Jackson (eds) *Critical Systems Thinking: Directed Readings*, Chichester: John Wiley.

Schein, E.H. (1999) *Organizational Learning: What is New?*, http://www.solonline.org/res/wp/10012.html, accessed 29 July 2009.

Schön, D. (1987) *Educating the Reflective Practitioner*, San Francisco: Jossey-Bass.

Schuler, R.S. and Jackson, S.E. (1999) 'Preface', in R.S. Schuler and S.E. Jackson (eds) *Strategic Human Resource Management*, London: Blackwell.

Schwartz, D.D. and Daylle, S. (2009) *Nice Girls Can Finish First: Getting the Results You Want and the Respect You Deserve . . . While Still Being Liked*, New York: McGraw Hill.

Schutz, W.C. (1973) *Joy: Expanding Human Awareness*, New York: Ballantine.

SCIE (2003) *SCIE Guide 1: Managing practice*, http://www.scie.org.uk/publications/guides/guide01/index.asp, accessed 5 March 2009.

SCIE (2004) *Learning Organisations: A Self-assessment Resource Pack*, http://www.scie.org.uk/publications/learningorgs/index.asp, accessed 29 July 2009.

Scottish Executive (2007) *Scottish Executive Guidance Notes: Completion of Corporate Action Plans 2007–8*, Edinburgh: Scottish Executive.

Secretary of State for Social Services (1974) *Report of the Committee of Inquiry into the Care and Supervision Provided in Relation to Maria Colwell*, London: HMSO.

Seden, J. (2008) 'Organizations and Organizational Change', in S. Fraser and S. Matthews (eds) *The Critical Practitioner in Social Work and Health Care*, London: Sage, pp. 169–85.

Selvini Palazzoli, M., Anolli, L., Di Blasio, P., Giossi, L., Pisano, I., Ricci, C., Sacchi, M. and Ugazio V. (1986) *The Hidden Games of Organizations*, New York: Pantheon (first published in Italian in 1981 as *Sel fronte dell' organizzazione*).

Senge, P.M. (1990) *The Fifth Discipline: The Art and Practice of the Learning Organization*, New York: Doubleday.

Senge, P. (1999) 'The Gurus Speak (Panel Discussion): Complexity and Organizations', *Emergence*, 1(1): 73–91.

Senior, B. and Fleming, J. (2006) *Organizational Change* (3rd edition), Harlow: Prentice Hall.

Shamir, B. (1995) 'Social Distance and Charisma: Theoretical Notes and an Exploratory Study', *Leadership Quarterly*, 6(1): 19–47.

Sheldon, B. (2001) 'The Validity of Evidence-Based Practice in Social Work: A Response to Webb', *British Journal of Social Work*, 31: 801–9.

Sheldon, B., Chilver, R., Elliss, A., Mosely, A. and Tierney, S. (2005) 'A pre-post empirical study of obstacles to, and opportunities for, evidence-based practice in social care', in A. Bilson (ed.) *Evidence-Based Practice in Social Work*, London: Whiting and Birch, pp. 11–50.

Shiba, S. (1998) 'Leadership and Breakthrough', *Centre for Quality of Management Journal*, 7(2): 10–22.

Shotter, J. (2005) 'Inside the Moment of Managing: Wittgenstein and the Everyday Dynamics Our Expressive-Responsive Activities', *Organization Studies*, 26(1): 113–35.

Shotter, J. and Katz, A.M. (1998) 'Living Moments', *Human Systems*, 9: 81–93.

Sidhu, J. (2003) 'Mission Statements: Is it Time to Shelve Them?', *European Management Journal*, 21(4): 439–46.

Simmons, L. (2007) *Social Care Governance – a Practice Workbook*, London: Social Care Institute for Excellence.

Simpkin, M. (1983) *Trapped within Welfare: Surviving Social Work* (2nd edition), London: Macmillan.

Skills for Care (2008) *Leadership and Management Strategy Update 2008: Transforming Adult Social Care*, Leeds: Skills for Care.

Skye, E., Meddings, S. and Dimmock, B. (2003) 'Theories for Understanding People', in J.

Henderson and D. Atkinson (eds) *Managing Care in Context*, London: Routledge.

Smedes, T. (2004) *Chaos, Complexity, and God: Divine Action and Scientism*, Leuven, Belgium: Peeters Publishers.

Smircich, L. and Morgan, G. (1982) 'Leadership: The Management of Meaning', *Journal of Applied Behavioural Science*, 18: 257–73.

Snook, S. (2001) *Friendly Fire*, Princeton, NJ: Princeton University.

socialworkscotland.org (2009) Home page, http://www.socialworkscotland.org.uk/, accessed 4 March 2009.

Sparrowe, R.T. (2005) 'Authentic Leadership and the Narrative Self', *Leadership Quarterly*, 16: 419–39.

Spillane, J. (2006) *Distributed Leadership*, San Francisco: Wiley.

Stacey, R.D. (1997) 'Excitement and Tension at the Edge of Chaos', in E. Smith (ed.) *Integrity and Change: Mental Health in the Marketplace*, London: Routledge.

Stacey, R.D. (2007) *Strategic Management and Organizational Dynamics: The Challenge of Complexity to Ways of Thinking about Organizations* (5th edition), Harlow: Pearson Education.

Stogdill, R.M. (1974) *Handbook of Leadership: A Survey of Theory and Re-search*, New York: Free Press.

Szabo, M. and Lambert, L. (2002) 'The Preparation of New Constructivist Leaders', in L. Lambert, D. Walker, D.P. Zimmermann, J.E. Cooper, M. Dale Lambert, M.E. Gardner and M. Szabo, *The Constructivist Leader* (2nd edition), Oxford, OH: Teachers College Press, pp. 204–38.

Taket, A.R. and White, L.A. (2000) *Partnership and Participation: Decision-making in the Multiagency Setting*, Chichester: John Wiley.

Taylor, C. and White, S. (2000) *Practising Reflexivity in Health and Welfare: Making Knowledge*, Buckingham: Open University Press.

Taylor, J.R. and Robichaud, D. (2004) 'Finding the Organization in the Communication: Discourse as Action and Sensemaking', *Organization*, 11(3): 395–413.

Thorndike, E.L. (1920) 'Intelligence and Its Uses', *Harper's*, 140: 227–35.

Thorpe, R. (2008) 'Introduction: Constructionist Approaches to Management Research', *Management Learning*, 39: 115–21.

Thorpe, R., Lawler, J. and Gold, J. (2007) *Leadership Literature: Systematic Review*, Northern Leadership Academy, http://www.northernleadershipacademy.co.uk/portal/server.pt/gateway/PTARGS_0_237_7044_504_1148_43/http%3B/NLAAS2/PublishedContent/Publish/nla_home/manager_content/doc_downloads/thorpe_lawler_and_gold_systematic_review_2007_branded_.pdf, accessed 17 August 2009.

Tourish, D. and Jackson, B. (2008) 'Guest Editorial: Communication and Leadership: An Open Invitation to Engage', *Leadership*, 4: 219–25.

Trist, E.L. and Bamforth, K.W. (1951) 'Some Social and Psychological Consequences of the Longwall Method of Coal Getting', *Human Relations*, 4: 3–38.

Troy, P. (ed.) (1999) *Serving the City: The Crisis in Australia's Urban Services*, Sydney: Pluto Press.

Tsoukas, H. (1993) 'The Road to Emancipation is through Organizational Development: A Critical Evaluation of Total Systems Intervention', *Systems Practice*, 6(1): 53–70.

Tsui, M. (2005) 'Functions of Social Work Supervision in Hong Kong', *International Social Work*, 48: 485–93.

Varela, F.J. (1992) *Ethical Know-How: Action, Wisdom and Cognition*, Stanford, CA: Stanford University Press.

Visser, M. (2007) 'Deutero-Learning in Organizations: A Review and a Reformulation', *Academy of Management Review*, 32(2): 659–67.

von Bertalanffy, L. (1950) 'The Theory of Open Systems in Physics and Biology', *Science*, 3: 23–39.

Waldrop, M.M. (1992) *Complexity: The Emerging Science at the Edge of Order and Chaos,* New York: Simon & Schuster.

Walter, I., Nutley, S., Percy-Smith, J., McNeish, D., and Frost, S. (2004) *Improving the Use of Research in Social Care Practice,* London: Social Care Institute for Excellence.

Watzlawick, P. (ed.) (1984) *The Invented Reality,* New York: Norton.

Watzlawick, P., Weakland, J.H. and Fisch, R. (1974) *Change: Principles of Problem Formation and Resolution,* New York: Norton.

Webb, S. (2000) 'The Politics of Social Work: Power and Subjectivity', *Critical Social Work,* 1(2), http://www.uwindsor.ca/units/socialwork/critical.nsf/982f0e5f06b5c9a285256d6e006cff78/6d7d850590867c4d85256ea700524df3!OpenDocument, accessed 17 August 2009.

Weber, M. (1947) *The Theory of Social and Economic Organization,* trans. T. Parsons, New York: Oxford University Press.

Weber, M. (1968) *Economy and Society: An Outline of Interpretive Sociology,* New York: Bedminster Press.

Weick, K. (1995) *Sense-Making in Organizations,* Thousand Oaks, CA: Sage.

Weick, K.E., Sutcliffe, K.M. and Obstfeld, D. (200) 'Organizing and the Process of Sensemaking', *Organization Science,* 16(4): 409–21

Weiss, W.H. (1999), 'Leadership', *Supervision,* January: 4–10.

White, S. (1998) 'Examining the Artfulness of Risk Talk', in A. Jokinen, K. Juhila and T. Poso (eds) *Constructing Social Work Practices,* Aldershot: Ashgate.

White, S. and Featherstone, B. (2005) 'Communicating Misunderstandings: Multi-agency Work as Social Practice', *Child & Family Social Work,* 10(3): 207–16.

Whittington, C. and Holland, R. (1985) 'A Framework for Theory in Social Work', *Issues in Social Work Education,* 6(1): 41–6.

Wilson, K., Ruch, G., Lymbery, M and Cooper, A. (2008) *Social Work: An Introduction to Contemporary Practice,* Harlow: Pearson Education.

Winograd, T. (2006) 'Shifting Viewpoints: Artificial Intelligence and Human–Computer Interaction', *Artificial Intelligence,* 170: 1256–8.

Winograd, T. and Flores, F. (1987a) *Understanding Computers and Cognition,* New York: Addison and Wesley.

Winograd, T. and Flores, F. (1987b) 'Understanding Computers and Cognition – a New Foundation for Design', *Artificial Intelligence,* 31(2): 250–61.

Worral, L. and Cooper, C. (2007) *The Quality of Working Life 2007: Managers' Health, Motivation and Productivity. Executive Summary,* London: Chartered Management Institute.

Wright, D. (2005) 'Embodying, Emotioning, Expressing Learning', *Reflective Practice,* 6(1): 85–93.

Wright, J.N. (2002) 'Mission and Reality and Why Not?', *Journal of Change Management,* 3(1): 30–44.

Yoder, J.D. (2001) 'Making Leadership Work More Effectively for Women', *Journal of Social Issues,* 57(4): 815–28.

Zaleznik, A. (1977) 'Managers and Leaders: Are They Different?', *Harvard Business Review,* 55(May–June): 67–78.

Index